Plans, Sections and Elevations

Key Buildings of the Twentieth Century

Richard Weston

Laurence King Publishing

LAURENCE KING

Published in 2004 by Laurence King Publishing Ltd
71 Great Russell Street
London WC1B 3BP
Tel: +44 20 7430 8850
Fax: +44 20 7430 8880
e-mail: enquiries@laurenceking.co.uk
www.laurenceking.co.uk

This book was produced by Laurence King Publishing Ltd, London

A catalogue record for this book is available from the British Library.

ISBN: 1 85669 382 1

Printed in China

Project managed by Anne McDowall
Designed by Godfrey Design
Drawings by Adrian Scholefield
Picture research by Mary-Jane Gibson

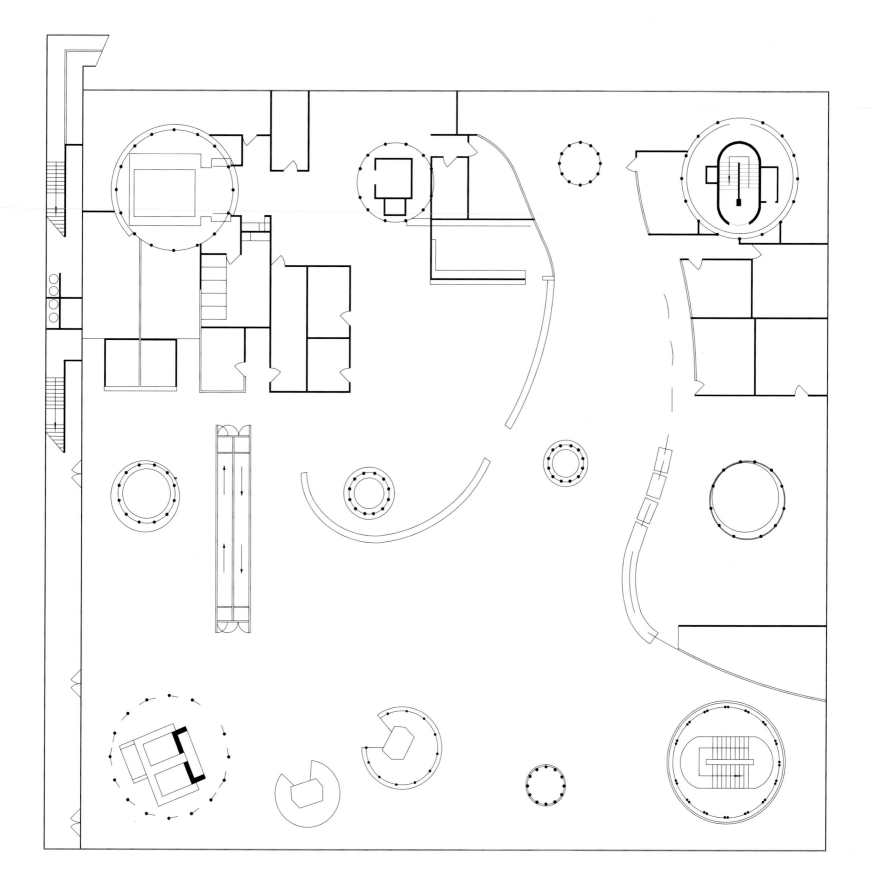

Contents

Introduction

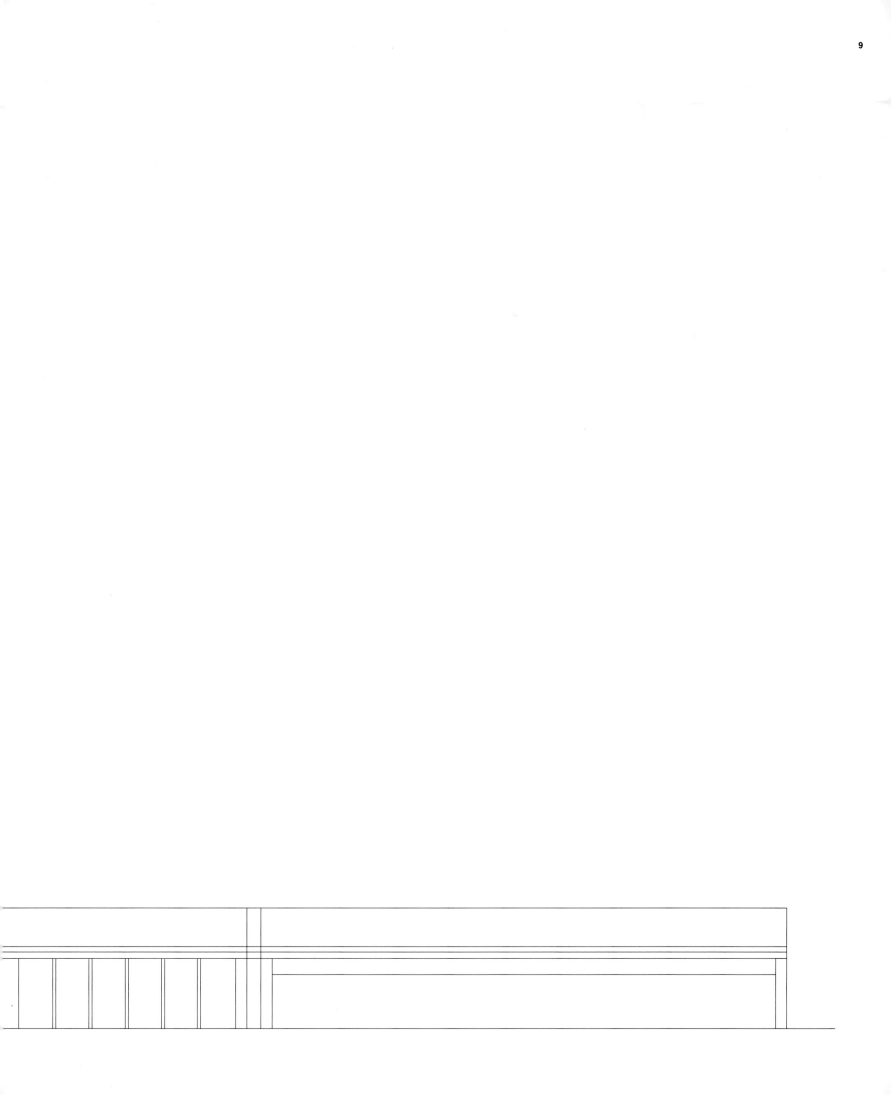

Guggenheim Museum

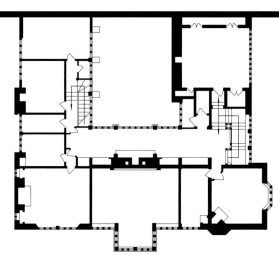

Deanery Garden

This book contains a representative collection of twentieth-century buildings, and as with all collections the choice of 'exhibits' posed two basic questions. What should be the criteria for selection? And how should the contents be organized and presented? The last is the more easily answered: the buildings are ordered chronologically, based on the date when design work started. This throws up some interesting surprises and juxtapositions, such as the early date of Frank Lloyd Wright's **Guggenheim Museum** (page 88) – although completed in the late 1950s, its revolutionary forms were established by 1945 – and 'the shock of the new' experienced by turning the page from Sir Edwin Lutyens's **Deanery Garden** (page 24) to Frank Lloyd Wright's **Larkin Building** (page 26). Organizing the material in this way also helps to suggest connections that stylistic or other narratives tend to obscure. Comparing Deanery Garden with Wright's con-

temporaneous Prairie Houses (represented by their most Modern version, the **Robie House**, page 34), for example, reminds us that there was more Beaux-Arts baggage in Wright's compositional methods than he cared to admit.

Each building is given the same space, and the plans, sections and elevations have all been drawn to a common style using CAD software. There are variations in detail – such as whether or not materials are indicated – to suit the building in question, but not to relate them back to the style of the architect's original drawings. This ensures legibility and consistency and meets the primary aim of producing a book in which to study the spatial organization of the twentieth century's key buildings. But it inevitably means that some drawings are less evocative than the originals on which they are based. One thinks, for example, of Aalto's finely textured plan of **Säynätsalo Town Hall** (page 100), or Utzon's rendered plan of **Sydney**

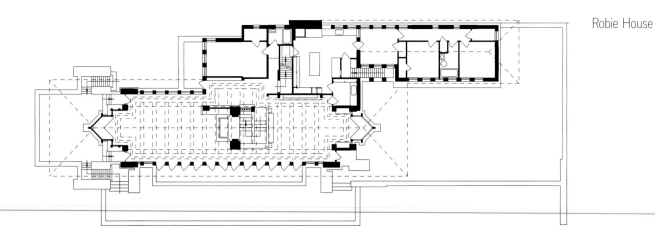

Robie House

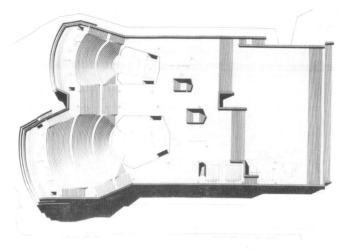

Opera House (page 126), which brought out the idea that the auditoria were 'carved' from a solid platform. A proper historical understanding of any building necessitates recourse to its original presentation, but this book will in almost every case provide a more complete description than those available in general histories.

It was decided not to include site plans for most of the buildings. This was partly for pragmatic reasons – they are often hard to come by in the literature, and their inclusion would generally mean that the floor plans had to be reduced in size. However, the reader should find that wherever matters of siting were of crucial importance in the design, either a site plan has been included or the essay discusses the relevant issues. We have made every effort to include sections and elevations for each of the buildings. In some cases, however, this proved impossible, and rather than extrapolate from photographs, with the inevitable approxima-

tions this involves, we have preferred to include only the plan. In the few cases where this is the case, the plan describes the essence of the architectural idea and spatial organization. All the drawings for each building are to the same scale unless otherwise indicated.

And so to the thorny question of what to include. From the outset, it was decided that only completed – but not necessarily extant – buildings would be featured. This eliminated several seminal projects that form part of any comprehensive history of twentieth-century architecture, in particular those made by Mies van der Rohe between 1919 and 1924, in which he proposed new expressive languages for glass, brick and concrete. It also means that the remarkable ideas explored in post-Revolutionary Russia could not be included. The bias in selecting buildings has been towards those that were innovative – stylistically, technically or programmatically – and especially those that sig-

Can Lis

Eiffel Tower

Roman Catholic Church, The Hague

nificantly affected the course of architecture. The aim has also been to include a wide range of architects, while doing justice to major 'masters'.

Finally, given that there can be no definitive list or canon, a few half-forgotten buildings are included that nonetheless seem to be of outstanding quality, such as Jørn Utzon's own house, **Can Lis** (page 174) and Aldo van Eyck's **Roman Catholic Church** in the Hague (page 152). The book also includes some architects who currently seem to be out of favour or fashion, such as Hans Hollein, whose **Mönchengladbach Museum** (page 172) is probably too tainted with traces of stylistic post-Modernism to appeal to many today.

Having suggested that one of the virtues of a collection such as this is the absence of the usual 'cause and event' explanations through which the invention and dissemination of architectural ideas are usually told, it will still be helpful to sketch briefly, and necessarily somewhat simplisti-

cally, the historical narrative of Modernity that underpins the book. The now widely accepted version of this story has deep and diverse roots, and it began at least several centuries ago, in the Renaissance, with two key developments.

Firstly, there was the gradual institutionalization of the separation between thinking and making, design and construction. This became explicit in the emergence of the role of the architect as an artist or professional, who worked independently of those who would build his (and eventually, her) designs. And secondly, the belief grew that designs should be based on reason and empirical evidence rather than on practices rooted in craft traditions and stylistic conventions. An unexpected pioneer of such an approach was Galileo, whose experiments to predict the performance of columns and beams based on quantifiable properties of construction materials could be said to have inaugurated an analytical mode of reasoning identical, in principle, to

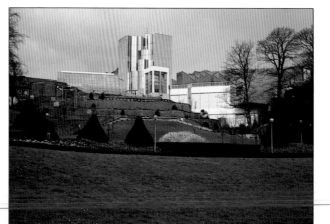

Mönchengladbach Museum

Unity Temple

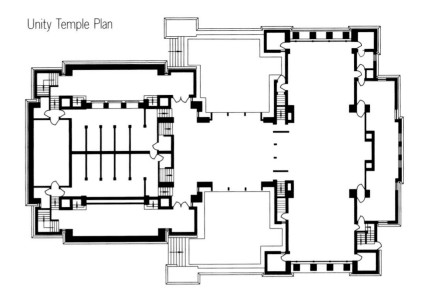

Unity Temple Plan

that of modern engineering. The growing specialization and difficulty of such technical knowledge meant that architects would increasingly lose control of substantial parts of their traditional domain of expertise, and it also helped to undermine the authority of the Classical tradition that was for so long the basis of European architecture.

By the mid-nineteenth century, with the Industrial Revolution in full swing and materials such as glass and cast and wrought iron, and later steel and reinforced concrete, becoming available in quantities, sizes and at a price that permitted their widespread use in buildings, the calls for a new architecture representative of the age began to be heard on all sides. Its first great monuments – Paxton's Crystal Palace, Eiffel's Tower, Dutert and Contamin's Galerie des Machines – were not the work of architects but of engineers, or, in Paxton's case, of a gardener of genius. While architects were still apt to debate which of a range of historical styles might

best suit the job in hand, the engineers were developing radically new forms that exploited the technical potential of the new materials.

It was in Chicago, not Europe, where a fully Modern architecture emerged – first with the development of the steel-framed skyscraper and then with Frank Lloyd Wright's 'destruction of the box' – a new conception of space that both treated the whole interior as a continuous spatial 'organism' and linked interior to out in a 'flowing' continuum. Emerging around the turn of the century in his Prairie Houses, this vision soon infused the workplace in the **Larkin Building** (page 26), and was seen at its most gloriously all-pervasive in **Unity Temple** (page 30).

Wright's work was soon published in Europe and made an immediate impact, but the extent of its influence remains unclear. *Fin de siècle* European architects were less innovative spatially, but they were exploring expressive possibilities suit-

Post Office Savings Bank

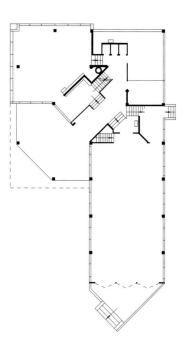

Bauhaus

Open Air School

ed to frame construction. Influenced by the ideas of the German architect and theorist Gottfried Semper, who conjectured that carpets hung from wooden frames had been the first form of spatial enclosure, buildings such as Otto Wagner's **Post Office Savings Bank** in Vienna (page 28) and Josef Hoffmann's **Palais Stoclet** in Brussels (page 32) treated stone as a lightweight cladding. In the 1920s the new ideas on space and its containment by a lightweight 'envelope' converged in the development of what would soon, at an exhibition held in New York's Museum of Modern Art in 1932, be christened the 'International Style'. It is represented here by such buildings as Johannes Duiker's **Open Air School** (page 52), Walter Gropius's **Bauhaus** (page 50, a hugely influential educational institution as well as building), Richard Neutra's **Lovell 'Health House'** (page 54), Le Corbusier's **Villa Savoye** (page 62), Mies van der Rohe's **Tugendhat House** (page 60) and Alvar

Aalto's **Tuberculosis Sanatorium** (page 66). In most of these buildings a grid of columns supports the floor slabs; space is articulated by free-standing screens or partitions; and the exterior is a taut skin in which large openings can be freely placed – by making the skin of glass, or the openings continuous and horizontal, the radical break from traditional construction was emphasized.

To its proponents, the International Style represented a lingua franca for the Machine Age. Freed of traditional stylistic trappings, buildings were to be designed 'functionally' as a direct response to the given brief, and to be amenable to industrial means of construction, both in principle and as a way of solving the massive housing shortages that were a major legacy of the First World War. Although these ideals were dominant for a while, an alternative sub-current ran through Modernism that challenged the supposed rationalism of the mainstream. Generally referred to as

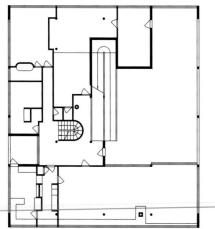

Villa Savoye

Palais Stoclet

Einstein Tower

Farnsworth House

Expressionism, these alternative ideals were vividly demonstrated just before the War in Bruno Taut's **Glass Pavilion** (page 40), and after it in Eric Mendelsohn's **Einstein Tower** (page 44). They are present again, suitably domesticated, in Hans Scharoun's **Schminke House** (page 72) and eventually burst forth — albeit largely stripped of the earlier metaphysical baggage — in his **Philharmonie Hall** in Berlin (page 124).

By the time the International Style had been named, its protagonists were already questioning the desirability of what Aalto called 'a rootless international modern architecture'. In the **Villa Mairea** (page 86), which was substantially complete by 1940, Aalto transformed the column grid into an abstraction of the Finnish forest, and incorporated references to Finnish vernacular traditions that would have been ridiculed a decade earlier. Frank Lloyd Wright's answer to the International Style, **Fallingwater** (page78), was also a vivid response to a unique site, while in Brazil Oscar Niemeyer developed an exuberant interpretation of Le Corbusier's style (**Niemeyer House**, page 112). He saw its sinuous curves as an echo of his country's tropical landscapes and plants, and of that devotion to 'the body of the beloved woman' ritualized on Copacabana beach.

Although the transformation was less dramatic than after 1918, the Second World War marked a major rupture in the development of Modern architecture. The spirit of the International Style took root in the USA, courtesy of such influential exiles as Walter Gropius and Mies van der Rohe, and Mies's steel-and-glass architecture — to which he first gave definitive expression in the **Farnsworth House** (page 92) — became the style of corporate America (as for example at **Lever House**, page 102) and, eventually, the world.

In California — where two gifted Austrians, Rudolf Schindler (**Schindler-Chace House**, page

Tuberculosis Sanatorium

Niemeyer House

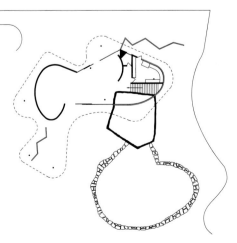

46), and Richard Neutra, had settled three decades earlier – international ideals melded with local traditions to produce some of the century's most seductively liveable houses. These ranged from such luxurious designs as Neutra's **Kaufmann Desert House** (page 94), built for the owners of Fallingwater, to the celebrated Case Study Houses: promoted by the visionary editor of *Arts and Architecture* magazine, John Entenza, these included the widely influential **Eames House** (page 90). In conjunction with comparable developments in Scandinavia, the 'Contemporary' style of California would influence lifestyles throughout the developed world.

With his great **Unité d'Habitation** in Marseilles (page 98), Le Corbusier signalled a radical break with his pre-war ideals. In place of space wrapped in a taut skin – epitomized by his **Swiss Pavilion** (page 70) – he offered a cliff of deep, cave-like dwellings framed in rough concrete and surmounted by a roof-garden that, for all the modernity of its functions – crèche, running-track, boiler-house – had the grandeur and mystery of the ruins of a past civilization. Having been erased from the curriculum at the Bauhaus, history was being rediscovered as a wellspring of invention. In the USA there was much talk of a 'New Monumentality' – with the leading critical propagandist of Modern architecture, the Swiss historian Sigfried Giedion, as an influential advocate.

Among many others, two of the most gifted architects of the new generation – Aldo van Eyck and Jørn Utzon – travelled widely in search of non-Western vernacular buildings and architecture, while Louis Kahn, a generation older but a late-developer, was transformed by the experience of touring the Mediterranean during his time as architect in residence at the American Academy in Rome. Van Eyck's **Amsterdam Municipal Orphanage** (page 120) – an accretion of small

Eames House

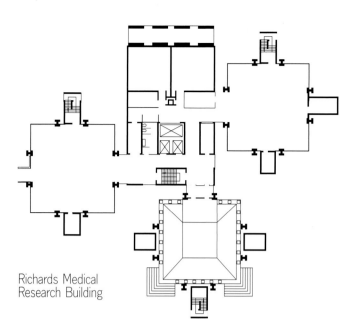

Richards Medical
Research Building

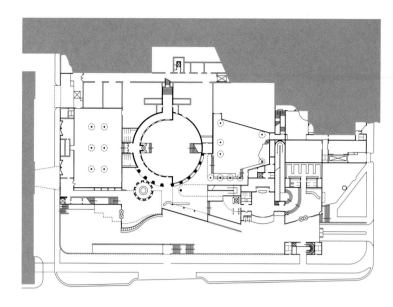

Staatsgalerie

'cells' — was directly inspired by the hive-like cas-bahs experienced in North Africa, while for Utzon the creative foundations for the future Sydney Opera House were laid atop the temple platforms of the Maya. In the work of both these architects, the creation of a concrete feeling of 'place', rather than the manipulation of abstract 'space', was to become a key aim.

Louis Kahn, trained in the French Beaux-Arts tradition, was determined to return architecture to more solid, permanent forms, and his key idea was that walls could be made substantial again by using them to accommodate a building's secondary spaces. Dividing his buildings into 'servant and served spaces' — as, for example, in the **Richards Medical Research Building** (page 128) — also gave Kahn a means to bring order to the bewildering complexity of modern building programmes, and in particular to the unruly pipes and ducts that their servicing demanded.

An influential teacher, Kahn proved an unlikely catalyst for one of the most controversial episodes in recent architecture, post-Modernism, for which the **Vanna Venturi House** (page 142) was the earliest, and remains perhaps the most persuasive, icon. Although post-Modernism's first manifestation in architecture was as a form of stylistic eclecticism, and more often than not Classically inclined, it was quickly allied to a broader critique of the foundations of Enlightenment thought, and therefore of Modernity itself.

Post-Modernism's most lasting manifestations within architecture were the rediscovery of interest in the city — vividly represented here by the change in James Stirling's work from the **Leicester Engineering Building** (page 116) to the **Staatsgalerie** in Stuttgart (page 182) — and the treatment of architecture as a language. The latter approach can be seen to embrace not only those, like Michael Graves (**Graves House**, page

Vanna Venturi House

Pompidou Centre

Koshino House

202), who turned to Classicism, but also fellow members of the New York Five, such as Richard Meier (**Atheneum**, page 180) and Peter Eisenman (**House VI**, page 178), who self-consciously revived the 'white' architecture of High Modernism. Even a building like the **Pompidou Centre** (page 168) seems, in retrospect, to be infused with nostalgia – for the future, and for its representation in seminal images of the avant-garde movements of early Modernism.

Just as it was being declared dead in the early 1980s, Modernism was the subject of renewed interest among many architects. Some of the most interesting developments came where it hybridized with local traditions and transformed to meet the demands of different cultures and climates, as for example with Tadao Ando in Japan (**Koshino House**, page 186), Glenn Murcutt in Australia (**Ball-Eastaway House**, page 192), and Ken Yeang in Malaysia (**Menara**

Mesiniaga, page 214). The 1980s also saw a succession of would-be avant-gardes, albeit with narrowly aesthetic revolutions in mind. The most concerted attempt to christen an emerging *zeitgeist* was the 'Deconstructivist Architecture' exhibition, held at the Museum of Modern Art in New York in 1988. But whereas the International Style had been a credible conflation of diverse talents, architects as diverse as Frank Gehry (**Gehry House**, page 184), Peter Eisenman (**Wexner Center**, page 200), Rem Koolhaas (**Kunsthal**, page 208), Bernard Tschumi and Zaha Hadid (**LF1, Landesgartenschau**, page 228) had little in common beyond a superficial shared interest in fragmented forms.

Recent architecture defies easy summary, partly, no doubt, because we are too close to it, and partly because we are living in a period of bewilderingly diverse trends and interests. The gravity-defying forms of Rem Koolhaas's masterly

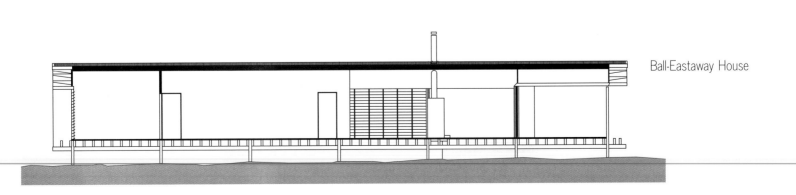

Ball-Eastaway House

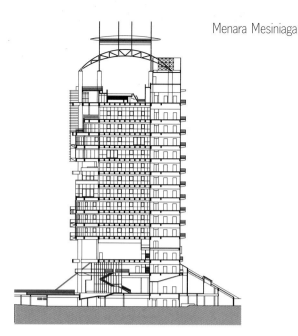

Bordeaux Villa (page 232), for example, can be seen as both a dazzling fulfilment of various tropes in Modernism, and a knowing commentary on them. Similarly, the immaterial 'liquid space' of Toyo Ito's **Sendai Mediathèque** (page 230) and Peter Zumthor's determination to ground his architecture in the 'facts' of construction – as, for example, in the **Thermal Baths** at Vals (page 204) – both draw on central strands of Modern architecture, while embodying very different attitudes to an age dominated by digital media.

From the point of view of the general culture, perhaps the most striking feature of architecture at the end of the century was the emergence of a global market for design talent. To function in this market architects need to develop a 'signature' style that differentiates them from their peers and guarantees that they will deliver a recognizable 'look' in response to a site and brief, almost regardless of location. The effects of this can be corrosive, as we see in the case of the architects of two of the most acclaimed buildings of the 1990s, Frank Gehry and Daniel Libeskind. Commissioned to repeat the magic of his **Bilbao Guggenheim Museum** (page 222) elsewhere, Gehry's forms have become increasingly overblown, while by recycling in other projects the supposedly site- and programme-specific language of his **Jewish Museum** in Berlin (page 218), Libeskind undermined the credibility of the original.

The buildings of the global superstars currently dominate the fashion-conscious public media, but historians of the future may well interpret them less as signs of things to come than as the clamorous manifestations of our own *fin de siècle*, with a legacy no more potent than the exotic indulgences of Art Nouveau a century before. As to what lies in store, the raw material for transformation is probably lurking elsewhere in this record of the first century of the 'tradition of the new'.

Jewish Museum

Bordeaux Villa

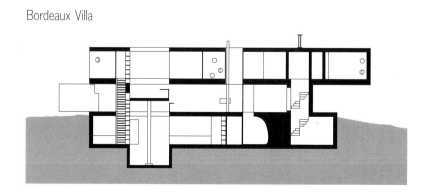

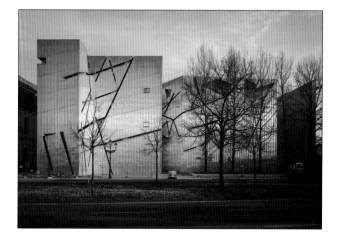

Buildings

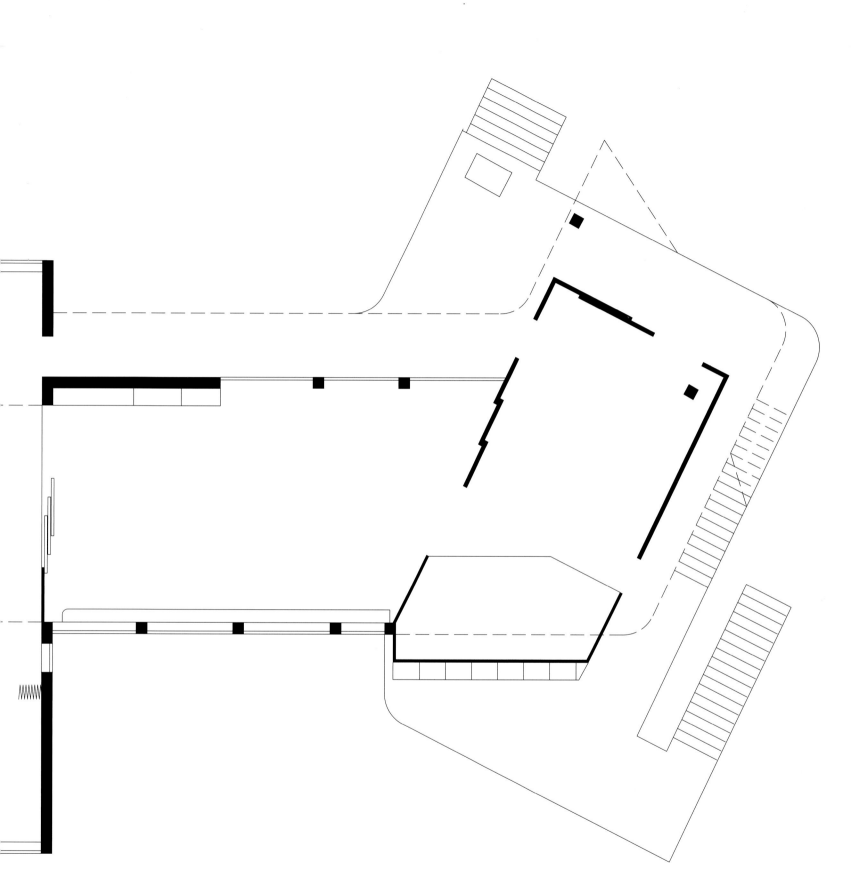

Glasgow School of Art

Charles Rennie Mackintosh, 1868–1928

Glasgow, Scotland; 1896–9, 1905–9

In 1896 the local firm of Honeyman and Keppie won a competition to design new premises for the Glasgow School of Art. The steeply sloping site was cramped and difficult and the budget modest: for an established firm the project was not prestigious, and the partners entrusted it to a young assistant, Charles Rennie Mackintosh. His design signalled the arrival of a major talent, and its development occupied him intermittently for 13 years.

Mackintosh's plan ranged the north-lit studios along the principal access street, with the library, lecture theatre, entrance facilities and staff accommodation projecting to the south. The symmetry is reinforced by the central entrance, and then seemingly wilfully denied. Four windows balance three, their sizes varying in an almost perversely 'honest' reflection of the arrangements within, while the elegant railings and walls re-establish symmetry — but in a way calculated to create a syncopated rhythm with the window-bays. Mackintosh's delight in such compositional subtleties found contemporary echoes in Lutyens (**Deanery Garden**, page 24).

The studio windows, with their exposed lintels and slender sections, are of almost industrial directness, whereas the iron brackets, with taut curves and elaborate junctions, confirm Mackintosh's affini-

ty with Art Nouveau. They are, however, functionally justified, primarily as supports for the window cleaners' planks, perhaps also as braces for the mullions. The main staircase and Museum offer similarly elegant examples of decorated construction. The paired beams that project to grasp the Voyseyesque newel posts are Japanese-inspired (the source also of the decorative motifs above the entrance railings), while the massive roof trusses, with their shaped timbers and tenon-and-dowel joints, are decidedly 'modern medieval' in feeling.

Due to limited funds, the west wing containing the celebrated library was not built in the first phase and Mackintosh was called back to it in 1905. Although the library occupies the cubic, double-height volume shown in the original design, the interior was totally transformed. A narrow gallery runs all around the space, but the columns that support it are placed some 1.2 metres (4 feet) further into the room, so that pairs of gallery beams have to project out to grasp the square timber sections. This expressive play on structure was demanded by the necessity of locating the columns on the lines of steel beams below, but, allied to the crisp detailing and subtly controlled natural and artificial lighting, it contributes to the complex articula-

tion of the space that makes it feel almost like an abstraction of a forest clearing. A similar sophistication is apparent in the west elevation. The doorway is a Mannerist exercise with missing keystone and complex mouldings, but the design is dominated by three narrow, square-gridded oriel windows that light the library. The lower sections are repeated across the room originally allocated to the School of Architecture in the studio wing, and all the windows are set in dressed stone, whereas the blank end of the north-lit studios is finished in rough stone — a change marked by a tiny setback in the wall plane. On the south façade, Mackintosh deployed similar windows, but here he placed them within the thickness of a roughcast wall. The calculated symmetry is broken by a small chimney and the dramatically cantilevered volume of the small greenhouse that provided flowers for drawing.

Mackintosh has frequently been claimed as a proto-Modern 'pioneer', but his work is firmly rooted in the values and methods of progressive, 'modern' practice as it was understood in the nineteenth century. He believed, with Voysey, that 'outside appearances are evolved from internal fundamental conditions'. And he applied these precepts with unrivalled rigour and inventiveness.

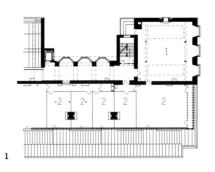

1 Second Floor Plan (Part)

1 Room over Library Balcony
2 Professor's Studio

1

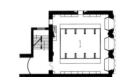

2 First Floor Mezzanine Above Library Balcony

1 Room over Library Balcony

2

3 Library Balcony

1 Library Balcony

3

4 First Floor Plan

1 Studio
2 Museum
3 Library

4

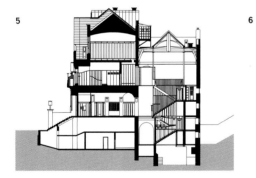

5

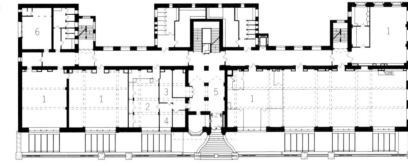

6

5 Cross Section (North-South)

6 Ground Floor Plan

1 Studio
2 Board Room
3 Shop
4 Office
5 Entrance Hall
6 Teacher's Room

7 Front Elevation

7

0 5 10 m
0 15 30 ft

Deanery Garden

Sir Edwin Lutyens, 1869–1944

Sonning, Berkshire, England; 1901

Born in 1869, Sir Edwin Lutyens was an exact contemporary of Frank Lloyd Wright. He began independent practice early, in 1889, and until his appointment in 1912 to design the Viceroy's House in New Delhi, India, country houses for self-made, adventurous clients formed the core of his work. Unlike Wright, however, Lutyens was not a radical innovator. His houses share the same basic plan, and the genesis of their architecture can be traced back through the work of Philip Webb to the country vicarages of William Butterfield.

Like several of the seminal Modernist houses built after the First World War, Lutyens's houses were designed mostly for weekend use. The development of the railways opened up hitherto inaccessible locations, enabling their owners to commute at weekends, and they frequently entertained large numbers of guests. The plans are hierarchically organized to provide discrete accommodation for the family, guests and staff. Lutyens typically favoured an H-plan, entered from the north via a large vestibule and with dining room, hall and drawing/sitting room ranged to the south.

Built within an old brick wall enclosing the north end of an orchard, Deanery Garden exhibits many of the typical features of Lutyens's early style. The plan is arranged symmetrically around an enclosed court, but entered off-centre via a low, groin-vaulted passage along the court's east side. This route extends out as the main axis of the garden. It is marked on the garden front by the massive chimney in the corner of the sitting room, while the underlying symmetry is reasserted by the large oriel window of the double-height hall. Like the house, the garden is organized into separate 'rooms', connected by intersecting paths and woven into a complex play of asserted and subverted symmetries, made more intricate by changes of level.

The integration of house and garden was central to Lutyens's work, and the gardens were normally planted by one of the most celebrated of English gardeners, Gertrude Jekyll, whose mastery of informal planting provided a perfect foil for the strong architectural framework. The pergola, designed to echo the circulation routes through the house, culminates in a rose arbour overlooking the orchard, where old roses trail through the trees. Exotic plants are confined mostly to the terraces, and much of the geometry of the garden is softened by the native plants Jekyll loved.

Extending the architecture into the surroundings was one of several means by which Lutyens sought to enlarge the apparent size of his houses. The subdivision into separate realms, typically arranged around single-banked circulation routes, generated a high ratio of external wall to enclosed space, and at Deanery Garden the three reception rooms are linked by double doors. These form a cross axis running from the fireplace of the dining room to the bay window in the sitting room, uniting the rooms into a single space. The spatial integration is by no means as complete as in Wright's Prairie Houses, but Wright's 'destruction of the box' retained traces of similarly axial planning.

The use of red Berkshire bricks, tiled roof and leaded lights reflects Lutyens's interest in vernacular buildings, which he spent time studying before entering George's office. Internally the brickwork is plastered, but the ashlar used to dramatize the groin vaults runs into the vestibule and staircase. The latter, typical of Lutyens's designs at this time, is of richly elaborated oak construction. Each dowel is expressed, and the space between the joists of the landing is left open to allow light down to the vestibule below. This delight in details, although indebted to the Arts and Crafts movement, arose more from a Mannerist love of exaggeration than from a concern with constructional 'honesty'.

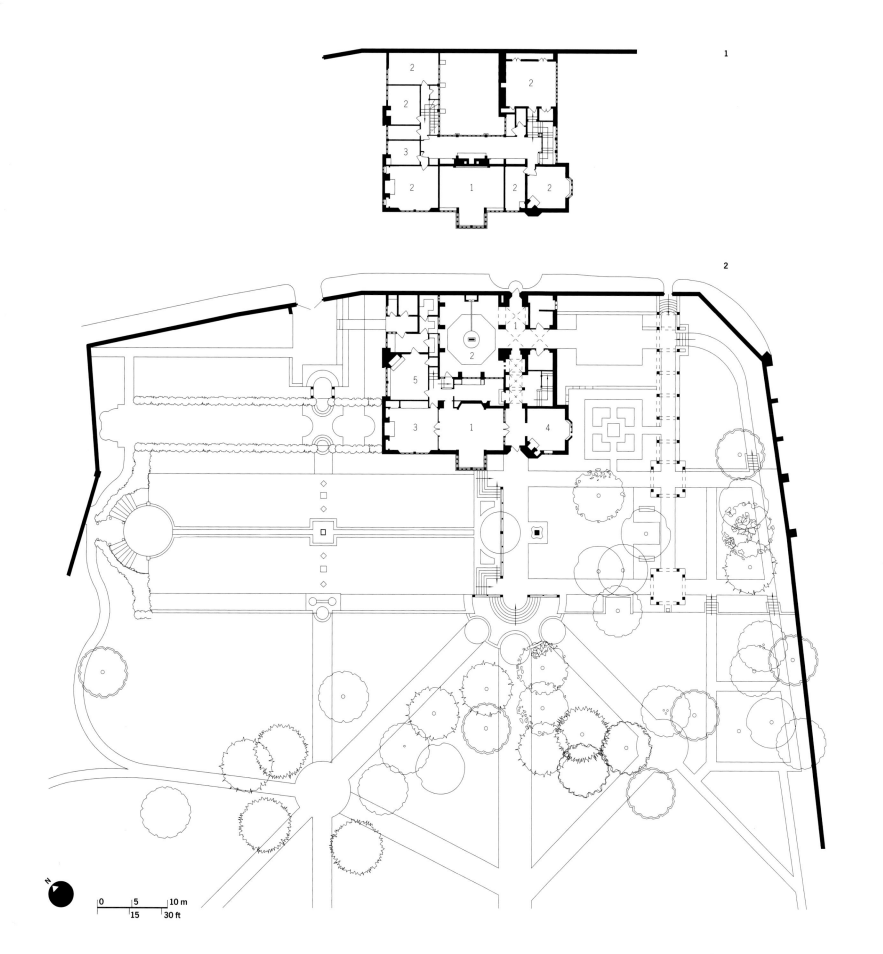

1

2

0   5   10 m
15   30 ft

Larkin Building

Frank Lloyd Wright, 1867–1959

Buffalo, New York, USA; 1902–6 (demolished)

By 1900 Frank Lloyd Wright had established a reputation in Chicago as a domestic architect of marked originality, and it was after seeing the earliest of his Prairie Houses that Darwin D. Martin, vice-president of the Larkin Soap Manufacturing Company, invited him to design a new administration building for their burgeoning mail-order business. It offered Wright the first opportunity to test his ideas on a large scale, and in a tough, urban context rather than in the leafy suburbs to which his 'organic' architecture might seem best suited. The site, locked between a railway and the company's manufacturing and storage facilities, was unprepossessing, and in response Wright made the building almost wholly introverted. No lover of the city, he was to follow much the same approach in almost all his urban commissions, such as those for the **Johnson Wax Administration Building** (page 82) and the **Guggenheim Museum** (page 88).

Wright described the exterior of the five-storey steel and reinforced concrete structure as 'a simple cliff of brick hermetically sealed', and planned the interior around a top-lit atrium — a pattern that would eventually become widespread in office buildings. Idealistically likening the workers to a great 'family gathering', he saw the building as a celebra-

tion of their collective effort. The frieze below the skylight was carved with suitably uplifting exhortations about the virtues of work and human solidarity, and in Wright's mind the central space clearly aspired to the scale and dignity of a cathedral nave.

Believing that space was the essence of architecture, Wright determined to free the 'great room' of the atrium of everything that might interfere with the enjoyment of its impressive volume. Stairs and services were placed in hollow piers at the corners of the building (the service ducts rise expressively above the stair towers), and these in turn were articulated from the main mass by narrow strips of glass, anticipating the comparable expression of 'servant and served' spaces in the work of Louis Kahn half a century later (**Richards Medical Research Building**, page 128). Similar hollow piers containing stairs were pulled out from one of the long sides to frame an annex housing lounges, bathrooms and the reception area. The main entrance slotted neatly into the gap between this ancillary block and the atrium, foreseeing the fully developed H-plan of **Unity Temple** (page 30).

The Larkin Company allowed Wright to treat the project, like his house interiors, as a *Gesamtkunstwerk*, in which every requirement was

to be re-thought and integrated as part of the whole. Filing cabinets, for example, were raised from the floor — for ease of cleaning and so as not to interrupt the continuity of space — and integrated into the spandrel panels around both the atrium and external walls: this arrangement provided a precedent for Mies van der Rohe's celebrated 1922 project for a Concrete Office Building. A similar raising of the WC cubicles was, according to Wright, the first time this almost ubiquitous feature of modern buildings was introduced.

The austere, strictly orthogonal forms of the Larkin Building, unrelieved by arises or mouldings at their corners, struck contemporary observers as excessively brutal and utilitarian, but to Wright they were a 'genuine and constructive affirmation of the new Order of this Machine Age ... a genuine expression of power directly applied to purpose, in the same sense that the ocean liner, the plane or the car is so'. We tend to associate such sentiments with the European Modernists of the 1920s, not with Wright, for whom Nature was an abiding inspiration. Such comparisons between architecture and 'machines' were becoming common in progressive circles around the turn of the century, but it was here that they first found compelling expression.

1 Office Area

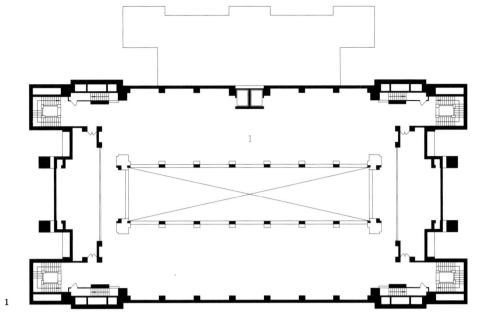

1 Office Area

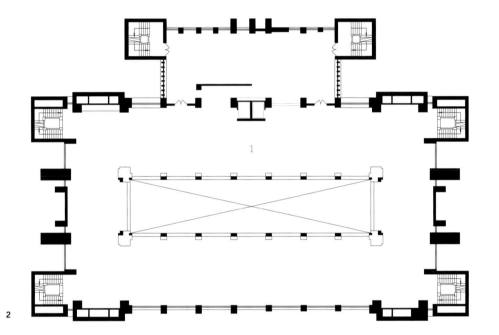

3 Ground Floor Plan

1 Office Area
2 Reception
3 Light Court
4 Entrance

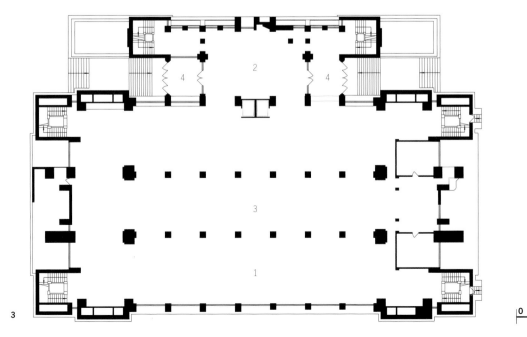

Post Office Savings Bank

Otto Wagner, 1841–1914

Vienna, Austria; 1903–12

Otto Wagner was the leading Viennese architect of his day and a distinguished teacher. As Professor of Architecture at the city's celebrated Academy, he influenced a talented younger generation, including Hoffmann, Olbrich and Plečnik, and was himself influenced by the radical ideas that culminated in the formation of the Vienna Secession in 1897.

The Post Office Savings Bank was a built exposition of ideas discussed in Wagner's 1896 book, *Modern Architecture*. Organizationally the building is not especially innovative: its fame rests on the cladding of the exterior, and on the interior of the banking hall. Cladding had become a key issue in the late nineteenth century, partly as a response to the replacement of loadbearing masonry walls with structural frames, and partly thanks to the development of ideas in Germany, above all in the work of Gottfried Semper.

In Semper's theory of 'The Four Elements of Architecture' the original role of providing enclosure is assigned to the 'wall fitter' or 'weaver of mats and carpets'. Even where solid walls became necessary for practical reasons, they should be treated, Semper argued, as the 'invisible structure hidden behind the true and legitimate representatives of the wall, the colourful woven carpets'. He identified

the cladding of a building with the dressing of the body, and used the same word, *Bekleidung*, for each. His consideration of fabrics in turn led him to formulate two principles: firstly, make a virtue out of necessity; and secondly, allow the material and process of fabrication to condition the end result.

The cladding of Wagner's bank presents a vivid illustration of these principles at work. Upper floors are clad with marble, the lower two with Swedish granite, and the entire façade is punctuated by what appears to be a grid of fixing bolts. In fact they are aluminium covers that make an ornamental virtue out of the hidden bolts used to retain the thin slabs while the mortar set. The bolt-heads could have been concealed, but, as Wagner pointed out, viewers familiar with the bolts and rivets of iron structures would understand them as fixings, making clear that the building is covered with thin slabs of stone. In *Modern Architecture* he had argued that the use of thin stone panels conspicuously 'bolted' to the façade was an essential feature of 'a modern way of building', not least because reducing the thickness of stone required meant that the finest materials could be afforded.

As in the works of Wagner's most famous students, such as Hoffmann's **Palais Stoclet** (page

32), the central banking hall can be seen as a *Gesamtkunstwerk*, in which every detail has been re-thought and integrated to form a seamless whole. But whereas in Hoffmann's work the logic of the total effect is predicated on strictly aesthetic grounds, here matters are rather more complex. The obscured glass lay-light roof, glass block floor and riveted steel structure would find many echoes throughout the twentieth century, most obviously in Chareau's **Maison de Verre** (page 64), and it is tempting to read them retrospectively as tokens of a potentially universal – even 'styleless' – Machine Age language to come. In fact, they are better understood in Semperian terms.

Like the diaphanous garments that clad the female body in Classical Greek sculptures, Wagner's glass surfaces seem to be designed to conceal as much as they reveal. As such, they belong to a very different world than the direct exposure of structure courtesy of transparent glass we encounter in much Modernist architecture. In this building they happily co-exist with Wagner's avowedly neo-Classical wooden furniture and the aluminium acroteria used externally along the cornice and attic storey. This symbiosis of old and new, traditional and synthetic materials was central to Wagner's mature style.

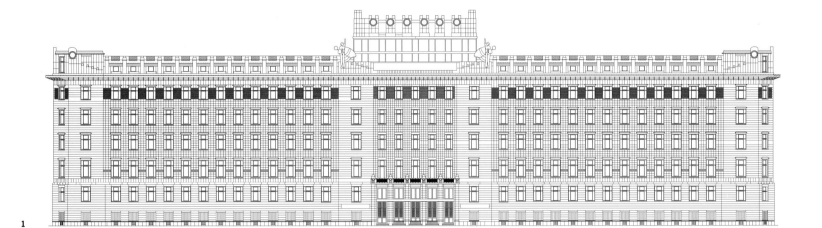

1

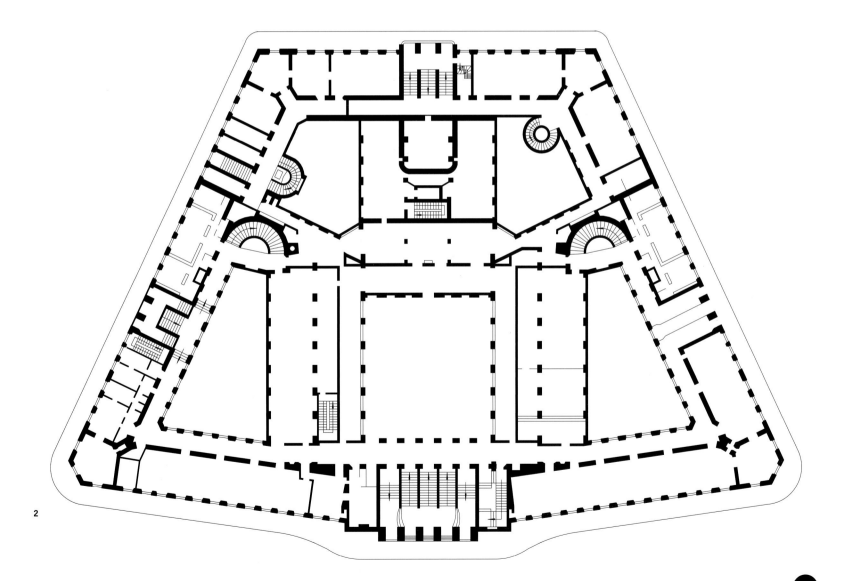

2

0   5   10 m
15   30 ft

Unity Temple

Frank Lloyd Wright, 1867–1959

Oak Park, Illinois, USA; 1905–8

As a member of the Unitarian church in Oak Park, Frank Lloyd Wright was a natural choice of architect for their new building. He had been raised in the faith and his uncle, Jenkin Lloyd Jones, was the most acclaimed Unitarian preacher in the area. The Unitarians' beliefs placed as much emphasis on reason as on faith. In response, Wright rejected orthodox models for church buildings, proposing instead a square auditorium in which the audience could gather around the preacher: this was, in his eyes, 'a frank revival of the old temple form'.

In addition to the main space for worship, the brief called for accommodation to serve the congregation's social and educational needs. Wright called this Unity House, and arranged the two elements either side of a shared entrance – a fully developed version of the bipolar plan implicit in the **Larkin Building** (page 26). The projects share other key features, from the introverted plan, designed to secure the peace of the interior on a busy corner site, to the provision of services in hollow piers and the block-like external massing. In Unity Temple, however, the exterior expresses rather than masks the internal organization, and it was here that Wright felt that the internal space first came through as the basis of the architecture.

The plan of the worship space is a perfect square that Wright deftly turned into a stubby Greek cross by the placement of the hollow service piers. Corner-stairs lead up to the balconies that occupy three sides of the square, and the fourth is filled by the pulpit, choir and organ loft. The central square is covered by a five-by-five grid of square skylights, while a clerestory around the arms of the cross – that stand higher than the stair towers – rings the space with daylight. The glass in the roof-lights is pale yellow, which Wright later explained as an attempt 'to get a sense of a happy cloudless day into the room'. This inner sanctum is reached by an exquisitely orchestrated sequence of changes in level, light and space, beginning with the paths that are partially sheltered by an overhanging roof plane. These lead up via short flights of steps to the raised platform and loggia that link Unity Temple and Unity House.

Entering the building, you find yourself in semi-darkness at the same level as Unity House but half a level below the main floor of the church, under which a semi-basement houses cloakrooms and storage. The view into Unity House is open and focused – as in a Prairie House – on a large fireplace, while that into the church is screened by a flat wall that directs you to the corner entrances. Turning twice through 90 degrees you discover the dark, subterranean passages Wright called 'cloisters', and from there narrow stairs lead up into the light. Wright masterfully completed the sequence by leading the congregation forward after the service, past the pulpit and down via stairs either side of it that were artfully hidden from view on entering by the same screen wall that controls your access.

Externally, Unity Temple is an almost monolithic construction of mass and reinforced concrete. Internally, in complete contrast, Wright transformed the entire volume into a purely plastic composition. By interweaving lines and planes and by masking or eliminating conventional expressions of load and support, ornament and construction, he removed all feeling of weight. The new unity of space, light and interpenetrating planes, wholly abstract in conception, was an apt expression of the Unitarians' religious and philosophical ideals. Formally it anticipated the mature expression of the Dutch De Stijl movement (as seen, for example, in the **Schröder House**, page 48), even if here, as in much of Wright's work, traces of Beaux-Arts symmetry and axiality continue to underpin the spatial order.

1 First Floor Plan	2 West Elevation	3 Ground Floor Plan	4 Section

1 Auditorium
2 Platform
3 Organ Space
4 Ceiling Light
5 Classroom
6 Sewing Room
7 Toilet
8 Storage

1 Cloister
2 Coat room
3 Foyer
4 Unity House
5 Classroom
6 Kitchen
7 Toilets
8 Storage
9 Terrace

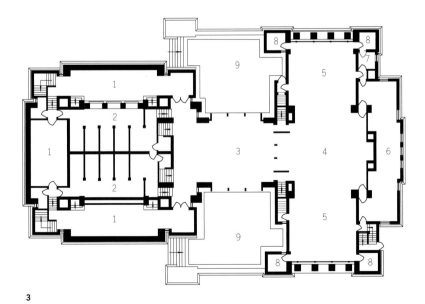

1

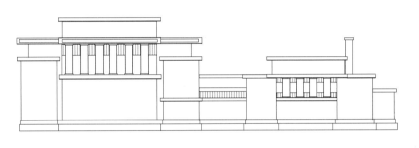

2

3

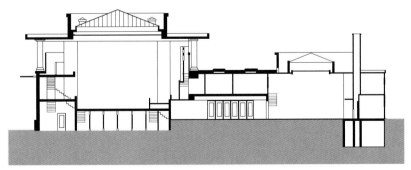

4

0   5   10 m
15   30 ft

Palais Stoclet

Josef Hoffmann, 1870–1956

Brussels, Belgium; 1905–11

In 1903, the architect Josef Hoffmann and artist Koloman Moser formed the studios and workshops known as the Wiener Werkstätte. In the spirit of William Morris, their programme stated that, 'We consider it our most noble duty to regain for the workers a joy in work and an existence worthy of a human being.' The Werkstätte was dedicated to the creation of *Gesamtkunstwerken*, total works of art, and the first opportunity to realize such a building came in Brussels courtesy of Adolphe Stoclet, a Belgian financier who had lived in Vienna, and his wife Suzanne. The brief was to create a house in which to exhibit their ever-growing collection of art and to entertain the artistic élite of Europe – the guest book contains the names of Diaghilev, Paderewski, Stravinsky, Cocteau, Anatole France…

The site, on the edge of the built-up area on the Avenue de Tervueren, a continuation of the prestigious Rue de la Loi, enjoyed fine views south. To take advantage of these, Hoffmann arranged the accommodation as an axially composed sequence of en-suite rooms forming a linear block facing the road. The major reception spaces are expressed as boldly projecting bays, establishing a subtle interplay of crossing axes that extends out into the garden. The planning was accomplished but not innovative,

still rooted in Classical principles, and what makes Palais Stoclet remarkable is Hoffmann's handling of surfaces and the sophistication of the interior.

Palais Stoclet was built of brick and clad in large, thin slabs of stone, a perfect example of 'the slablike treatment of the surface' that Hoffmann's teacher, Otto Wagner, had proposed as a mark of Modern architecture. The size of the slabs showed that they must be a thin veneer, not an ashlar wall, and like Wagner, who had famously used exposed fixings like 'nails' on the **Post Office Savings Bank** in Vienna (page 28), Hoffmann was at pains to emphasize that this was cladding not solid masonry. He did so by marking corners and framing openings with thin metal profiles that appear like tautly stretched ropes. The result is striking, even disconcerting, completely undermining the visible interaction of load and support that had underpinned the formal expression of much previous architecture. In Palais Stoclet the windows are no longer holes in a wall but rectangular surfaces on – and in some cases actually in front of – the wall. The volumes read as compositions of planes, emphasizing the geometric purity of the design, and the effect is so light as to feel almost surreal. Hoffmann exploits the planar quality to dramatic effect in details such

as the covered seating area carved out of the garden elevation, where the sagging soffit and façade above seem to hang languorously and, thanks to the doubling of the mouldings, appear almost ready to slide down like a giant gate.

The sumptuous interiors were designed collaboratively with Hoffmann's Secession colleagues, and in lesser hands could have been oppressive. The refinement and control, however, are masterly. The dining room walls, for example, are recessed in three stages: dark Portovenere marble and macassar wood cabinets project furthest, recessed above them is a band of light Paonozzo marble, and above and behind that are mosaic decorations by Klimt. Less opulent but no less remarkable was the ample main bathroom, with its walls of pale marble inlaid with strips of black marble and malachite and purpose-made furnishings and silver toilet articles.

More completely than any other building, arguably, Palais Stoclet exemplified the *fin-de-siècle* ideal of the aestheticization of life over which the architect and artist assumed control, transforming the dwelling from a setting for normal, everyday life into a higher realm consecrated by art. Early visitors reported that the Stoclets lived out this vision, achieving perfect harmony with their surroundings.

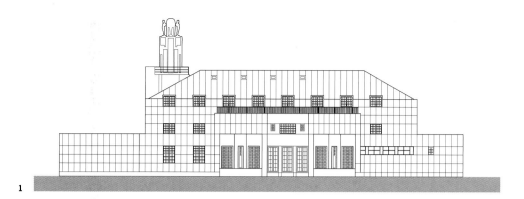

1

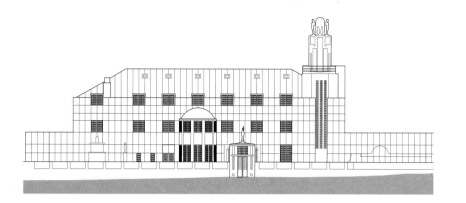

2 Front Elevation

2

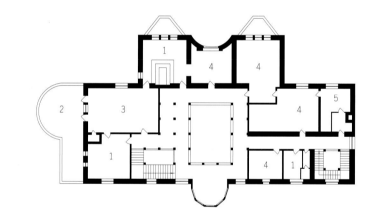

3 First Floor Plan

1 Bathroom
2 Terrace
3 Bedroom
4 Children's Room
5 Ladies' Room

3

4 Ground Floor Plan

1 Entrance Hall
2 Terrace
3 Drawing Room
4 Lavatory
5 Stage
6 Music Room
7 Men's Room
8 Dining Room
9 Hallway
10 Cloarkroom
11 WC
12 Breakfast Room
13 Pantry
14 Kitchen
15 Servants' Room
16 Servants' Dining Room
17 Courtyard
18 Garage
19 Coal
20 Larder
21 Meat Room

N

4

0	5	10 m
	15	30 ft

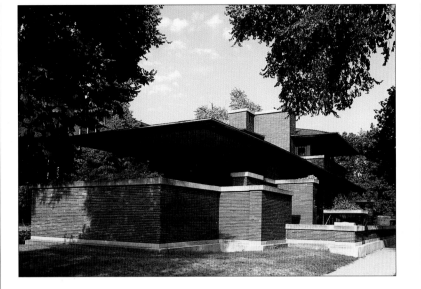

Robie House

Frank Lloyd Wright, 1867–1959

Chicago, Illinois, USA; 1908

The Robie House represents what Wright came to regard as the most extreme and conclusive development of what he christened the Prairie House, a type that crystallized six years earlier with the building of the Willits House. There, the major ground floor rooms in the cruciform plan were overlapped to form a continuous space around a central fireplace. Although radically innovative, the axial organization nonetheless retained traces of the Beaux-Arts system, and can interestingly be compared with a more overtly traditional design such as Lutyens's **Deanery Garden** (page 24). The openness, however, was unprecedented, as was the idea – already encountered in **Unity Temple** (page 30) – that the internal spatial organization should come through in every aspect of the exterior.

Frederick Robie was a typical Wright client, an inventor who made bicycles and car parts in his father's firm. He bought a site in south Chicago that was tighter than the suburban plots Wright was used to working with. It demanded three floors of accommodation rather than the usual two, but at first sight Robie House appears to have a single, elevated level with a small addition emerging from the overhanging roofs. In fact there is also an almost invisible ground floor, like a basement above ground.

The house hugs the ground, yet, thanks to the judicious use of hidden steelwork and massive cantilevers, the elevated brick walls and deeply undercut roofs feel as if they can defy gravity. The pervasive horizontality is reinforced by the exposed stone foundations and lines of copings and subtly stressed by the long Roman bricks laid in thick, plain mortar beds; the narrower vertical joints are also suppressed, by being pointed in coloured mortar to match the brick. Wright's attention to detail was total and nothing was allowed to contradict the horizontality – he saw 'the strong earth-line' as an expression of home and symbol of freedom in the American landscape.

The Robie House plan has traces of the classic cruciform type, but to fit the site it was transformed into a long room, set against a service block and with a vestigial cross-axis marked by the entrance – located out of sight around the back to ensure privacy, to avoid breaking up the street frontage and to heighten the sense of arrival. The large fireplace is in its familiar place at the heart of the house, sunk into the floor to imply vertical continuity and opened above to allow an almost uninterrupted horizontal flow of space between the living and the dining room.

Both ends of the main volume terminate in pointed prows framed by staggered piers and the perimeter is enclosed by a ribbon of doors and windows, all glazed with leaded lights of Wright's design. The composite effect is the dissolution of solid enclosure and the framing of space by folding planes – what Wright would later call 'the destruction of the box'. Artificial lighting, heating and ventilation are integrated seamlessly into the design: pierced wooden grilles above the windows conceal lamps that cast a dappled light onto the floor, while small globes are suspended from the oak strips that weave their way across the ceiling to reinforce the feeling of a folded plane floating overhead.

Contemporary observers nicknamed the house a 'ship of the prairie', and in it Wright subjected the traditional image of the house – still secure in his 1893 Winslow House design – to a series of formal transformations. The dwelling is reinvented as abstract planes defining shifting geometric shapes in which traditional distinctions between wall and window, inside and out, cease to be valid. The real prairie may have been physically distant from Wright's Prairie Houses, but he captures its openness through spatial and formal continuity. This process reached its high-point in the Robie House.

1 Section

2 First Floor Plan

1 Living Room
2 Dining Room
3 Guest Room
4 Kitchen
5 Servants' Quarters

3 Ground Floor Plan

1 Billiard Room
2 Playroom
3 Garage
4 Service Yard

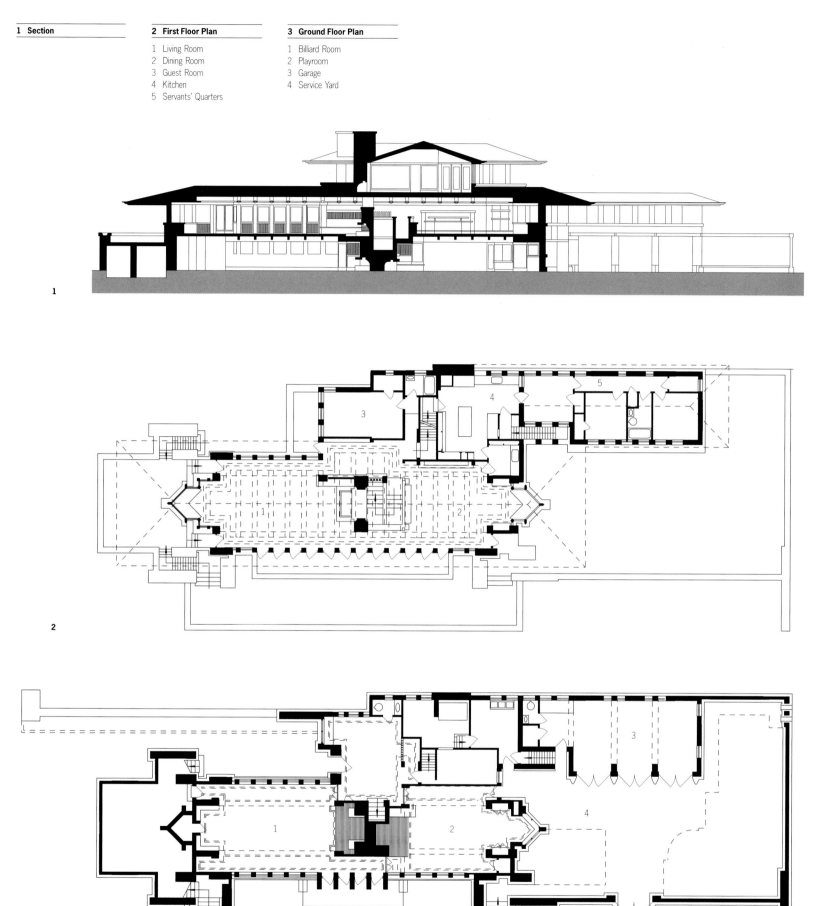

1

2

3

N

0		5		10 m
	15		30 ft	

Turbine Factory

Peter Behrens, 1868–1940

Berlin, Germany; 1908–10

In 1907, designer-turned-architect Peter Behrens was appointed as 'artistic adviser' to the giant electrical company Allgemeine Elektricitäts-Gesellschaft (AEG). He was given total control over the company's visual image, with authority to advise on everything from the design of letterheads and electrical kettles to entire buildings. The following year he began work on what was to prove his masterpiece.

From today's perspective the brief was hardly promising: a vast steel-framed shed, robust enough to support the 100-ton loads carried by the pair of vast, travelling cranes used in the assembly of the massive turbines. But at the time great significance was attached to turbines as quintessentially modern sources of power and, sited at the corner of AEG's extensive works in Berlin, the new building would act as the showpiece for the entire complex.

Built in two phases, the finished factory is over 207 metres (679 feet) in length. The structure was designed by the engineer Karl Bernhard as an asymmetrical, three-pinned arch, restrained by tie rods. The largest structural section rises from impressive pin-joints that punctuate the long street frontage – external tokens of the imposing mechanical work within – and then arches over to reach the apex of the roof. There, a further pin-joint connects

it to the smaller members that spring from the junction with the lower, two-storey section to the rear. The bare structural necessities worked out with the engineer were only the starting point for Behrens. Contrary to nineteenth-century expressions of iron construction, such as Paxton's Crystal Palace, he wanted to make out of the necessary construction an emphatic mass, not a dematerialized network of slender structural members and transparent glass. The upper sections of the arches are fabricated as open lattices, but the vertical sections, riveted from flat plates, appear reassuringly solid. Along the public side elevation, their solidity is emphasized by inclining the glazing, and concrete panels below it, to follow the tapering inner profile of the structure.

On the temple-like front elevation, the concrete panels are wrapped around the corner and stacked to fill the entire height of the building up to the underside of the roof. The joints are marked by iron bands and, like the glazing of the side elevations, the vertical profile follows the tapering structure to yield a pair of inward-leaning pylons framing a vertical screen of steel-framed glass, the vertical members of which support the polygonal gable. The latter lies in the same plane as the glass and is framed by a concealed iron truss. The other two

elevations were left to Bernhard and emerged as more direct expressions of the constructional facts. On the building's two public elevations, Behrens insisted on an essentially Classical expression of the building as a solid, corporeal form. The result was decidedly ambiguous: although the concrete infill panels were detailed to suggest their role as infill, their heaviness suggests a load-bearing role, and few people looking at the building's exposed corner are likely to appreciate that the massive-looking concrete pylons are non-structural. But in fact the solid body of the roof rests on the steel structure set back from the corner, and the concrete could have been replaced with versions of what would soon be established as the iconic expression of the 'destruction of the box', the corner window.

The importance of the building was that it brought the utilitarian factory firmly into the domain of architectural tradition. To Behrens, a monumental statement of the institutions of an industrial civilization could be achieved only by embracing Classical values, even if this necessitated the radical inversion of Classical norms implicit in a factory modelled on a Greek temple in which the corners are intended to be read as infill, not structure, and the central void is emphatically not an entrance.

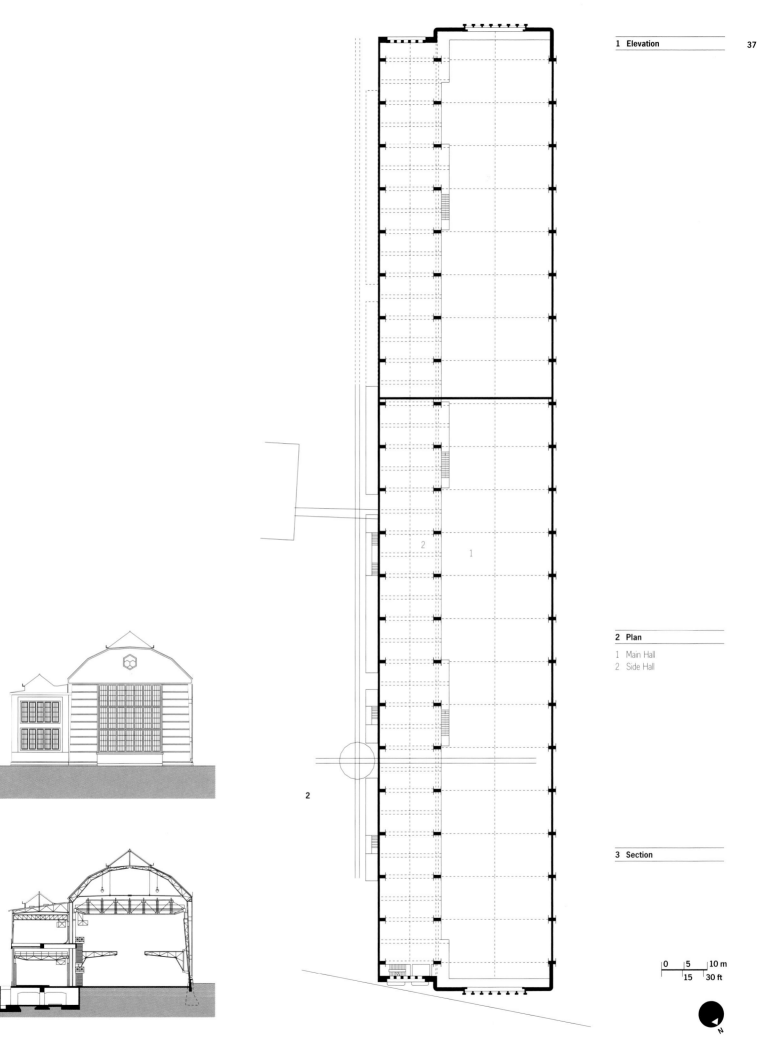

2 **Plan**
1 Main Hall
2 Side Hall

3 **Section**

0   5   10 m
  15   30 ft

Casa Milá

Antoni Gaudí, 1852–1926

Barcelona, Spain; 1906–10

Born into a relatively poor family, plagued by illness, and increasingly devoted to a conservative Catholic faith, Antoni Gaudí was an unlikely architectural revolutionary. As a student he devoured the ideas of John Ruskin while Viollet-le-Duc's great *Dictionnaire*, an exhaustive account of French Gothic, became his bible. And as a young architect, he embraced the popular neo-Gothic manner before exploring Moorish influences, mixing cheap rubble with exotic-looking ceramic tiles in the Casa Vicens (1888).

Gaudí's originality grew out of his love for, and critique of, Gothic structure. He regarded the flying buttresses developed to resist the outward thrust of the ceiling vaults as makeshift 'crutches', and resolved to find a way to do without them. Gradually the idea of leaning columns emerged and, once mastered, became the leitmotif of his mature work.

Casa Milá, a large apartment building, presented Gaudí with major practical challenges. Occupying a typical chamfered corner in Barcelona's celebrated grid-plan laid out by the engineer Alfonso Cerdá, the site was — at some 1,000 square metres (over 10,000 square feet) — both large and deep. Externally, Gaudí all but eliminated the corner, absorbing the three, normally distinct, frontages into a continuous, rippling mass of stone, its

smooth forms emphasized by the endlessly inventive wrought-iron balcony fronts, designed by his most gifted assistant, Josep Maria Jujol. The façade had thereby been transformed into a deeply indented zone in which traditional distinctions between wall and window no longer apply. It became known locally as La Pedrera, 'the quarry', but despite the marked stratification, any resemblance to an actual quarry was slight. The only real models were to be found in Gaudí's earlier work, most obviously the sinuous bench that frames the elevated plaza in the Güell Park — echoed here on the roof.

The plasticity of the exterior extended to every part of the design — indeed it is perhaps better seen as the out-working of an inner formal impulse. In place of the familiar square patios of conventional apartment buildings, Gaudí deployed two rounded light-wells that grow outwards as they rise, like giant funnels designed to draw down light and air. And on the roof — which resembles an undulating landscape beneath the sky — Gaudí transformed the chimneys and air ducts into giant, playful figures whose forms seem, to modern eyes, to look simultaneously back to ancient cultures and forward to Modernist sculptures or to the aliens of science fiction films.

Casa Milá is far from just a *tour de force* of form-making, however. As if in anticipation of the underground garage to come, the basement houses cars, while the variety of apartment plans above is remarkable, changing both laterally and from floor to floor. Gaudí was able to achieve this by eliminating load-bearing walls and replacing them with a system of columns and piers. The result is, however, far from the Modernist 'open plan' with its systematic column-grid and floor plates. Here, erratically placed leaning columns support steel beams, and from these spring the shallow vaults of the rooms. The undulating façade is both a plastic composition in its own right and a more or less direct transcription of the rising and falling ceilings of the rooms within, which feel like cells in an organic whole.

Commenting on Casa Batlló, a smaller apartment building completed just before Casa Milá, Gaudí declared that 'the corners will vanish, and the material will reveal itself in the wealth of its astral curves; the sun will shine through all four sides, and it will be like a vision of paradise'. Almost a century later, organic forms are again a subject of interest in architecture, but nothing achieved in recent years comes close to rivalling Gaudí's inventiveness or rigour in integrating plastic form and structure.

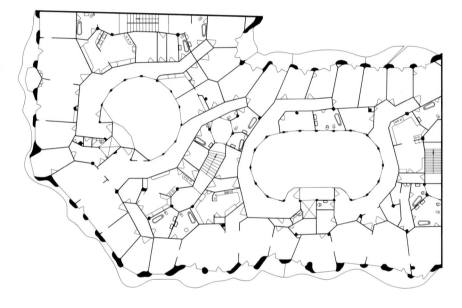

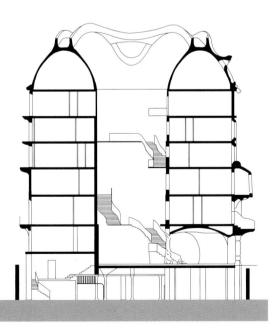

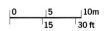

Glass Pavilion

Bruno Taut, 1880–1938

Deutscher Werkbund Exhibition, Cologne, Germany; 1914 (temporary pavilion)

Founded in 1907, the Deutsche Werkbund promoted better design through the joint efforts of artists, craftsmen and manufacturers. It was an uneasy alliance of those who advocated an outright commitment to industrialization and those who believed in the value of individual artistic expression. Nowhere did this produce a more startling result than in this Glass Pavilion, designed by Bruno Taut for the Werkbund's first exhibition.

Taut's client was the association of German glass industries, who wanted a structure to demonstrate the potential of different kinds of glass in architecture. For Taut, the commission transcended commercial aspirations, offering the opportunity to give expression to the vision of a Glass Architecture that had become central to the Expressionist circle of which he was a leading member. *Glasarchikektur* was, in fact, the title of a book published the same year by the poet Paul Scheerbart: aphorisms from it were inscribed on the vestigial entablature around the building, and Scheerbart's ideas also inspired the ritualistic composition of the interior. For Scheerbart, opening rooms to 'the light of the sun, the moon, and the stars … through every possible wall' was a way to 'bring us a new culture'. Unlike centuries of 'brick culture' that had hemmed peo-

ple in, the 'glass environment' was, he believed, the means by which to 'transform mankind'.

Externally, the faceted, diagrid structure of the cupola is calculated to recall the complex geometry of nature, while exploring its symmetrical internal composition must have felt like negotiating the inner passages of a mysterious glass body. The raised, quasi-sacred level under the cupola was reached via the pavilion's best-known features – glass-treaded staircases screened by glass-block walls. The surviving black-and-white photographs give only a pale impression of the 'cosmic' central space, bathed in coloured light that was reflected and multiplied by a seven-tiered water cascade. From under the cupola, visitors embarked on a protracted rite of passage through narrow spaces lined from floor to ceiling in coloured glass mosaics. These led to a small projection room and then, rather unceremoniously, out into the real world.

1914 also saw the founding, by Taut, of the magazine *Frühlicht* (Dawn's Light). It acted as a focus for his Expressionist circle and the iconography of glass on which they drew can be traced back to accounts of Solomon's Temple in the Bible and Koran. It was also steeped in the medieval aesthetic tradition that equated 'beautiful' with 'lucid',

'luminous' and 'clear': one of Taut's early drawings for the Pavilion describes it as having been made in the spirit of a Gothic cathedral. Writing about it, the critic Adolf Behne suggested that the 'longing for purity and clarity, for glowing lightness, crystalline exactness, for immaterial lightness, infinite liveliness, found in glass a means of fulfilment'. And four years later, in the aftermath of war, he said that 'building with glass … would be the surest way of transforming the European into a human being'.

The passion for glass found its most extravagant expression in Taut's book *Alpine Architecture*. Published in 1919, it envisaged embellishing the Alps with glass structures lit by coloured beacons, a monumental work of construction to counter the destruction of war. The Glass Pavilion itself can be seen as a prototype of such structures, and in Taut's thinking, like a Gothic cathedral, it was also a model for the *Stadtkronen* (city crowns) he believed should form the symbolic focus of communities. Just such a structure, in a woodcut by Lionel Feininger, figured on the cover of the Bauhaus manifesto published by Walter Gropius in 1919, but two years later the tide turned decisively against the quasi-medieval devotion to craft in favour of industrial design.

1

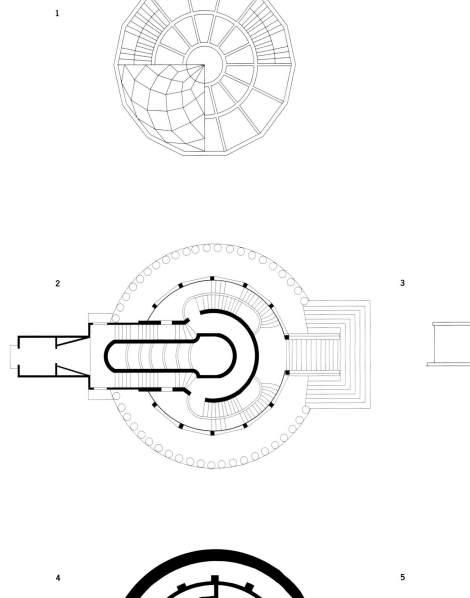

2

3

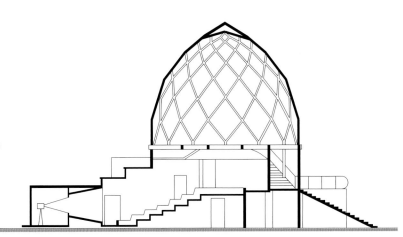

4

5

Stockholm Public Library

Erik Gunnar Asplund, 1885–1940

Stockholm, Sweden; 1918–27

Throughout Europe following the First World War there was an almost wholesale rejection of individualistic expression, epitomized by Art Nouveau, and of overtly national variations of that style – developed, most famously, in Catalonia, but also extensively in eastern and northern Europe. For many, Classicism was seen as representing the timeless core of European values, and the most original development of the Classical language came in the Nordic countries. First revealed to the wider world in Paris at the 1925 Exhibition of Decorative Arts, where it was christened 'Swedish Grace', this fascinating but short-lived style, now generally known as Nordic Classicism, was largely written out of architectural history, only to be re-evaluated in the 1980s. Gunnar Asplund was its leading exponent, and the Stockholm Public Library his major achievement, before, like many of the young Classicists, he embraced the new ideas developing on the Continent.

In Sweden in 1918 a public library was a novel building type and Asplund was originally appointed to research the brief and prepare a competition programme. He visited the USA, where public libraries were most widely developed, thanks to the efforts of philanthropists such as Andrew Carnegie, and as his work progressed it became clear that he was best equipped to carry out the job. The basic form of the building, quickly established, was starkly neo-Classical: a centralized composition, circle within square.

The site was on a prominent corner at the junction of one of Stockholm's major thoroughfares, Sveavägen, with Odengatan, and the design went through two distinct phases. Initially, Asplund envisaged a free-standing building with a dome crowning the circular lending room and tall porticoes on three sides framed by pairs of Corinthian columns. The interior would have been flooded with light through multiple arched openings in the dome – complete voids where coffers might have been expected – and the difficulty of entering such a centralized space was to have been solved by admitting visitors from below, up a long scala regia, almost into the centre of the room.

As part of a larger urban proposition, Asplund then decided to place the building on a platform, occupied by shops, that extended laterally to make a connection to a new urban park along Sveavägen; to the side, along Odengatan, he envisaged a low market building, but this remained unrealized. As the design progressed, Asplund pared away many of the overtly Classical features and ornament. The dome disappeared, replaced by an upwards extension of the cylinder to form a projecting drum. The porticoes were reduced to tall, Egyptianate portals and the entrance corridor and stair were narrowed and lined with high walls of black polished stucco – a deliberately dark preparation for the light-filled lending hall. Hanging at its centre, and the focus of attention as you ascend, is a huge, glowing bowl-shaped chandelier. The room is lined with three tiers of books, arrayed in exquisite wooden cases; above, white-painted walls of rough stucco rise sheer and bright below a ring of clerestorey windows.

By the time he finished the library, Asplund was becoming aware of the radical ideas emanating from Germany. His embrace of what would be known as Functionalism was immediate, and the large sheets of glass and abstract treatment of the shop-fronts in the base, completed in 1928, reflect the new style. The result is far from incongruous, because their forms were indebted to the same 'timeless' ideals typified by Classicism. With their emphasis on basic architectural values – clarity of form, proportion and geometry – and preference for immaterial, seemingly weightless effects, the formal tropes of Nordic Classicism had much in common with those advocated by the Modernists.

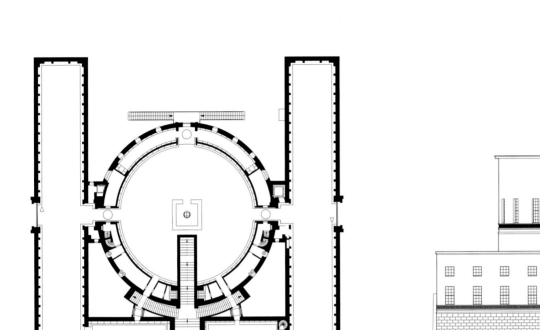

1

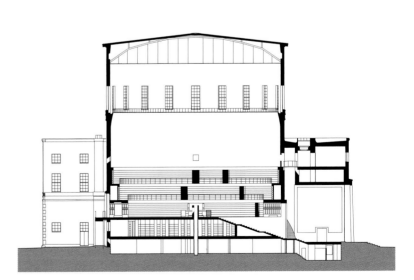

2

3

4

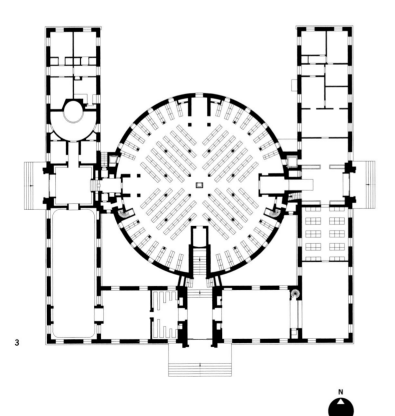

N

0   5   10 m
15   30 ft

Einstein Tower

Eric Mendelsohn, 1887–1953

Potsdam, Germany; 1919–24

Mendelsohn's Einstein Tower is one of the most celebrated achievements of the so-called Expressionist movement that flourished in Germany and The Netherlands in the years either side of the First World War. The term Expressionism is notoriously imprecise, used both to denote works characterized by spiky, jagged or curvilinear forms, which are often described as 'anti-rational', and also to suggest that such forms are expressive of a particular, often heightened, state of emotion – an idea that found extended theoretical support in Wilhelm Worringer's seminal *Abstraktion und Einfühlung* (Abstraction and Empathy), published in 1907.

Two influences played a major part in Mendelsohn's development. Firstly, the work and ideas of the leading Belgian practitioner of Jugendstil, Henry van de Velde, who believed that buildings and furniture should be conceived as 'living organisms' that express the play of internal forces through their structure – a position close to that of Antoni Gaudí (**Casa Milá**, page 38). And secondly, the *Blaue Reiter* (Blue Rider) group of artists, with whom he came into contact in 1911 while in Munich. Their intuitive approach to form-making had 'cosmic' overtones, and the most

influential among them, the Russian Wassily Kandinsky, was a leading advocate of abstraction as an expression of spiritual values.

The first manifestations of Mendelsohn's ideas were produced in the most improbable of circumstances – while he was serving in the First World War trenches. The sketches he made there captured the basic forms of a series of buildings – an observatory, film studio, railway station – in a few calligraphic lines that suggest the continuity of a single formal impulse expressed in what he liked to call a 'dynamic' form. His first opportunity to build these ideas could hardly have been more felicitous: the Einstein Tower was an observatory commissioned by the leading astro-physicist Erwin Finlay-Freundlich and, as its name implies, was intended as a monument to the most revolutionary theory in modern science.

The links between energy and mass postulated by the Special Theory of Relativity reinforced Mendelsohn's conviction that Modernity must be expressed through dynamic forms. His early sketches for the tower had little of the force of his wartime studies, but these quickly gave way to drawings intended to convey the feeling that the tower was shedding mass as it appeared almost

to grow out of the landscape, like some strange plant or geological formation – although, judging by contemporary reactions, this interpretation seems to have been lost on all but Mendelsohn's own circle. The leaning, gravity-defying forms were to be made possible by reinforced concrete, but in the final building, much to Mendelsohn's disappointment, economies dictated that it had to be combined with large areas of rendered brickwork.

The functional armature of the building – a vertical shaft housing a solar instrument, known as a coelestat, that reflected rays of sunlight into a horizontal, underground laboratory – was determined by the scientific requirements, but in developing the spaces around it Mendelsohn had great freedom. The forms he created appear to have been swept back by some invisible force, giving the impression that the building itself is in motion. Believing that science and industry could be new sources of cultural energy, Mendelsohn saw the Tower as a demonstration of the machine's potential to become the 'constructive element of a new, living organism'.

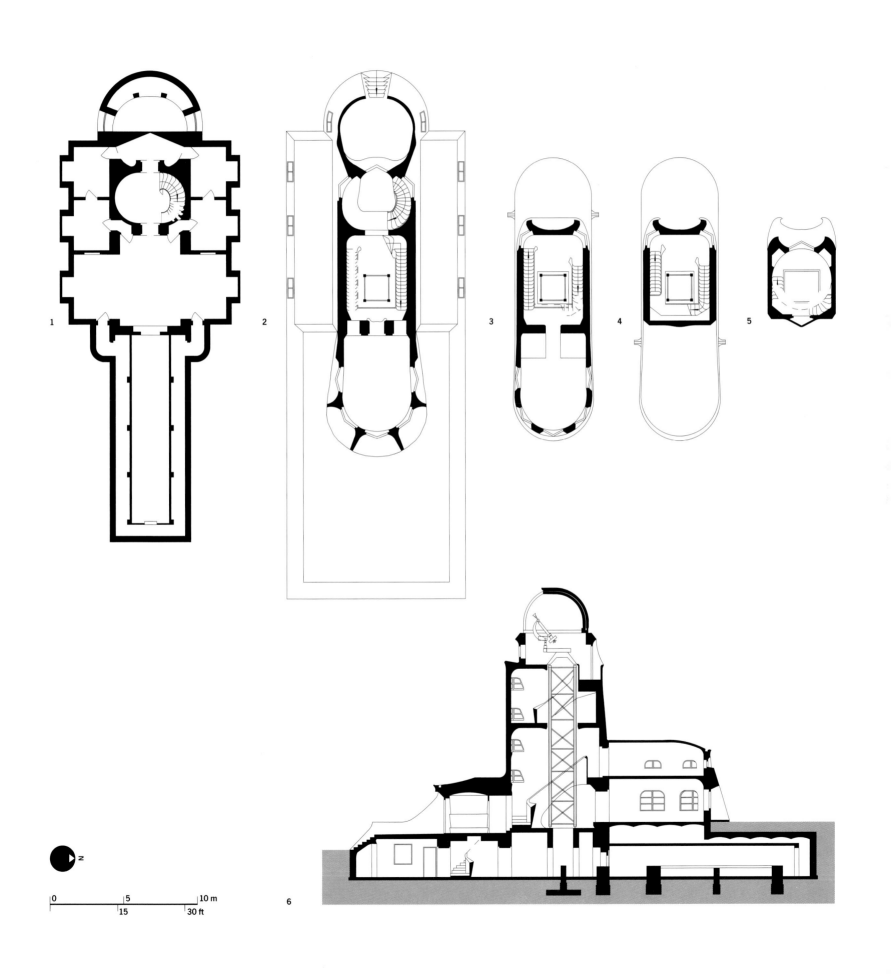

1

2

3

4

5

6

0   5   10 m
    15   30 ft

Schindler-Chace House

Rudolf Schindler, 1887–1953

West Hollywood, California, USA; 1921–2

Viennese-born Rudolf Schindler looked first to Adolf Loos as his mentor and then, after discovering his work through the Wasmuth portfolios in 1910, to Frank Lloyd Wright. On the eve of the First World War he decided to leave for America, and three years later, in 1917, started working for Wright at his Taliesin home and studio in Wisconsin. In 1920 he was despatched to California by Wright to assist on one of his most important commissions, the Hollyhock House. In response to the benign climate, Wright designed it to be as much 'outside as inside', with the main bedroom – which Schindler detailed – conceived as a tent-like space hovering among the trees.

After moving to California, Schindler also got to know the work of Irving Gill who, like Wright, originally hailed from Chicago. Inspired by the local Spanish mission buildings, Gill built several cubic, whitewashed, flat-roofed, asymmetrical houses that were totally devoid of ornamentation. All these early influences, filtered through the floating world of Japan, can be discerned in Schindler's first and arguably finest building, a double-house built for himself, his wife and their friends Clyde and Marian Chace on North Kings Road, West Hollywood, in 1921–2.

The inspiration to live in a radically new kind of house sprang from a camping and horse-riding trip the Schindlers took in Yosemite Valley. They wanted a house as open to nature as a tent, and after pooling resources with the Chaces decided that each couple should have an L-shaped wing. Explaining the design in a letter to Pauline Schindler's parents, who were to lend most of the funds, they pointed out that each couple would have 'large studio rooms – with concrete walls on three sides, the front open (glass) to the outdoors – a real California scheme. On the roof two "sleeping baskets" are provided – for open-air sleeping – with temporary covers for rainy nights.'

The open garden fronts were fitted with large sliding doors, above which two cantilevered beams supported an overhanging roof, sliding light fittings and movable partitions. The varied roof levels, rooftop sleeping baskets and close integration between the rooms and patios produced a complex, three-dimensional interlocking of house and garden. The 'honest' exposure of natural finishes and materials, expressed timber structure and *shoji*-like panels of the interior were deeply marked by Japanese influence, and no doubt the planning, too, owed something to the echelon

arrangement of Japanese houses such as the Katsura Detached Villa in Kyoto. The comprehensive spatial integration of internal and external space was, however, new: a response to the climate as well as to emerging architectural ideas, it anticipated the relaxed Californian lifestyle that blossomed after 1945 – epitomized by such designs as the **Eames House** (page 90) and Neutra's **Kaufmann Desert House** (page 94).

Schindler went on to develop a formal language based on wood framing and stucco and produced a steady stream of fine domestic projects into the early 1950s. Only the Lovell Beach House of 1922–6, however, rivalled the poetry and originality of the Kings Road houses, but when Lovell came to build a far larger, permanent house in the Hollywood Hills, he turned – in circumstances that remain contentious – to Schindler's friend Richard Neutra. The **Lovell 'Health House'** (page 54) was destined to become one of the earliest and most important International Style buildings in America.

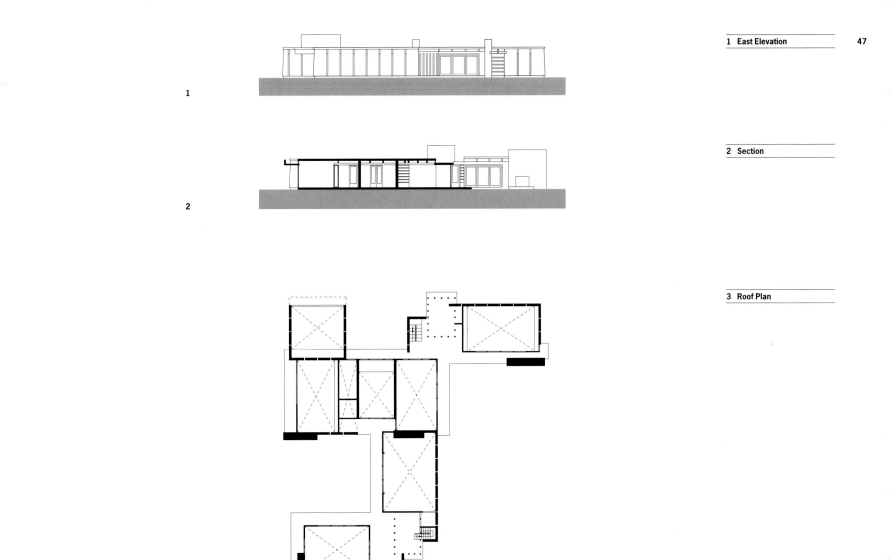

1

2

3

4

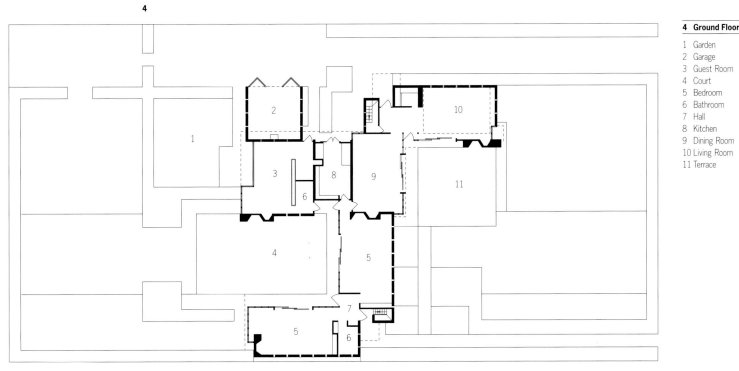

4 **Ground Floor Plan**

1 Garden
2 Garage
3 Guest Room
4 Court
5 Bedroom
6 Bathroom
7 Hall
8 Kitchen
9 Dining Room
10 Living Room
11 Terrace

```
0      5      10 m
   15     30 ft
```

N

Schröder House

Gerrit Rietveld, 1888–1964

Utrecht, The Netherlands; 1924

Like many of the greatest twentieth-century houses – including the **Villa Savoye**, **Villa Mairea** and **Farnsworth House** (pages 62, 86 and 92) – the Schröder House evolved out of a close relationship between the architect and a female client. In this case the client, Truus Schröder-Schräder, was a young widow who had been married to a rather staid solicitor but preferred to socialize with the Dutch avant-garde. She was widely read in the arts and philosophy and already knew Gerrit Rietveld well. Rietveld had trained as a furniture maker before studying architecture part-time, and came to fame thanks to the adoption of his Red and Blue Chair of 1918 by Theo van Doesburg, founder of the Dutch De Stijl movement, as a perfect – if largely unwitting – example of the aesthetic ideals he advocated.

Following her husband's early death, Mrs Schröder-Schräder decided to build a house in which her children could be educated by mixing freely with the artists and intellectuals she entertained. She acquired a small plot at the end of a short terrace of brick houses: it originally looked out over open country, but is now close to a major road. To enjoy the views, she chose to live at first floor level; and to circumvent the building regulations, the ground floor was designed with relatively conventional rooms, plus a built-in garage – novel at the time, especially as she didn't have a car! – while the radically innovative first floor was left open and labelled simply 'attic' on the submission of the plans to the local authority.

Rietveld organized the open-plan space around a tight, winding staircase, lit through the flat roof by a cubic skylight. In the rear corner, tucked against the party wall, was Truus's room, which could open into the living area via a folding door. The rest of the space could be completely open, or subdivided by thin sliding partitions into living space, a room for her two girls, and one for her boy. With a craftsman's eye for detail, Rietveld redesigned everything in light of the abstract formal principles explored in his furniture. The windows, framed by differently coloured strips of wood, could be either closed or secured fully open at 90 degrees to the façade so as not to introduce a jarring diagonal – in the strict De Stijl system, only horizontals and verticals were permitted, and assumed cosmic significance as representative of the feminine/earth and masculine. Broad sills were provided for ornaments and plants, and furniture was built-in or of Rietveld's design.

Every detail reflected the organizing principle of the house: the definition, but not containment, of space by sticks and planes. To emphasize their autonomy they were variously coloured, and either free standing or slipped past one another to avoid conventional corners. To open the interior to the garden and countryside, columns retreated from the corners, and these could be completely dissolved by opening the windows. The result reflected the attention to detail of a *Gesamtkunstwerk* like the **Palais Stoclet** (page 32), but was wholly modern in the abstraction of its formal language. It was also liberating and receptive to ordinary living.

The Schröder House was the first building to match the post-war dream of a new world rebuilt on new aesthetic, social and political principles. To both client and architecct, clarity and simplicity were articles of faith as well as artistic means. Truus Schröder-Schräder's ideas about the family, the role of women in society and the shared responsibilities of individuals were central to the making of her house, and Rietveld's unsurpassed achievement was to create an environment in which simple acts like closing partitions or raising and lowering a table assumed ritual significance as part of a conscious celebration of daily life.

49

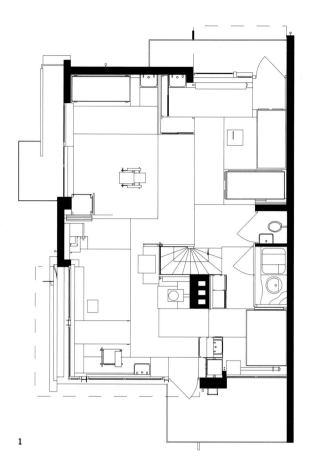

1

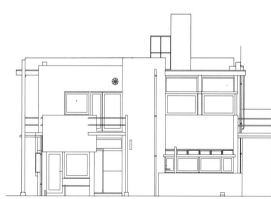

2

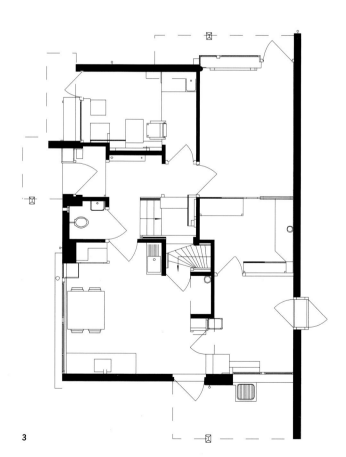

3

4

5

1 First Floor Plan

2 Section

3 Ground Floor Plan

4 Southeast Elevation

5 Southwest Elevation

0   5   10 m

15   30 ft

Bauhaus

Walter Gropius, 1883–1969

Dessau, Germany; 1925–6

Founded in Weimar in 1919, the Bauhaus was intended, according to its first director, Walter Gropius, to forge a new 'unity between the arts'. Formed by amalgamating an existing Arts and Crafts school with the city's Academy of Fine Arts, it was new primarily in name and ideals, and initially the latter had as much to do with medieval crafts and the Wagnerian concept of the total work of art (*Gesamtkunstwerk*) as they did with the kind of industrial design with which 'Bauhaus' later became almost synonymous. These ideals, represented on the cover of the founding proclamation by Lyonel Feininger's celebrated woodcut of a Socialist 'future cathedral', proved too radical for the conservative city of Weimar. Things came to a head in 1923 with the Bauhaus's first Open Exhibition, and two years later the institution was moved to Dessau, a more progressive and rapidly expanding industrial town.

Gropius began work almost immediately on the design for the Bauhaus's new home, and what emerged in just over a year was the first large-scale demonstration of the potential of the new architecture. The plan was functionally zoned into a pinwheel-composition of three blocks bridging a road. To one side was the Technical College, housing a variety of classrooms, small laboratories and other teaching spaces. Facing it, linked by the auditorium and canteen, were the Workshop (studio) Block, wrapped all round in a curtain of glass, and a six-storey tower of residential accommodation. The interior, from colour schemes and signage to furniture and fittings, became a living demonstration of Bauhaus principles and capabilities. The furniture, designed by Marcel Breuer, presented the first large-scale use of tubular steel, while the similarly inventive light fittings were produced by the metal workshop under the direction of Max Kraals and Marianne Brandt. The architecture also provided an impressive demonstration of the building as machine, courtesy of the ranks of small sash windows opened, at identical angles, by a system of chains and pulleys.

Contemporary reactions, in a Germany where the seeds of Nazism were beginning to sprout, were predictably mixed, but among committed Modernists Gropius's building was immediately hailed as a major triumph. To the Russian writer Ilya Ehrenburg it seemed to be 'cast of one piece like a persistent thought … its glass walls, which form a transparent angle, united with the air and yet separated from it by a distinct will'. With its set-back columns and continuous gridded skin of glass, the Workshop Block was no longer a solid, hollowed-out mass but a vast cage of space, filled with natural light by day and glowing like a magical box of light by night.

In his account of the building, Gropius emphasized that by rejecting the traditional symmetrical façade, the building demanded that you walk right around it to understand its composition. This, combined with the complex, unexpected views through, and reflections in, the glazed envelope made it for Sigfried Giedion a prime example of what he called 'space-time' and 'simultaneity' in architecture, visual effects produced by the 'hovering relations of planes and the kind of "overlapping" which appears in contemporary painting'. The links Giedion claimed to modern physics may now seem tenuous, less so the comparisons he made between the Bauhaus and the complex, shifting effects of Cubist paintings.

In his short book entitled *The New Architecture and the Bauhaus*, Gropius wrote, 'Our ambition was to arouse the creative artist from his otherworldliness and reintegrate him into the workaday world of realities: and at the same time to broaden and humanize the rigid, almost material mind of the businessman.' His vision influenced generations of art and design educators, but as an architect he never came close to equalling his canonical achievement in the Bauhaus at Dessau.

1 West Elevation

2 First Floor Plan

Bridge (Administration Building)
1 Hall
2 Library
3 Typing
4 Waiting Room (Technical School)
5 Administration
6 Conference room
7 Director
8 Bauhaus Waiting Room
9 Telephone
10 Lecture Room

Technical School
11 Staff Room
12 Vestibule
13 Classroom
14 Lockers
15 Materials
16 Workshop for Preliminary Course
17 Weaving Workshop
18 Master
19 Wardrobe
20 Washroom

Studio Wing
21 WCs
22 Studio

3 North Elevation

4 Ground Floor Plan

Technical School
1 Laboratory
2 Classroom
3 Physics Room
4 Hall
5 Porch
6 Lockers
7 WCs
8 Darkroom

Workshop Building
9 Display Room
10 Materials
11 Master
12 Room for Foreman
13 Cabinet-making Workshop
14 Machine Shop
15 Room for Veneer Work
16 Washroom

Single-storey Block and Studio Wing
17 Kitchen
18 Pantry
19 Vestibule
20 Serving Counter
21 Student Room
22 Canteen
23 Terrace
24 Stage
25 Auditorium

5 East-West Section

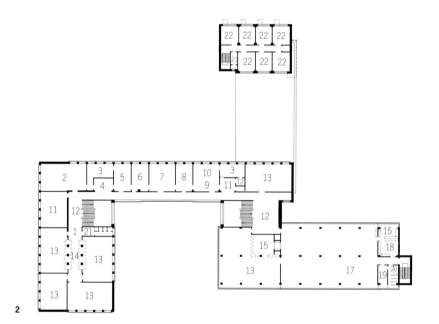

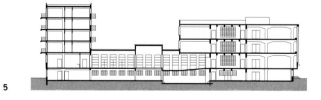

Open Air School

Johannes (Jan) Duiker, 1890–1935

Amsterdam, The Netherlands; 1927–8

Despite dying young and leaving behind a relatively modest body of work, Jan Duiker occupies a special place in Modern architecture. His primary motivations were social rather than aesthetic, and through his writings and buildings he argued for a healthier world based on hygiene, light and air. He campaigned for better housing for the poor and against all purely aesthetic movements, whether Modern, like De Stijl; historicist, like the conservative Delft School; or – his particular enemy – Expressionist, like the Amsterdam School.

Duiker's first competition project, made with his long-term collaborator Bernard Bijvoet in 1917 for the State Academy in Amsterdam, was deeply marked by Frank Lloyd Wright's **Larkin Building** and **Unity Temple** (pages 26 and 30). The design won, but remained on the drawing board. By 1924, when they came to design a house in Aalsmeer and a laundry in Diemen, Duiker and Bijvoet had moved decisively towards a Modernist position. Duiker joined the radical, Amsterdam-based 'De 8' group and shared their manifesto belief that 'for the time being it would be better to build something ugly and functional, than to erect "façade architecture" to front inferior floor plans … De 8 is non-aesthetic.'

In 1926 Bijvoet left The Netherlands temporarily to work with Pierre Chareau on the **Maison de Verre** (page 64), but despite this must have had some involvement in the design of the Open Air School as he signed the plans dated 12 May 1927. The brief was a response to the belief that an open-air school would provide a better environment 'for the healthy child' and Duiker's first proposal was prepared without a specific site in mind. When a site was found, it was in the courtyard of a perimeter housing block, with a separate entrance building to one side. The school itself went through six transformations, during which the rotated diagonal emerged, the columns were displaced from the corners to the centres of the sides, and the number of outdoor classrooms was reduced.

Both the plan and structure bear an uncanny resemblance to several of Louis Kahn's designs, including the **Richards Medical Research Building** (page 128), but unlike Kahn a quarter of a century later, Duiker's aim was an expression of extreme lightness. By placing the stair, cloakrooms and toilets in a smaller, rotated square – its corners defined by the central columns of the larger squares – and by projecting the stair landings and

toilets beyond this inner square, Duiker achieves a remarkable integration of the bipolar 'butterfly' plan.

The placement of the columns at the centres of the sides of the squares also recalls the arrangement Mies van der Rohe adopted in his 50x50 House project and at the National Gallery in Berlin. It allowed the exposed, cantilevered beams to taper to almost nothing at the corners, where the lightness is further enhanced by cantilevering the floor slab out from the beams and by exposing its edge beyond the solid spandrel panels. Steel glazing bars and doorframes of astonishing slenderness originally completed the effect. Sadly, their replacement by more robust sections robs the building we see today of much of both its liberating lightness and the faceted, crystalline quality that once gave the school an air of machine-like precision as impressive as many more renowned examples of early Modern architecture.

1 Courtyard Level Plan	2 First Floor Plan	3 Section	53

1 Gymnasium
2 Classroom
3 Open Air Classroom

1 Classroom
2 Open Air Classroom

1

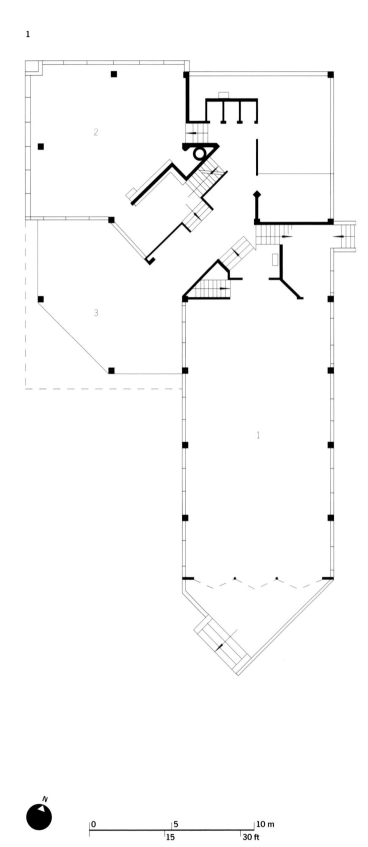

2

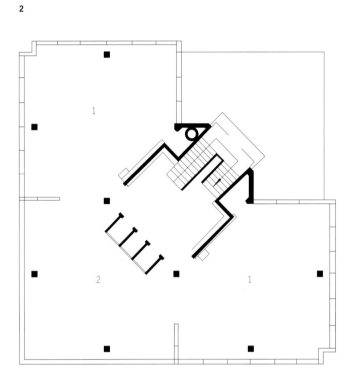

3

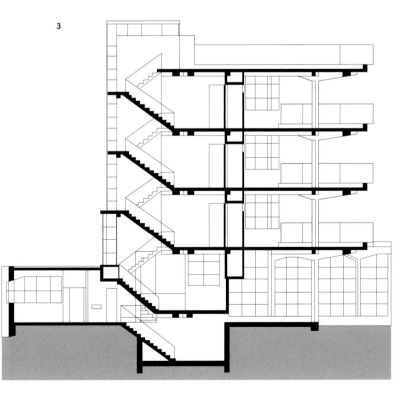

0   5   10 m

15   30 ft

Lovell 'Health House'

Richard Neutra, 1892–1970

Los Angeles, California, USA; 1927–9

Like his friend Rudolf Schindler (**Schindler-Chace House**, page 46), Richard Neutra was born in Vienna, where he worked for Adolf Loos (**Müller House**, page 68). After two years with Eric Mendelsohn (**Einstein Tower**, page 44) in Berlin, he emigrated to the USA in 1923, where he worked for Holabird and Roche in Chicago. While there he met Louis Sullivan and his hero Frank Lloyd Wright. In 1927, towards the end of a two-year association with Schindler, he built one of the first Modernist buildings in America – the Jardinette apartments – and took on this commission for a large house for Philip Lovell. A fanatical advocate of natural remedies, vegetarianism, exercise and nude sunbathing, Lovell wrote a popular column on health in the *Los Angeles Times*. Schindler, who had designed Lovell's Beach House, claimed Neutra had stolen his client, something Neutra – probably accurately – fiercely denied. Whatever the truth may be, the commission was to make Neutra's name.

Lovell owned a steeply sloping plot in the Hollywood Hills, and to Neutra part of the project's appeal lay in creating a 'wide-open filigree steel frame, set deftly and precisely by cranes and booms into this inclined piece of rugged nature'.

He planned the house on two-and-a-half floor levels, with entry at the upper, street level. The arrangement of rooms and masses was relaxed and rambling, a feeling reinforced by carrying some of the solid bands into the landscape as walls and screens, and by suspending open balconies and sleeping porches from the edges of the structure. Most impressive of all, perhaps, was the stairway off the main entrance hall (shown above). Enclosed by a wall of full-height casement windows looking out over Los Angeles, it was wittily lit by Model-T Ford headlamps, their clear covers replaced with translucent glass.

Exploiting the site to the full, Neutra designed a varied sequence of living areas. An intimate sitting space, like a Modernist version of an inglenook fireplace, was tucked under the stairs; the cave-like library nestled back into the hill; and the living and dining areas, courtesy of the light steel frame, appeared almost to take flight from the land. Doubting the capacity of local contractors to rise to the challenge of building such an innovative design, Neutra acted as the general contractor, controlling a range of subcontractors through detailed specification and regular on-site supervision.

The bolted steel frame was prefabricated in portable elements and took only 40 hours to erect. The infill panels were made of either steel or 'gunite' concrete sprayed onto a wire lath. The balance of solid and void was beautifully judged, and the southwest elevation – one of the iconic images of Modern architecture – was among the most satisfying created anywhere using the new architectural language. More relaxed in its asymmetry than many European designs, it suggested the dynamic balance of a De Stijl painting, and the design's impressive consistency was marred only by the flagstone fireplace – a hangover from Neutra's admiration for Wright.

Following its completion, Lovell promoted his house vigorously in his 'Care of the Body' column. He announced that he and Neutra would be present on four successive Sunday afternoons to lead tours and in response 15,000 members of the public flocked to see it. Most were both amazed and bemused by the modernity of its design and the 'Health House', as it was soon known, became an instant star.

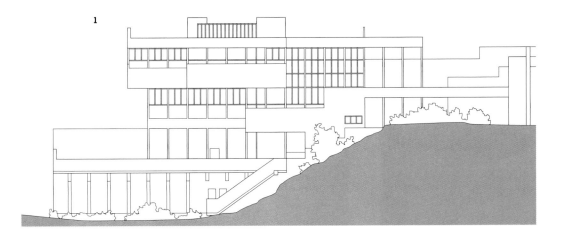

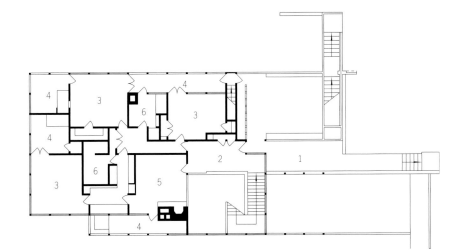

2

2 Entrance Level Plan

1 Entrance Terrace
2 Entry
3 Living Room
4 Sleeping Porch
5 Study
6 Bathroom

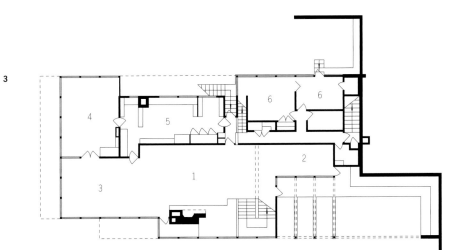

3

3 First Floor Plan

1 Living Room
2 Library
3 Dining Room
4 Porch
5 Kitchen
6 Guest Room

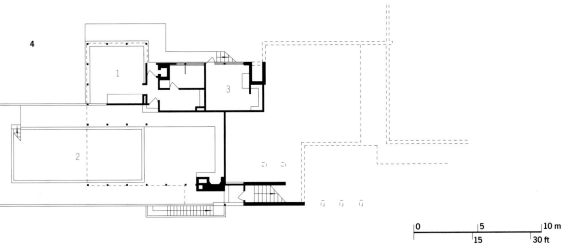

4

4 Ground Floor Plan

1 Porch
2 Pool
3 Laundry Room

```
0        5        10 m
   15        30 ft
```

N

Church of the Sacred Heart

Jože Plečnik, 1872–1957

Vinohrady, Prague, Czech Republic; 1927–31

Born in Slovenia, and educated in Vienna in Otto Wagner's studio at the Fine Arts Academy, Jože Plečnik was among the most original twentieth-century exponents of the Classical tradition. He moved to Prague in 1911, where he devoted the next decade almost entirely to teaching as head of the School of Applied Arts. In 1918, when Czechoslovakia gained independence, he began work on transforming Prague Castle into the Presidential Residence. The following year he was invited – in a letter signed by 29 distinguished architects – to submit a proposal for this church, after a competition had failed to yield a satisfactory proposal. He continued to work on both projects after returning to Slovenia in 1920.

Located in the Prague suburb of Vinohrady ('Vineyard Hills'), the Church of the Sacred Heart is sited in the leafy main square. The spacious nave has neither aisles nor side chapels and is a tall, square-ish volume focussed on the main altar placed at the centre of the east wall. The square-coffered ceiling of dark, polished timber conceals a steel structure, and the space is lit by 32 square clerestorey windows that wrap around three sides of the space in a white-rendered band above the brick walls – although less complex, the room

brings to mind Wright's **Unity Temple** (page 30). The most striking element of the composition is the slender, 42-metre (138-foot) high clock and bell tower flanked by pyramidal pylons. The enormous glass clock face is criss-crossed by a ramp, lightening the mass of the tower while lending it the monumental scale of a traditional cathedral west front – Plečnik's aim was to lock the church into the city.

Externally, the church is characterized by the striking contrast between the dark, richly textured and largely blank base, made of clinker bricks and projecting stone blocks, and the white-plastered upper stages and door and window surrounds. The brickwork terminates in a deep, outward leaning cornice of a type favoured by the exponents of Czech Cubism before the First World War, and this canted form is echoed in the more overtly Classical window and door surrounds – although here, as throughout his work, Plečnik's Classicism is free and inventive.

The expressive use of materials is almost certainly derived from the ideas of the nineteenth-century architect-theorist, Gottfried Semper, who noted that in antiquity textiles were used on special occasions to enhance the significance of archi-

tecture. Here, Plečnik has chosen to 'dress' the church's white walls with an 'ermine robe': this symbol of royal dignity, and dress of a Cardinal, is represented by the richly textured, and textile-like, brick walls. It could also be that, alert to the newly independent nation's search for identity, he intended to give architectural expression to the kind of formal structure that Bartók identified in East European folk music: the more 'primitive' brick base echoes the 'ancient layer', while the Classically ordered superstructure – like the second layer of song – has a strict rhythm and architectonic order.

Long neglected by mainstream architectural history, Plečnik was eagerly appropriated by post-Modernists as a precursor. His immersion in tradition was, however, of a different order to theirs: although intensely personal in expression, his designs were rooted in the unpretentious craft of building and had nothing in common with the cult of personality that dominated so much work produced in the late twentieth century.

1 Gallery Level and Reflected Ceiling Plan

1 Organ and Choir Gallery
2 Clock Tower
3 Store

2 South Elevation

3 Plan

1 Entrance Terrace
2 Narthex
3 Nave
4 Altar
5 Crossing beneath Clock Tower
6 Baptism Hall
7 Sacristy
8 East Entrance

4 West-East Section

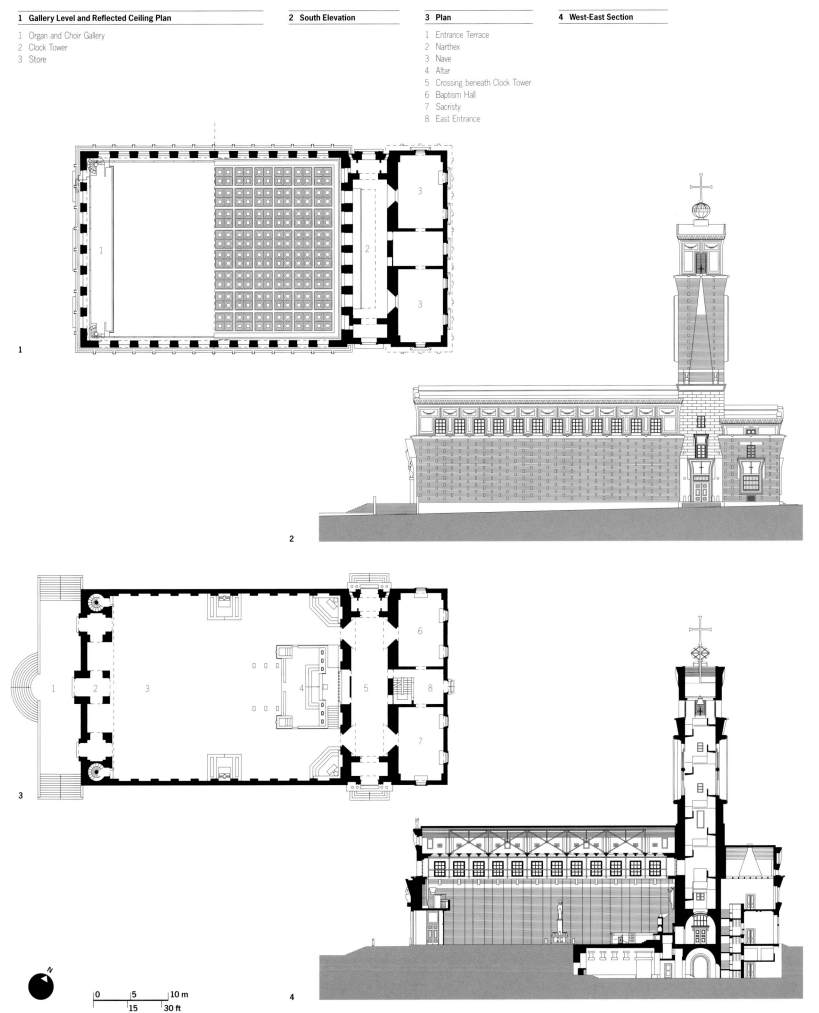

0 5 10 m
15 30 ft

Barcelona Pavilion

Mies van der Rohe, 1886–1969

International Exposition, Barcelona, Spain; 1928–9 (demolished)

Demolished in 1930, shortly after the close of the 'International Exposition' for which it was built as the German exhibit, Mies van der Rohe's Barcelona Pavilion was, until its rebuilding in 1986, known only through drawings and black-and-white photographs. Despite this, it acquired an almost mythical status: several historians and critics declared it 'the most beautiful building of the century'.

Mies's brief was demanding but open-ended: to advertise, a decade after the First World War, the virtues of a newly democratic, culturally progressive Germany. It should, in the words of the Commissioner, Georg von Schnitzler, give 'voice to the spirit of a new era'. Mies's response was radical. Unlike conventional national pavilions, there would be no trade exhibits, only the structure, a single sculpture and purpose-designed furniture – the iconic 'Barcelona Chair' would find its way into more prestigious corporate interiors than any other design.

The lack of conventional accommodation enabled Mies to treat the Pavilion as a continuous space, melding inside and out into a unified whole variously modulated by the roof plane and changes of material. The design was predicated on an absolute distinction between structure and enclosure – a regular grid of cruciform steel columns

interspersed by freely placed planes. In practice, the design had to be adapted to Barcelona's nineteenth-century craft traditions and the real structure was a hybrid in which some planes also acted as supports. This hardly mattered: what you perceive is a crystal-clear demonstration of a radically new way of building, and of an equally radical conception of space.

For Modernist critics, the Barcelona Pavilion was the ultimate example of spatial abstraction, free of context and dependent upon the distinction between structure and enclosure that Mies heightened by choosing opulent, reflective and/or highly figured materials for the wall planes – onyx, travertine and two green marbles, and by using different kinds of glass – green, grey, white and clear. The reflective surfaces were multiplied by the large pool that greeted visitors and by a darker, enclosed one at the other end. Framed by walls, it was here that Mies placed the classical statue by Georg Kolbe: like the waterlilies in the larger pool, it provided a stable, figural counterpoint to the deliberately insubstantial surfaces all around.

More recent interpretations, mostly written since the 1986 rebuilding, have focussed on the interrelationships between building, site and visitor. Caroline Constant, for example, has argued that the

spatial composition should be understood in terms of the formal tropes of a Picturesque garden rather than those of a traditional building. And to Robin Evans, the reflective columns, clad in polished chrome, appear to be struggling to hold the 'floating' roof plane down, not to be bearing its weight. He points out that by choosing a ceiling height of three metres (ten feet), Mies deliberately placed the visitor's eye level almost exactly half way between floor and ceiling. The biaxial symmetries that were ruthlessly banished from the free plan now multiply bewilderingly in section – an effect most evident in the Rorschach blot-like figures created by the matched veneers of the onyx wall.

Far from being context free, the design can also be interpreted as a commentary on its setting – Mies himself chose the site, after rejecting the one he was offered. Screened by a row of Ionic columns, the Pavilion acted as the gateway between the eclectic architecture of the main exhibition and the 'Spanish Village' occupying the hill behind it. At the opposite end of the long plaza in front of it was Barcelona's own neo-Renaissance pavilion. Standing on a low podium, like the stylobate of a Greek temple, Mies's design offered itself as a commentary on the exhausted language of Classicism.

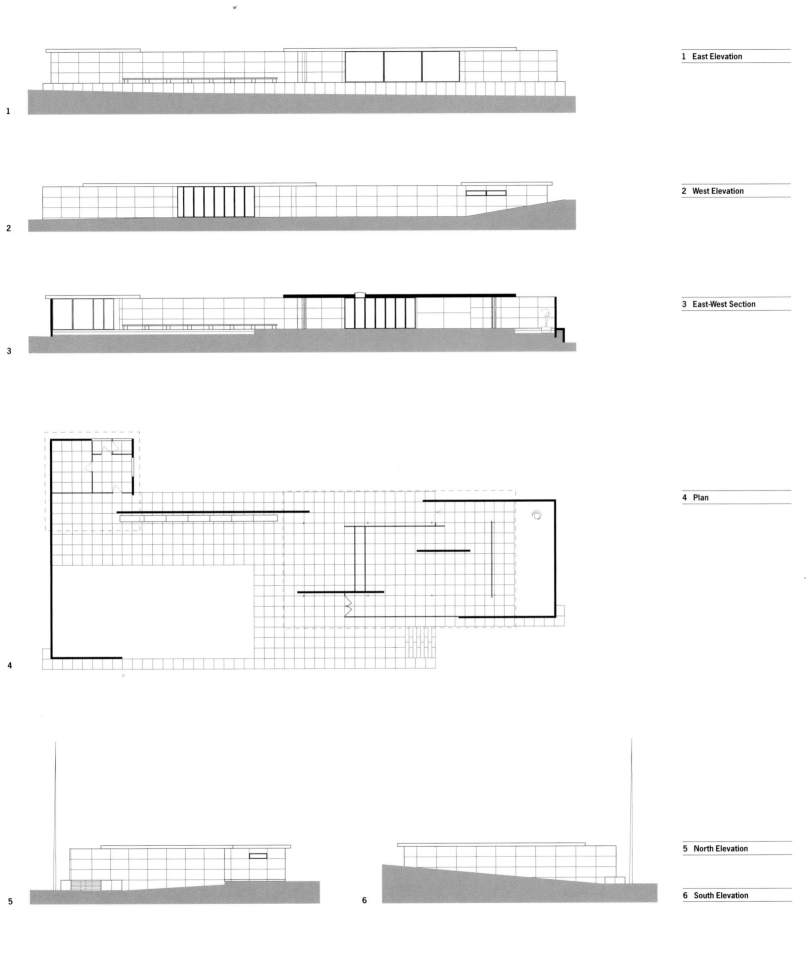

1 East Elevation

2 West Elevation

3 East-West Section

4 Plan

5 North Elevation

6 South Elevation

| 0 | 5 | 10 m |
| 15 | 30 ft |

Tugendhat House

Mies van der Rohe, 1886–1969

Brno, Czech Republic; 1928–30

Commissioned by Greta and Fritz Tugendhat, heirs of German-speaking Jewish industrialists, Tugendhat House occupies a large sloping plot facing south over parkland towards the city of Brno. On arriving, you are presented with a picturesque view of a nearby fortress, framed by the closed volumes that contain the private realm of the bedrooms. The entrance is tucked out of sight between plain walls and the milky white semi-circular glass enclosure of the main stair. With travertine floor, full-height translucent glass and dark, Palisander-veneered doors and wall panelling, the entrance hall has a semi-public feel: calm and quietly opulent.

Descending via the broad dog-leg stair you emerge into a truly vast living space. Directly ahead, filling the short side, is the winter garden – a captured landscape bursting with plants – and to the right, glimpsed between free-standing planes, is a long wall of cast glass. This runs the full 24-metre (79-foot) length of the space and is designed so that two large sections can disappear at the touch of a button. They descend into the basement, transforming the living area into an open verandah overlooking the garden. In the evening it can be transformed again by the large curtains that feel more like sliding partitions.

Although the living floor can be experienced as a continuous, flowing space in the manner of the **Barcelona Pavilion** (page 50), Mies articulates the traditional 'rooms' of a bourgeois house – for dining, living, study, music and plants – at a relatively modest scale. The primary sub-division is effected by a semi-circular wall of highly figured red- and brown-streaked macassar and a straight plane of onyx, and the space is further punctuated and divided by the polished cruciform columns, variously coloured textiles and meticulously placed furniture, all of which was designed by Mies – some of it, like the Brno Chair, especially for the house. Materials – emerald green leather, ruby velvet and white vellum – are luxurious and colourful, and each piece had its appointed place: despite the potential 'flexibility' of the open space, Mies's vision has as much in common with a *Gesamtkunstwerk* like the **Palais Stoclet** (page 32) as it does with the freedoms of Le Corbusier's *plan libre*.

Believing that 'a clear structure is the basis of the free plan', Mies maintained the regularity of the column grid throughout the interior; a few columns are replaced by walls, but for the most part the grid reads clearly as a counterpoint to the free-standing partitions and furniture. The floor was finished in ivory-coloured linoleum that by day assumes an almost identical tone to the white ceiling. As in the Barcelona Pavilion, the ceiling height is contrived to ensure that eye level is poised half way between floor and ceiling planes, enhancing the feeling of a 'floating world' of reflective surfaces and luxurious materials transfigured by light.

The interior's marked aesthetic quality, combined with the idealized dialogue with the landscape, inspired a contemporary critic to remark that Mies here showed how to 'elevate oneself above purely rational and functional thinking . . . into the realm of the spiritual'. Completed within a year of each other, the Barcelona Pavilion and Tugendhat House effectively signalled Mies's break with the functionalist, socially driven wing of German Modernism: increasingly, he would be preoccupied by the search for new spatial models and the expression of construction.

Faced with the rise of Nazism, the Tugendhats fled their house in 1938. It was eventually taken over by the Communist authorities and during the 1960s the living room was used as a gymnasium to help rehabilitate disabled children. It was restored, minus the original furniture and many of the fittings, in the late 1980s.

1 East Elevation

2 North Elevation

3 South Elevation

4 Second Floor Plan

5 First Floor Plan

0   5   10 m
  15   30 ft

N

Villa Savoye

Le Corbusier, 1887–1965

Poissy, France; 1928–30

Built as a weekend house in the then leafy Paris suburb of Poissy, the Villa Savoye represents the culmination of Le Corbusier's Purist style of the 1920s, the ideas of which had been published in the magazine *L'Esprit Nouveau* and widely disseminated in the hugely influential book, *Vers une architecture* (Towards a New Architecture), published in 1923. Spatially, the design exploited to the full the possibilities of concrete frame construction, which Le Corbusier had proclaimed as the 'Five Points of a New Architecture':

1. Columns (he called them *pilotis*) raise the house in the air, freeing the ground for people and vehicles.
2. A roof garden on the flat roof replaces the ground lost by development.
3. Extending the *pilotis* through as a structural frame enables partition walls to be freely arranged in what he called the *plan libre*, or free plan.
4. Disposing windows as required by the interior creates a free façade.
5. Long horizontal windows — *fenêtres en longueur*, or ribbon windows — give a more even distribution of light (in fact the technical argument was dubious).

Formally, the house can be seen as a reinterpretation of a Classical, centralized plan, such as Palladio's Villa Rotonda: the plan is similarly four-square and the house addresses the horizons through continuous ribbon windows. But in place of a central room, to give a focus and sense of closure, Le Corbusier places a ramp, the basis of what he called the *promenade architecturale*. Similarly, the square is defined by a classically incorrect four-by-four bay system (there is a column, not an open bay, at the centre), but the house is not exactly square, being extended by cantilevers along the direction of approach to imply a major axis.

The entrance is on the far side of the house and is approached via a curving glass screen whose radius was determined by the turning circle of a Voisin car, inviting the kind of provocative comparison between architecture and engineering Le Corbusier made in his writings. You enter at the centre of the curved screen and are greeted by the ramp that rises and turns. As it does so, views open invitingly across the terrace, through the corner of the living room and out to the landscape framed by the ribbon window. The living room itself opens to the terrace via almost 10 metres (32 feet) of full-height glazing, half of which can be slid aside using a hand-crank. The architectural promenade continues from the terrace via the ramp and arrives, on axis with a framed view towards the

Seine, in a 'solarium'. Although planted, it feels like the deck of a ship, an image Le Corbusier prompts with the funnel-like enclosure of the stair and white-painted, steel-tube handrails. Here, surrounded by geometric forms, you experience what he called 'architecture's purest gift, mathematical lyricism'.

Although the architectural order, posited by the column grid and latent symmetries, recalls the disciplines of Classicism, in the spirit of the new freedom of planning it is everywhere responsive to patterns of use and to the presence of the observer. Notice, for example, how the ramp is framed by two rows of columns, not divided by them as the grid would suggest, and that these are then doubled to mark a place of arrival. Elsewhere, individual columns step aside to free a room or move slightly to engage with a partition: free-standing columns are always round, engaged ones square.

In the Villa Savoye, the quintessentially Modernist de-centring of the composition — marked by the column grid, reinforced by disposing the principal spaces around the edges of the composition (as if spun out by the ramp) and expressed by ribbon windows — is used to suggest a pervasive movement, upwards and outwards, towards the landscape and the sky, towards nature.

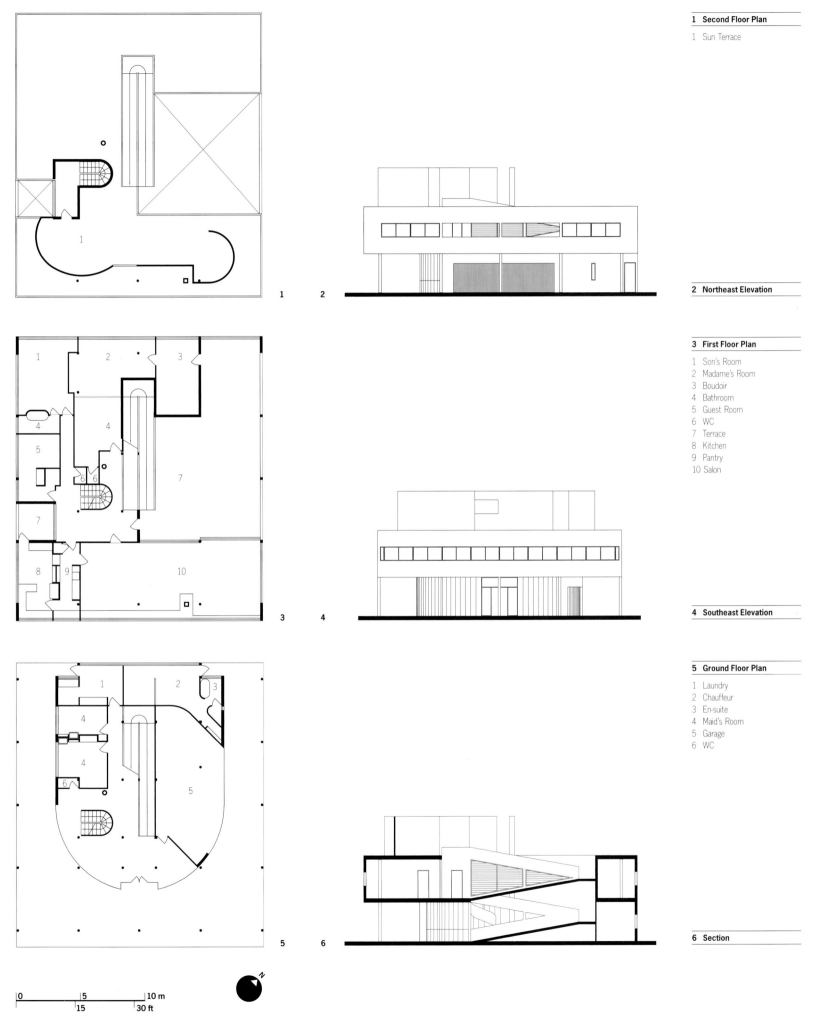

1 Sun Terrace

2 Northeast Elevation

3 First Floor Plan

1 Son's Room
2 Madame's Room
3 Boudoir
4 Bathroom
5 Guest Room
6 WC
7 Terrace
8 Kitchen
9 Pantry
10 Salon

4 Southeast Elevation

5 Ground Floor Plan

1 Laundry
2 Chauffeur
3 En-suite
4 Maid's Room
5 Garage
6 WC

6 Section

0   5   10 m
15   30 ft

Maison de Verre

Pierre Chareau, 1883–1950, and Bernard Bijvoet, 1889–1979

Paris, France; 1928–32

Designed by the interior and furniture designer Pierre Chareau with the help of the Dutch architect Bernard Bijvoet, the Maison de Verre offered a strikingly new interpretation of the Modernist vision of the house as a 'machine for living in'. The client was a leading gynaecologist, Dr Dalsace, and his brief called for a combination of private house and medical clinic. The site was a private court in a quiet part of Paris, and the house is wedged in between and under surrounding apartments.

The elevations that give the house its name are made largely of the glass bricks that were then associated with public lavatories and pavement lights. Laid in four-brick-wide panels, they establish the 91-centimetre (36-inch) module that controls dimensions throughout the design. The blocks might have had utilitarian connotations, but their use was supremely sophisticated, suggesting a delicate veil that appears to hang in space, filtering the light and screening the private interior from the world: critics were understandably quick to liken it to the gridded paper screens of traditional Japanese houses.

The delicate balance Chareau strikes on the façades between utilitarian materials and exquisitely refined abstraction is in marked contrast with the main structure inside. Made of industrial steel I-sections painted with red lead, the columns are forge-beaten, plated together and over-sized. Technically obsolescent, they might have escaped from a nineteenth-century factory – but not quite, as they are civilized, if not exactly domesticated, by a revetment of thin slabs of slate fixed to their flat faces. The thick edges of the galvanized steel warm-air ducts laid over the floor beams are similarly visible, beneath a thin coating of studded-rubber flooring.

The interior bristles with fascinating technical and visual details: balustrades double as bookcases, a frankly nautical stair is designed to lift up and away when not needed, and electrical wires pass through exposed metal conduits onto which the switches are mounted. In contrast to the deliberately over-sized column sections, the full-height doors were fabricated with utter economy of means from a single piece of bent sheet-metal; industrial Duralumin was used to make sleekly efficient wardrobes and drawers; and the bathrooms are screened by curving panels of finely perforated aluminium – an idea that found many imitators when the Maison de Verre was re-evaluated in the 1980s.

Toiling away in his workshop to perfect his endlessly innovative interior, Chareau saw the project as 'a model executed by craftsmen with the aim of industrial standardisation'. In fact, it was too singular for that, and far too dependent upon the skills and values of craftsmen devoted to achieving the highest standards in the quality of their work. Not trained in the complex business of anticipating and resolving in advance the many, potentially conflicting, problems that arise in the course of designing and building, Chareau did not aspire to the 'integrated whole' that is generally judged a hallmark of fine architecture. Instead he chose to work additively, addressing difficulties piecemeal as they arose and finding often striking solutions to them – hence the exposure of services and the Maison de Verre's fascination for subsequent generations of designers to whom elaborate detailing became a means of enriching architecture and resisting the growing divide between thinking and making.

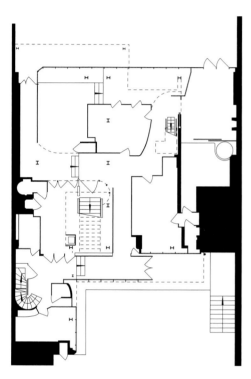

1

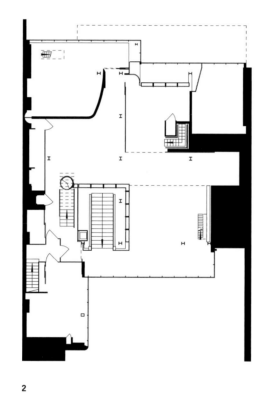

2

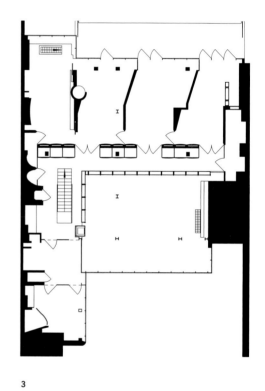

3

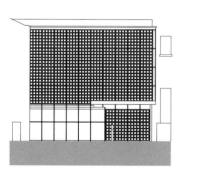

4

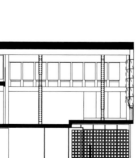

5

0   5   10 m

15   30 ft

Tuberculosis Sanatorium

Alvar Aalto, 1898–1976

Paimio, Finland; 1928–33

Until the advent of penicillin, there was no cure for tuberculosis, and the preferred treatment was to expose patients to as much sunshine and fresh air as possible. This medical regime accorded perfectly with the Modernists' belief in the health-giving properties of 'sun, space and greenery' – epitomized by Le Corbusier's *Ville Radieuse* – and the sanatorium became a favoured building type for functionalist design. The stepped terraces of the celebrated Swiss establishments were most widely known, but in terms of architectural distinction only the Zonnestraal Sanatorium at Hilversum (1926–8) by Johannes Duiker and Bernard Bijvoet rivalled this by Alvar Aalto at Paimio. Acclaimed by Sigfried Giedion, secretary of the CIAM (*Congrès Internationaux d'Architecture Moderne*), it secured Aalto's place among the Modernist elite.

The plan is functionally zoned, with separate, clearly articulated blocks for the hospital's various activities. To maximize sunlight, the patients' rooms face southwest and are ranged along single-banked corridors. As the flat Finnish landscape made a stepped section impracticable, the roof was used as a terrace – offering spectacular views across the surrounding forest – and each corridor led to an open sun-deck, stacked and dramatically can-

tilevered, like the branches of a tree, from a spine wall. The result was a striking demonstration of the structural potential of reinforced concrete construction, but with the sanatorium's later conversion into a conventional hospital, the open structure was glazed in to form additional wards.

Internally, the design was marked by exceptional attention to detail as Aalto took the opportunity to re-think and re-design everything. The rooms, most shared by two patients, were designed with the needs of a person in bed in mind: the source of heat was in the ceiling, from which light was also reflected gently down from a wall-mounted uplighter. To avoid disturbing the other patient, the wash-basins were designed – not entirely successfully – to be quietly splash-proof, and, for ease of cleaning, the wardrobes were suspended from the walls and given round corners in case patients should happen to knock against them.

The sanatorium also gave its name to the first in a long line of superb bent-wood chairs designed by Aalto. Developed with the doctors, it was intended to flex to assist the patients' breathing, but its aesthetic qualities alone were to secure its status as a classic of Modern design. In retrospect, like the many other purpose-made elements of the inte-

rior, not to mention the organic forms of the entrance canopy, the Paimio Chair can be seen as anticipating Aalto's humanist critique of much so-called functionalist design. Epitomized by a preference for natural over machine-made materials and for combining organic and rectilinear forms, Aalto's mature style – represented here by **Seinäjoki Library** (page 148) – was to prove hugely influential. But in the sanatorium he showed himself to be an equally persuasive exponent of what would become known as the International Style.

Visitors are still greeted by an iconic Modernist device – a glazed lift shaft. Adjacent to this Aalto placed cantilevered balconies whose structure tapers expressively in response to the load, like those on Duiker's **Open Air School** (page 52) in Amsterdam that may well have inspired them, while beyond range ribbon windows as impressive as any built by Le Corbusier. The structural heroics of the sun-decks are echoed in the staff dining room, where Aalto suspended a large mezzanine floor on steel tubes, and the whole interior is pervaded by health-giving light, most powerfully, perhaps, in the stairs, down which it spills through huge areas of glazing: even the effort of climbing was made to feel part of the cure.

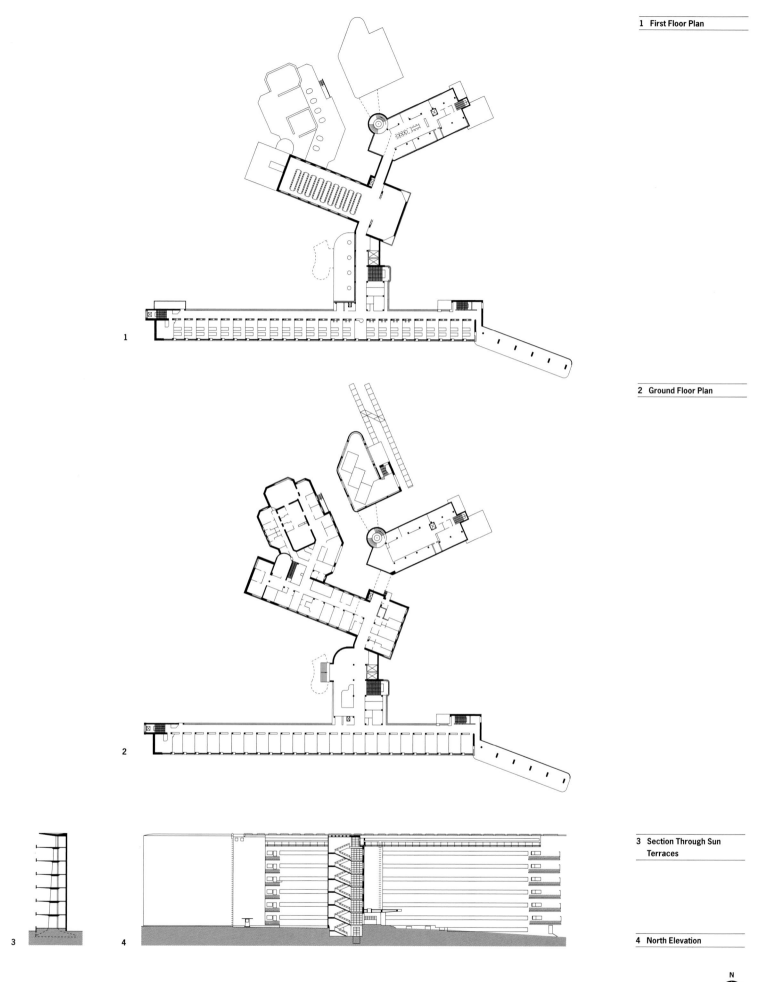

1

2 Ground Floor Plan

2

3   4

3 Section Through Sun
    Terraces

4 North Elevation

N

0	10	20 m
	30	60 ft

Müller House

Adolf Loos, 1870–1933

Prague, Czech Republic; 1930

Adolf Loos came to attention as an acerbic critic of Art Nouveau, and in place of the work of self-conscious designers he commended the study of the everyday products of crafts and modern engineering. He detested the work of the Wiener Werkstätte, epitomized by Josef Hoffmann's **Palais Stoclet** (page 32), and the exterior of his Steiner House, completed in 1910, was the most austerely abstract built anywhere by that time. Spatially, however, it was relatively traditional, and the severe, white-rendered exterior was in marked contrast to the panelled walls and exposed oak beams of the interior. For Loos, this radical disjunction was a response to the anonymity of the modern city, and it became central to his vision of the house as a shelter for the psyche as well as the body.

Shortly before the First World War Loos began to have the germs of a spatial idea that blossomed after it: 'This is the great revolution in architecture,' he declared, 'the planning of a building in volume.' He called his 'plan of volumes' a *Raumplan* and viewed the building-cube as a void to be filled with rooms of different volumes not just areas. 'I do not design plans, façades, sections,' he explained in 1933, the year of his death, 'I design space … there are merely interconnected

spaces, vestibules, terraces. Every room needs a specific height – the dining room a different one from the pantry – therefore the floors are on varying levels. After this one must connect the spaces with one another so that the transition is unnoticeable and natural, but also the most practical.'

The Müller House, built in Prague in 1930, represents the most complete realization of the *Raumplan*. At first, the plan, organized around a central stair, appears straightforward, almost traditional. But it requires only brief inspection to sense the complexity that lies in store. The main stair, for example, is only reached after passing through an anteroom, turning left up seven risers onto a landing before the main hall, and then turning right and rising another half-level to reach the core. The interior verges on the labyrinthine: few rooms share the same 'floor' and the identity of each is reinforced by varied proportions and unique surfaces.

The latter were grounded in Loos's commitment to the theory of cladding articulated by Gottfried Semper. Tracing the origins of architecture back to animal skins or carpets hung from a timber framework, Semper argued that masonry walls must always be clad to evoke these primitive origins. To emphasize that his finishes were only

skin deep, Loos favoured veneers of highly figured stone and wood, deploying them both to assert the uniqueness of each room and to create an appropriate atmosphere. The library, for example, is clad with dark mahogany, the ladies' boudoir with glossy lemonwood.

The highly individual treatment of the rooms produces an extraordinary intensity, and to hold the entire composition together the claddings of the various spaces are wrapped and folded onto adjacent walls and floors. The passages and other transitional spaces are not, however, allowed their own identity: the wall surface, for example, may be 'borrowed' from a room ahead, the floor run through from the one you have left, and the ceiling be a projection down from the space above.

Experienced as a series of distinct, richly elaborated episodes, the interior of the Müller House cannot be understood in terms of conventional architectural order and defies adequate description by plans and sections: what matters most in this architecture cannot be represented. For Loos, this was a means of resistance to the reduction of architecture to drawing. Passionately committed to the continuity of craft traditions, he described himself as a builder, not a designer.

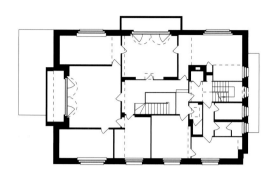

1

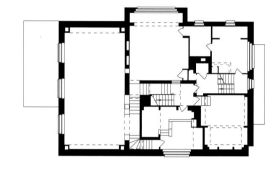

2

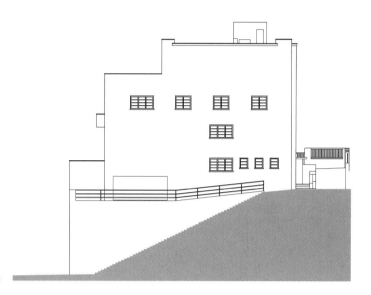

3

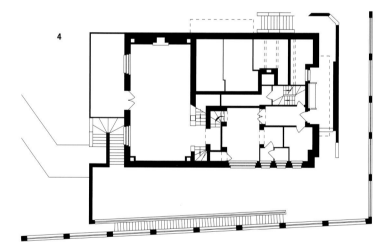

4

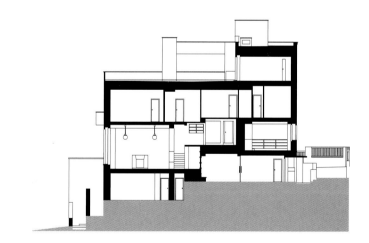

5

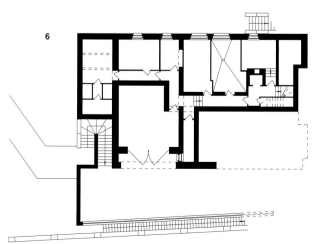

6

0   5   10 m
15   30 ft

N

Swiss Pavilion

Le Corbusier, 1887–1965

Cité Universitaire, Paris, France; 1930–1

The Swiss Pavilion occupies a crucial place in Le Corbusier's work, marking the summation of key ideas of the 1920s and anticipating his mature expression. A hostel for Swiss students at the Cité Universitaire in the south of Paris, it consists of two principal elements: a rectangular, steel-framed slab housing the student rooms, and a low, single-storey block containing the communal accommodation, from which the stair and lift rise to service the slab above. This is elevated on concrete pilotis to 'liberate' the ground, and its roof provides a solarium for the students and rooms for the maids.

In essence, the Swiss Pavilion was a large-scale demonstration of the 'Five Points of a New Architecture', which received their definitive, house-sized expression in the **Villa Savoye** (page 62). What makes this design significant is the way in which Le Corbusier adapted these principles to the scale of a collective block. The account of the building in the second volume of his *Œuvre Complète* emphasizes, both visually and in words, the importance of the pilotis as part of his vision of a modern urbanism, adapted to the needs of traffic. Far from being an isolated building, he saw the Swiss Pavilion as a prototype for the housing blocks of his ideal 'Radiant City', in which the ground would be developed as a continuous park, criss-crossed by a network of paths and minor service roads and traversed by elevated highways.

In discussing the Villa Savoye, we noted the correspondence between elements of the plan and a guitar in a Cubist painting: in the Swiss Pavilion the interplay between painting and architecture becomes altogether richer. Le Corbusier's paintings were ignored by many of his most fervent admirers. To him, however, they were vital experiments in the 'patient search' for form, and in the plan of the Swiss Pavilion we see a new freedom in giving shape to the individual elements of the composition, and a corresponding precision of formal organization, characterized by the layering and interdependence of shapes, that can best be described as 'painterly'. Visually, the most striking features of the Pavilion, when seen in the context of the buildings of the 1920s, are the almost collage-like combination of disparate materials – dressed stone, random rubble, glass bricks and a wonderfully elegant steel and glass curtain wall – and the replacement of spindly columns by massive, sculptural piers: in the office they were apparently referred to, almost inevitably, as 'dog bones'.

The sculptural pilotis give expressive force to the task of supporting the slab and anticipate the even more expressive *béton brut* underpinnings of the **Unité d'Habitation** in Marseilles (page 98). Their forms are unmistakably organic, and as such are at one with the free, curvilinear plan of the single-storey block and with such details as the aerofoil-shaped pier at the base of the stair. The latter is covered with large square photographs, whose subject matter is revealing: vastly enlarged microscopic close-ups of natural forms – plants, minerals, etc. – and aerial views of uninhabited landscapes are dominant, whereas the 'Machine Age' imagery found throughout his early books is almost entirely absent. Nature had always vied with the machine as a presiding metaphor of efficient design and in the Swiss Pavilion Le Corbusier made it clear that it was destined to become a major inspiration in his work.

1   Refectory
2   Office
3   Kitchen
4   Director's Office
5   Shower Room
6   WC
7   Bedroom
8   Kitchen and Dining Room
9   Hall

1

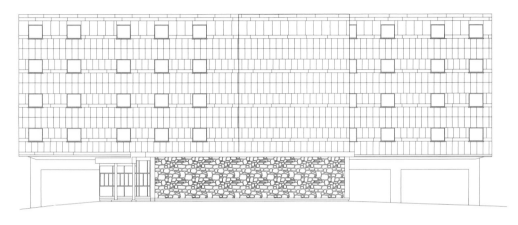

2

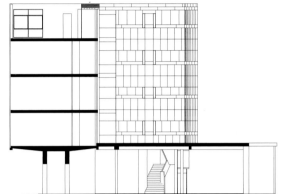

3

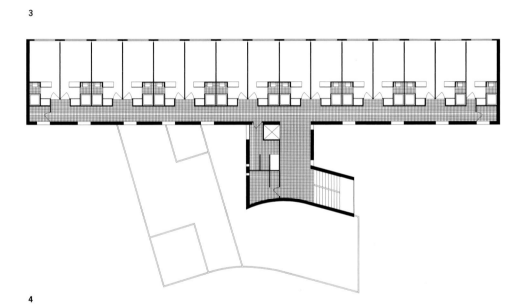

4

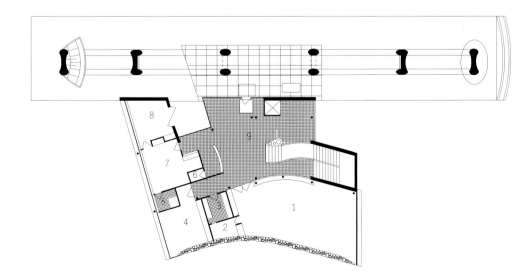

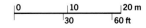

Schminke House

Hans Scharoun, 1893–1972

Löbau, Germany; 1932–3

Hans Scharoun was one of the leading exponents of the strand of Modernism pioneered by Hugo Häring and generally referred to as Organic Architecture. Häring's approach was epitomized by the project for a 'house shaped by use and movement' that he published in 1923 – the same year as Mies van der Rohe's far better known project for a Brick Country House. Whereas Mies's design was a field of space articulated by free-standing planes – an experiment en route to the **Barcelona Pavilion** (page 58) – and gave no hint as to how it might be inhabited, Häring showed every piece of furniture to illustrate how his walls literally wrapped themselves around tables and chairs to create specific places. Rejecting all aesthetic dogma, Häring also rejected Le Corbusier, seeing him as a representative of 'Latin Classicism', determined to impose geometric forms on life rather than to allow them to grow 'organically' – as in nature – by wrapping 'light constructions, with elastic and supple materials' around the needs of the client's brief and in response to the site.

Although deeply influenced by Häring's ideas, Scharoun was by no means unresponsive to the visual power of Le Corbusier's work – an early

sketch for the Schminke House shows the owner's car sweeping up under a projecting terrace, suggesting a likely debt to the **Villa Savoye** (page 62). Despite sharing a similar formal language to the Purist villas, however, in almost all other respects Scharoun's design can be seen as the antithesis of Le Corbusier's ideals. Whereas Le Corbusier exploited the tension between a complex programme and geometric form, Scharoun allowed the exterior to expand and contract in response to spatial and functional pressures.

The clients for the house were the wealthy industrialist Fritz Schminke and his wife. Their site, near the Czech border, was challenging, enjoying a spectacular distant view to the northeast, and being entered from the south. In response, Scharoun placed the main body of the house facing south, but turned the east and west ends to run parallel to the site boundaries. This neatly aligned the solarium at the eastern end towards the view – a direction Scharoun labelled *Blickachse* (view axis) on some of the plans. The main stair was then aligned on this same diagonal, creating a dynamic element at the centre of the plan, enriching the pattern of movement through the house, and establishing the shifted geometry

as a second orthogonal system that works in counterpoint to the east-west alignment of the main body of the building.

Although the spaces flow together in the Modern manner, they are also clearly identified as well-defined territories designed for specific activities: a bay is pushed out to create a place for the dining table, while a free-standing fireplace gives focus to the living room, around whose perimeter are long runs of built-in seating. The lighting is similarly varied and responsive: a ceiling light for the dining table; place-lamps for the piano, hearth and sofa; and spotlights for bookshelves and flowers. The thrust to the right introduced by the diagonal shift is exploited to create a progression towards the sun and view that culminates in the fully glazed solarium and winter garden on the ground level and the terrace of the master bedroom above. Below, on the garden side, the ground falls away dramatically, leaving the house and terraces to soar free above the landscape.

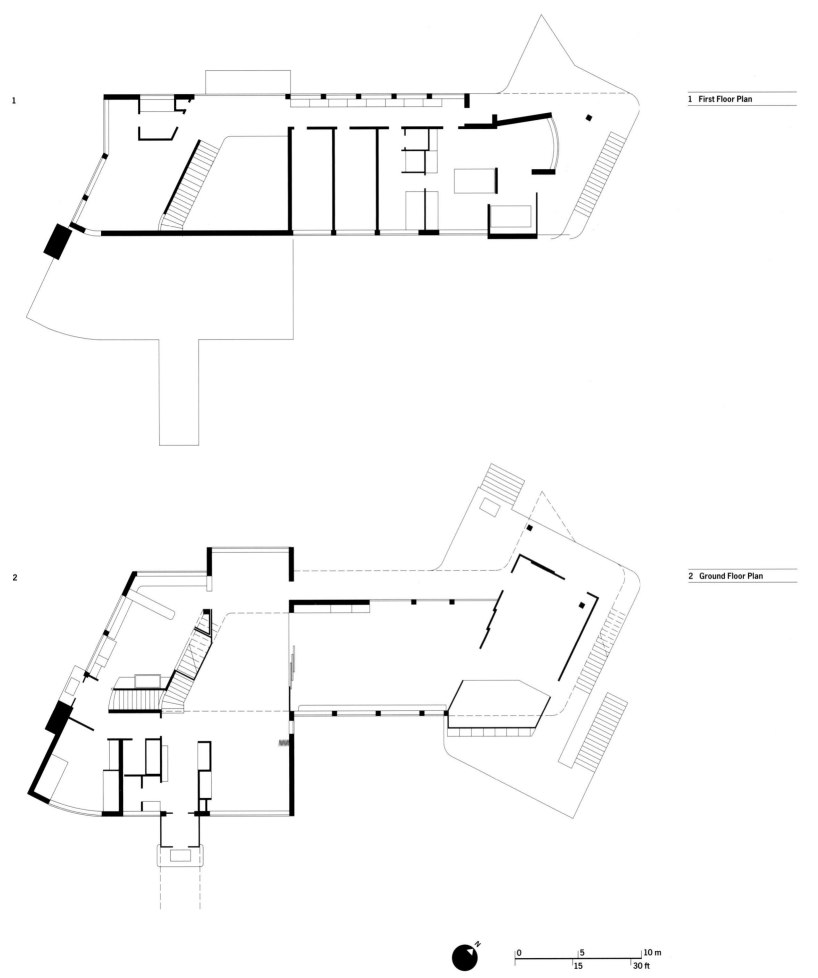

1

2

0   5   10 m
15   30 ft

Casa del Fascio

Giuseppe Terragni, 1904–43

Como, Italy; 1932–6

The Casa del Fascio is the defining achievement of Italian Rationalism, a Modernist movement begun in 1926 by young graduates of Milan Polytechnic. Styling themselves Gruppo 7, they sought to fuse the abstract language of Modernity with the Classical ideals of the Mediterranean. This synthesis proved acceptable to Mussolini and his declaration that Fascism was 'a house of glass' found its most potent expression in Terragni's masterpiece.

The Casa was the local headquarters for the Fascist party. Housing administrative offices and acting as a centre for propaganda and political and social 'education', it was allocated a prominent site opposite the large piazza in front of Como Cathedral on a site defined by the city's Roman grid. Terragni initially organized the accommodation around an open court, but this evolved into a double-height atrium. The centre of a nine-square plan, it is top-lit by glass blocks or lenses set in a matrix of concrete and surrounded on all four sides by offices and meeting rooms accessed from open galleries.

Like Mies van der Rohe's **Barcelona Pavilion** (page 58), the Casa del Fascio stands on a low podium, the steps up to which are the first element of a protracted transition between inside and out. You pass first through a rudimentary porti-

co defined by five free-standing external columns, then a screen of glass doors – these could be electrically operated to open simultaneously, permitting the ceremonial exit of the militia onto the piazza. Beyond the doors lies a transitional zone before the first row of columns that marks the foyer proper: one storey high, this runs between the main stair and a monument to the Fascists' March on Rome in 1922. Finally, you reach the hall itself, a cubic space of startling abstraction from which almost all indications of 'up' and 'down' have been removed.

The abstraction is almost as complete as that of Rietveld's **Schröder House** (page 48), but whereas exponents of De Stijl proceeded from abstract form to material construction, Terragni worked in the opposite direction. The early designs for the Casa were more conventionally building-like – walls pierced with openings – but in the final project Terragni made no distinction between structure and infill. All surfaces are clad in the same Bolticino marble, and the completed building reads as a complex composition of planes and voids designed to suggest the spatial composition within and to affirm the building's links to tradition.

The front, although asymmetrically Modern, is simple and monumental, a multi-storied colonnade

whose recessed layers – glazed screen at ground floor, loggia at the top – subtly indicate the presence of the atrium. The rear façade is carved away at the centre, its residual structural frame intended to recall, perhaps, the garden façade of a Palladian villa. The southern façade is the most closed, and in his presentation of the scheme in the magazine *Quadrante* in 1936, Terragni included solar diagrams to explain his efforts to avoid over-heating. The north-facing façade is the most complex. Here, the atrium is projected onto the wall plane and its geometry is used in turn to control the dimensions of the openings to left and right, permitting a subtle balance between a statement of both the overall tripartite division and the disposition of rooms within.

At first sight, the Casa del Fascio suggests a solid cube that has been hollowed out, with thick walls and deep-set windows. But this perception quickly gives way to a reading of a structural frame and layered planes: what at first appeared to be individual, framed windows are now seen as glass screens running behind the frontal planes of stone. Declining to choose between an architecture of the wall and that of a structural frame and infill, Terragni offered a uniquely potent synthesis of tradition and Modernity.

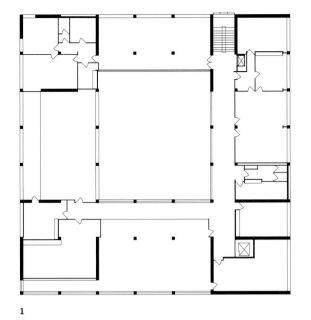

1

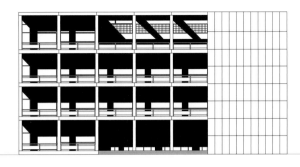

2

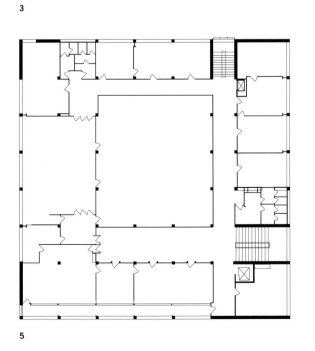

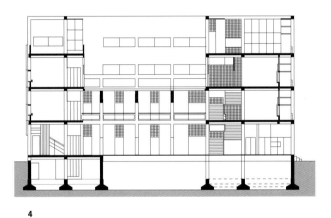

3   4

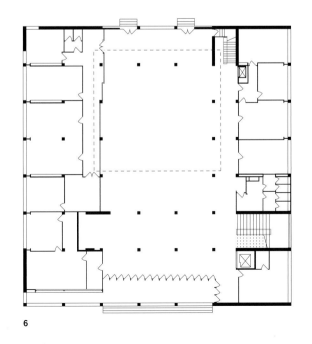

5   6

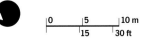

N

0   5   10 m
   15   30 ft

Gothenburg Law Courts Annex

Erik Gunnar Asplund, 1885–1940

Gothenburg, Sweden; 1934–7

This project's complex history began in 1913, when Asplund won the competition to alter and extend the Law Courts in Gothenburg with a design of National Romantic inspiration. This evaded the difficult problem of adding to a Classical design by proposing a total transformation of the existing building and integration of the extension to form a new whole. Through a succession of subsequent schemes, of overtly Classical design, Asplund gradually developed the idea of the extension as an attached pavilion whose composition deferred to the existing building while maintaining an identity of its own.

The façade we see today, arrived at as late as 1936, after construction had begun, is a masterly reconciliation of old and new, Classical and Modern. The internal structure of floor slabs and columns is expressed as an abstract, gridded frame — reminiscent of Terragni's contemporaneous **Casa del Fascio** (page 74) — while the asymmetrical pattern of windows subordinates the extension to the old building and, simultaneously, hints at the internal organization. The two right-hand end windows of the 'old' building are, in fact, new, and the four new openings with bas-reliefs above them are asymmetrical not only within the

whole, but also within themselves. They also mark the most important rooms on the front façade and delineate the size of the atrium within.

The interior underwent a similarly comprehensive transformation. Asplund originally envisaged glazing over the courtyard of the existing building, but as the idea of a distinct extension developed, he proposed a separate atrium for the extension, at first circular, then square. The final solution leaves the existing courtyard open, but integrates it into a fictive inside-outside space by linking it to the new atrium via a glass wall. The superbly refined detailing of this space combined exposed structure and other overtly Modern features, such as the free-standing glass lift shaft, with plywood panelling, timber handrails and bentwood furniture. Its impact was immediate and widely felt: here, in essence, was the basis — developed almost in parallel in the work of Aalto — of that 'humane', 'natural' Scandinavian style that would be so widely emulated in the '50s and '60s.

Asplund's sensitivity to the needs of the building's users is everywhere apparent. The main stair from ground to first floor — in Classical terms, the *piano nobile* — is a single flight of unusually low pitch: the necessarily slow ascent to

the courts was calculated to calm frayed nerves. The other floors are served by a dog-leg stair that disappears upwards, as if to heaven, into a glazed slot. Finished in blue leather, its lowest step, extended to match the semi-circular landings, seems to curve round in greeting, while the slender steel balusters bend as if in response to the weight of your body.

The courts themselves are, by the standards of most countries, remarkably informal. Potato-shaped in plan — their limp curves are worlds apart from Aalto's dynamic use of curves — and with asymmetrically arranged furniture, they present a radically modernized vision of justice. The judiciary are seated only slightly higher than the rest of the court, with the presiding judge at the same level as the rest, while distinctions between the accused, lawyers and the public are drawn only by the furniture.

1

2

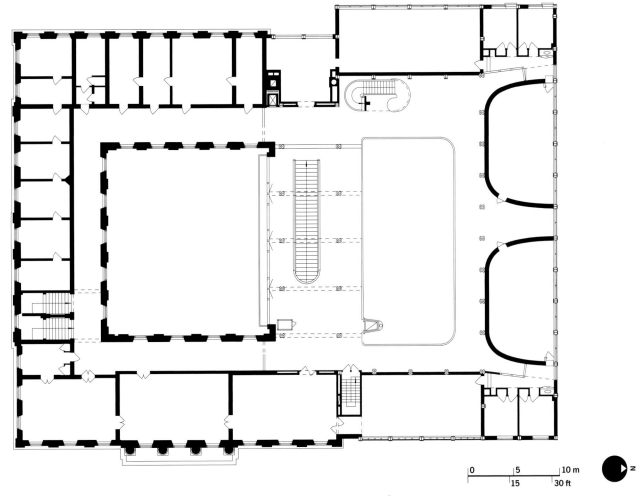

3

0   5   10 m
15   30 ft

N

Fallingwater

Frank Lloyd Wright, 1867–1959

Bear Run, Pennsylvania, USA; 1935–7

Edgar and Liliane Kaufmann, owners of the Kaufmann Department Store in nearby Pittsburgh and clients for Fallingwater, were introduced to Frank Lloyd Wright through their son, Edgar Jr., who had started work the previous year as an apprentice at Wright's combined office and school, the Taliesin Fellowship. They owned 1,600 acres of land in the Allegheny Mountains and to their surprise Wright selected an unlikely site dominated by a stream and small waterfall, adjacent to a large boulder that had become Edgar's favourite resting-spot on their many visits. The idea of building the house 'to the music of the stream' apparently occurred to Wright on his first visit, but the design took nine months to mature and he famously only committed his ideas to paper after his clients announced that they were going to drop by a few hours later to see how the plans were progressing!

Structured as a series of reinforced concrete trays, cantilevered from a rock ledge next to the stream, the house is supported by orthogonally arranged loadbearing walls and piers. They were made of local stone, specially quarried nearby and laid in irregularly coursed horizontal beds, the thinner of which project to form narrow ledges. The result, as Wright intended, recalls the eroded bed-ding planes of sedimentary rock more than conventional masonry. As in the Prairie Houses, the living room moves from a relatively dark entrance and hearth to open terraces, towards which you gravitate, drawn by the sound of falling water. The hearth is the surface of an enormous boulder – Edgar's former resting-spot – that emerges through the shiny flagstone floor like a rock in a stream.

The terraces cantilever dramatically more than five metres (16 feet) out over the stream and the main room not only opens out but up – through a glazed concrete trellis – and down, through a sliding glass hatch onto a concrete staircase, hung by steel bars and descending to the stream. Wright thought it could be deepened for swimming, but it was as much an excuse to create the symbolically necessary connection to the water. Above and to the rear of the living room, the bedrooms pinwheel around the central chimney, each a miniature of the space you have left, with its own fireplace and floating terrace.

Wright described the house as 'an extension of the cliff' and anchored it back with a concrete trellis that continues the plane of the first floor tray through the rear stone wall. One of the beams forms a semi-circle to wrap around the trunk of a tree, emphasizing the integration with nature: thus framed and contrasted, you notice how the ridges on the tree's bark are echoed in the striated surfaces of the stones behind. Wright always regarded concrete as a liquid material, and the parapets have correspondingly rounded edges. Just as the walls were metaphoric rocks, in Wright's mind the concrete elements corresponded with the water. He wanted to coat them with gold leaf, so they would come alive by responding to light flashing from running water or flickering through foliage, but it proved too extravagant for even this most enthusiastic of his clients and he settled for a suitably autumnal peach-coloured paint.

Throughout his life Wright was fascinated by natural processes, especially the large-scale ones of geology. He thought of stone as 'the basic material of our planet', which reveals the laws of 'cosmic change', and Fallingwater was designed as an image of flux. At one end of the time-scale, the structure and volumes of its dynamic composition evoke the processes of transformation and erosion that affect rocks, while at the other, by heightening our awareness of the flickering forest light and sounds of moving water, they provide a vivid reminder that life is perpetual change.

The guest wing (added later) is connected to the main house by a semi-circular canopy.

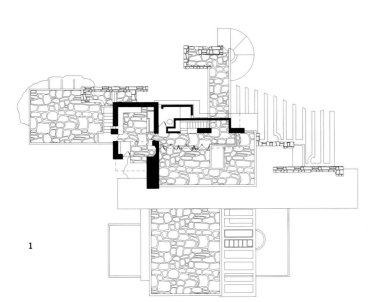

1

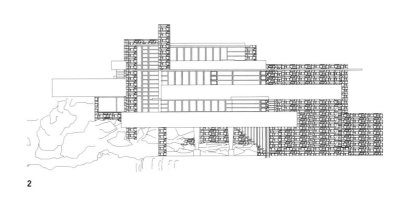

2

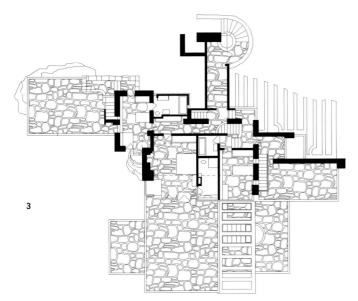

3

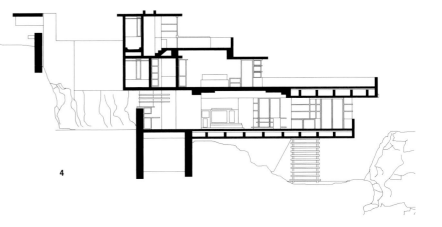

4

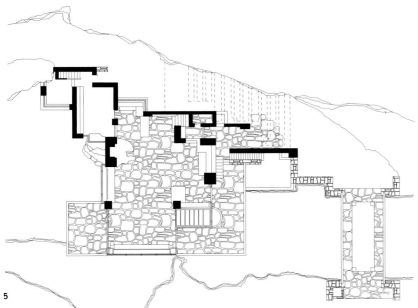

5

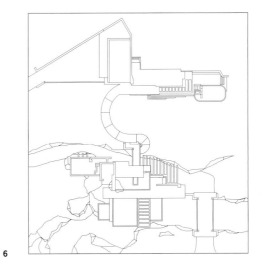

6

| 0 | 5 | 10 m |
| 15 | 30 ft |

Jacobs House

Frank Lloyd Wright, 1867–1959

Madison, Wisconsin, USA; 1936

During the late 1920s Frank Lloyd Wright developed a vision based on what he called 'Ruralism' – the opposite of Le Corbusier's *Urbanisme*, the title of a 1924 book, translated five years later as 'The City of Tomorrow'. Whereas Le Corbusier envisaged apartment blocks in a continuous green park crisscrossed by elevated highways, Wright proposed a radically restructured suburbia. He designed prototype houses for a variety of incomes, naming the most basic 'Usonians', and in 1936 built the first of many – for journalist Herbert Jacobs and his wife.

At 125 square metres (1,350 square feet) the Jacobs House is, by American standards, small for a three-bedroom home. Loathing the convention of placing a dwelling in the centre of its plot, Wright developed an L-shaped plan to frame the garden. He positioned the house close to the boundary, with only the high-level windows to the bedroom corridor visible to public gaze, and a place for the car conveniently close to the entrance under the shelter of a carport – a Wright invention. At the heart of the plan, between the fireplace and the bathroom, is the kitchen, which, for reasons of economy, was designed like a ship's galley. To one side, the dining and living areas form a continuous living space, articulated by brick piers and enclosed

by long runs of book-shelving and a screen of glazed opening doors, while to the other, the three bedrooms form a staggered tail of accommodation served by a single-banked corridor.

Wright believed that a constructional system formed the basis of any genuine architecture, and for the Jacobs House he used a cheap and highly efficient combination of masonry and timber. The service core is framed by solid walls, but for the most part the perimeter was either glazed or of a board and batten sandwich panel of extreme thinness – in long runs, the bookshelves were essential to help ensure structural stiffness. The stripes of the horizontal battens control the vertical dimensions, while in plan the houses were laid out on a 1.2 x 2.4-metre (4 x 8-foot) module to suit the standard sizes of plywood sheets: the grid is marked in the painted concrete floor slab as a reminder of the underlying discipline.

The overhanging roof prevents unwanted solar gains in summer but allows in the low winter sun to warm the interior. The brick walls and concrete floor – into which heating pipes were embedded – act as a 'thermal flywheel', releasing the heat absorbed during the day as free warmth in the evening. Wright's use of underfloor heating was

novel, inspired, he said, by Japanese and Korean examples. But he may well have known of a 1907 book by the Englishman Arthur Henry Barker that promoted a revival of this ancient technique.

Wright thought of the garden as the most important 'room' in the Jacobs House: in organic architecture, he said, 'we have no longer an outside and an inside as two separate things. Now the outside may come inside, and the inside may and does go outside.' He rejected air-conditioning: in a 1954 book, *The Natural House*, he wrote that 'whether people are fully conscious of this or not, they actually derive countenance and sustenance from the "atmosphere" of the things they live in or with. They are rooted in them just as a plant is in the soil.'

Environmentally conscious before its time, the Jacobs House attracted considerable interest as a solution to the 'small house problem'. The January 1938 issue of *Architectural Forum* magazine was devoted to it, and in his article Wright made no claims about its beauty, but pragmatically stressed the practical, cost-saving benefits of his methods. Although modest in scale, and far less spectacular than the **Robie House** or **Fallingwater** (pages 34 and 78), the Usonians deserve to rank among Wright's finest achievements.

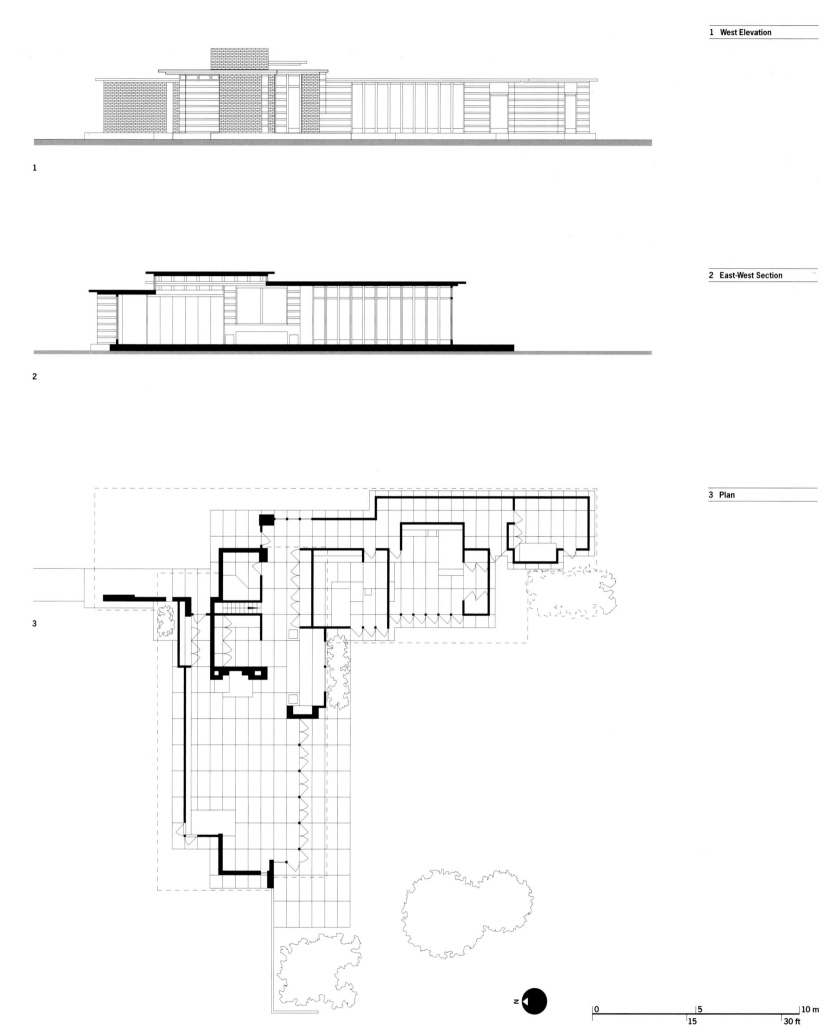

1

2

3

N

0		5		10 m
	15		30 ft	

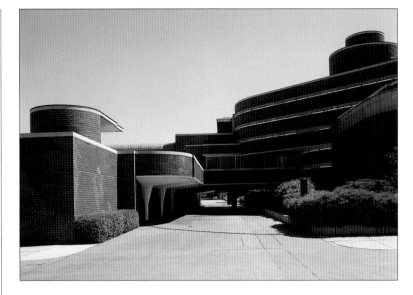

Johnson Wax Administration Building

Frank Lloyd Wright, 1867–1959

Racine, Wisconsin, USA; 1936–9

Thanks to the efforts of designers like Raymond Loewy and Norman Bel Geddes, the 1930s in America became known as 'The Streamlined Decade'. Developed to help vehicles move through air or water with least resistance, streamlining was extended to everything from refrigerators to staplers. The Johnson Wax Administration Building was, in part, Wright's response to this all-pervasive sense of fluidity; in it he achieved his most powerful inversions of traditional constructional forms.

Although the almost suburban site was far more appealing than the tough surroundings of the **Larkin Building** (page 26), Wright again opted for a wholly introverted organization. Here, a top-lit space akin to the nave-like atrium of the earlier building acted as an entrance hall, its height dramatically enhanced by being entered from under the low, spreading carport. Beyond lay one of Wright's – and the century's – great spaces: a forest of mushroom columns rise from pin-joints cast in bronze and taper gently outwards to meet the circular crowns that branch from the slender shafts. Wright had projected something similar in 1931, for the Salem Capital Journal newspaper plant, but the forms were so novel, and appeared so delicate, that the building inspectors insisted

their strength be proved by a physical test. Never one to doubt his own ideas, Wright famously sat under the trial column as it was stacked with sand-bags to more than ten times the design load!

The interior is suffused with light. It pours down through the gaps between the lily-pad column tops and twice rings the space, courtesy of a slot below the soffit of the surrounding balcony and the curved glazed corner – a kind of 'anti-cornice' by which Wright destroys any lingering sense of conventional, box-like enclosure. To glaze all these openings, Wright developed a system of Pyrex tubes. The result, as described by Henry-Russell Hitchcock, the first major commentator on Wright, gives 'a certain illusion of sky seen from the bottom of an aquarium'. Visually, the tube-glazing was a beguiling invention, but technically it proved fraught. In the days before flexible sealants, the caulking in the joints cracked under thermal stresses, enhancing Wright's reputation as a master of leaks and leading to much of the glass being replaced with shaped plastic sheeting.

Externally, Wright opted for a combination of smooth red engineering bricks and red sandstone, capped by rounded copings of concrete set flush with the wall surfaces. The bedding joints of the

brickwork were raked to emphasize the flow and horizontality of the smooth, rounded forms – seen at their most fluent in the sweeping perimeter of the upper 'penthouse' offices. The result, as Hitchcock was quick to point out, was far more like some great machine for working in and, as such, more convincing than anything achieved in Europe. Inside and out, the building projected a business-like air of efficiency while creating a calm, relaxed atmosphere for the employees.

To Wright, a great place of work like the Johnson Wax building made the company one of the few institutions capable of uniting scattered non-spatial communities created by the motor car. He persuaded his clients to include some communal facilities in the building, such as a squash court and a 250-seat auditorium. Intended, presumably, for films, lectures and meetings, it was sited on the mezzanine level and, as a mark of its social importance, occupied a central, axial position in relation to the adjacent 'cathedral' of work. The company's investment was well rewarded: when the building opened in 1939, it generated so much publicity in newspapers, magazines and on television that Johnson Wax were able to claim that it had effectively paid for itself.

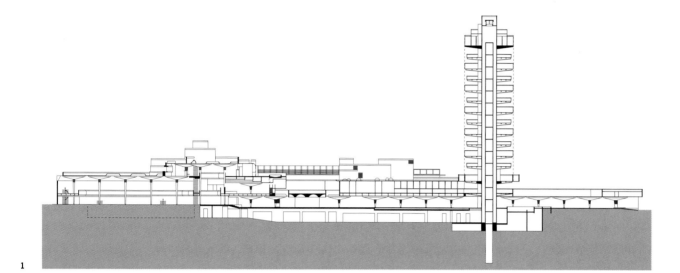

1

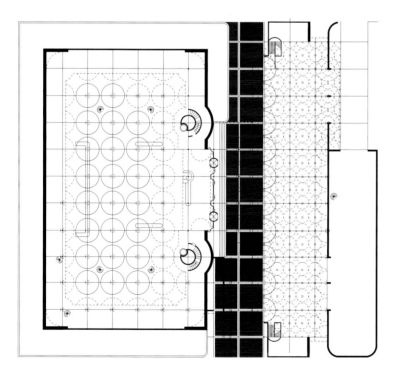

2

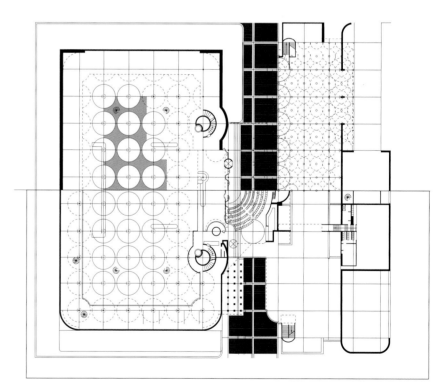

3

0 5 10 m
15 30 ft

N

Baker House

Alvar Aalto, 1898–1976

Massachusetts Institute of Technology, Cambridge, Massachusetts, USA; 1937–40

Alvar Aalto survived the stringent wartime economy in his native Finland by making regular trips across the Atlantic to teach as a visiting professor at the Massachusetts Institute of Technology (MIT). These trips continued after the War, at which time he began to reflect more deeply on the issues that seemed to him of overwhelming importance in developing a more humane modern architecture: 'How can one subdue a machine without destroying it, how can one preserve industry without "industrializing" man?' Ever loyal to his native country, Aalto suggested that recent Finnish successes with timber-framed, prefabricated houses illustrated how the 'flexible standardization' of nature could be emulated using industrial means.

Through his work at MIT, Aalto also came into contact with a burgeoning debate about 'a new monumentality' in architecture – an issue addressed in print by Sigfried Giedion and Louis Kahn, among others – and in 1937 the Institute gave him the chance to build a response to the issues of technology, monumentality and humanism by commissioning him to design Baker House, a large dormitory for senior students. The chosen site on Memorial Drive was long and relatively narrow and ran parallel to the adjacent Charles River.

Despite his reputation as an intuitive designer whose ideas emerged from soft-pencil sketches, Aalto presented the project as an exercise in rational design. In a series of comparative studies, he illustrated the advantages and disadvantages of various more conventionally 'functional' volumetric arrangements, evaluating each in terms of sun, view and privacy. His point was that while the serpentine, double-curved form he chose might appear 'irrational', a formal echo of the meandering river rather than a logical solution to the problem, in fact it made best use of the site by affording nearly every room both sunlight and a view of the river. It seems unlikely, however, that these studies played a part in the genesis of the design. They were intended, rather, as a critique of orthodox Modern architecture of the Bauhaus kind – an example of which, a new graduate student centre, was being designed up the road at Harvard by Walter Gropius and The Architects Collaborative.

The serpentine plan generated a variety of room shapes, which the students soon named 'coffins, pies, and couches', and was set against an orthogonal, diagonally aligned, two-storey block containing the communal facilities. The main corridor was broad and varied, swelling and narrowing

in response to the density of use or to accommodate informal sitting areas, and Aalto's choice of stairs – a cantilevered pair that cascaded, *scala-regia*-like towards the main entrance – gave the elevation facing the campus a distinctive, and decidedly monumental, quality. The stairs were originally to have been tile-hung, but stucco had to be substituted to save money.

For the brick walls, Aalto chose a rough clinker brick that came in a surprising variety of colours and irregular shapes. He asked that even the most erratically formed ones should be used – some are literally banana shaped and appear to be on the brink of falling out of the walls – and also specified that the bedding joints should be more deeply recessed than the vertical joints. The result is brilliantly alive, a vivid demonstration of 'flexible standardization' that reminded MIT's Dean of Architecture and Planning, William Wurster, of Florence. Aalto was doubtless delighted.

1

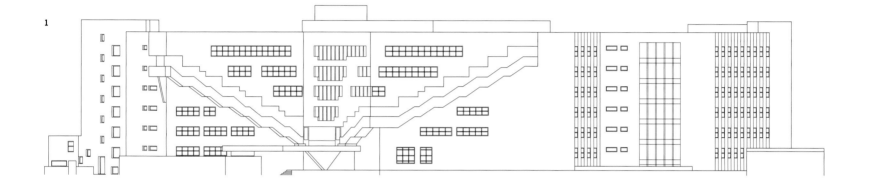

2

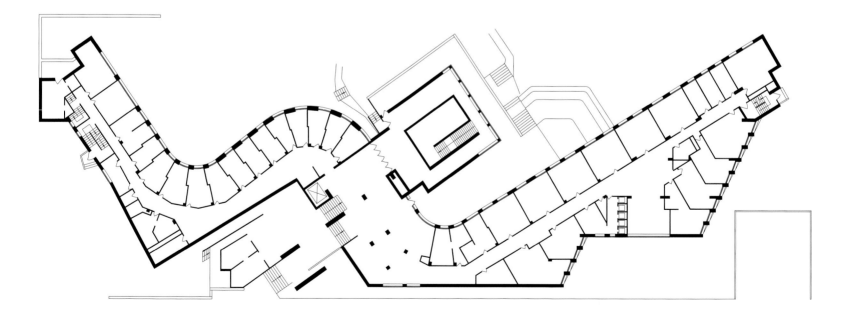

0   5   10 m
  15   30 ft

Villa Mairea

Alvar Aalto, 1898–1976

Noormarkku, Finland; 1937–40

Built for industrialists Harry and Maire Gullichsen, the Villa Mairea is a grand version of the summer cottages valued throughout the Nordic countries as opportunities to retreat to nature. The clients asked Aalto for a house that was both contemporary and Finnish and this inspired him to produce a unique and radical synthesis of modernity and tradition. His starting point was a wooden farmstead and the house is conceived less as a single structure than as a grouping of buildings, earth mounds and planting to frame a courtyard.

Traditionally, the first building to be erected was the sauna, and in the Villa Mairea it can be seen as the first element of a composition that grows in technological sophistication around the courtyard to culminate in Maire's cantilevered first floor studio. During the 1920s she had studied painting in Paris and perhaps in allusion to this her studio is clad with subtly moulded boards that have the same profile as those Aalto used on the Finnish Pavilion at the 1935 Paris World's Fair. With its grass roof and wooden walls, the sauna appears thoroughly traditional, but unlike vernacular forms its roof is flat and the cladding has the sophistication of a Japanese tea-house. Similar complexities occur throughout the house: the cov-

ered dining terrace, for example, recalls a single-storey fragment of the stripped-down concrete frame of the archetypal Modern house, but its grass roof on timber boarding drains to a wooden gutter hollowed from a log.

Internally, Aalto combines a modern open plan with memories of the traditional *tupa*, the large living room of farmhouses in which poles at ceiling level defined areas for different activities. In the Villa Mairea, Aalto places the entrance space at a lower level, changes the floor finishes so that they become progressively more domestic and intimate – from stone through tiles to timber boarding and rugs – and contrasts a 'flowing' living space with a more formal setting for dining.

Most radical is the treatment of the columns. The grid is regular, but 'to avoid all artificial architectural rhythms', as Aalto put it, no two columns are alike. All but one – a reinforced concrete column in the library – are circular steel sections and painted black, but they are individualized by being variously doubled or trebled, wrapped with rattan singly or in pairs, or clad with birchwood strips. In place of the 'clear structure' that Mies saw as essential to the free plan, Aalto gave his clients an abstraction of the Finnish pine for-

est, an image rendered all the more vivid by the fact that the bark of mature pine trees peels away along part of their height to reveal a golden core.

The tree-like columns recall their natural origins and are complemented by the 'forest light' Aalto creates in the undulating screen that fills the slot between the library's bookcase partitions and the ceiling. Glass alternates with solid, curved panels, so that when low sun, or artificial light, spills out it recalls sunlight through trees. The twin-stemmed white column supporting the studio can be seen as a metaphoric birch tree at the edge of the 'pine-forest' within. The inclined half is structurally redundant, and the engineer asked for it to be omitted – like several 'painterly' touches in the building, it was reinstated at Maire's insistence.

In the Villa Mairea, Aalto used the technique of collage to combine fragments designed to bring to mind memories of nature, traditional Finnish buildings and more exotic sources: Japan most obviously, but also Italy – the white surfaces are lime-washed brickwork, not render. By 'naturalizing' the column grid, Aalto weakened the inherent structure of the main living area so that it appears to open and close: as in a forest, you feel as though you are the moving centre of the space.

3 First Floor Plan

1 Studio
2 Maire's Bedroom
3 Upper Hall with Fireplace
4 Harry's Bedroom
5 Terrace
6 Children's Hall/Playroom
7 Children's Bedrooms
8 Guest Rooms

5 Ground Floor Plan

1 Swimming Pool
2 Sauna
3 Winter Garden
4 Living Room
5 Library
6 Dining Room
7 Entrance Hall
8 Main Entrance
9 Staff Rooms
10 Office
11 Kitchen

1

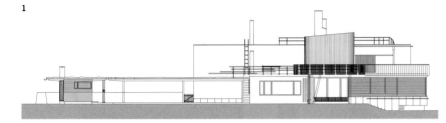

2

3

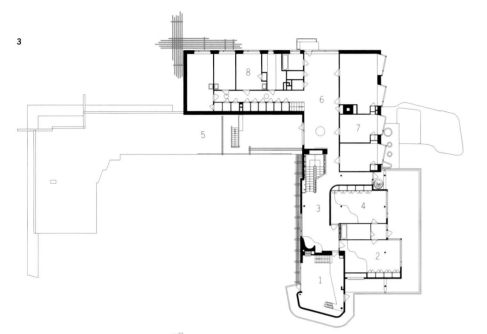

4

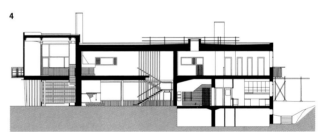

5

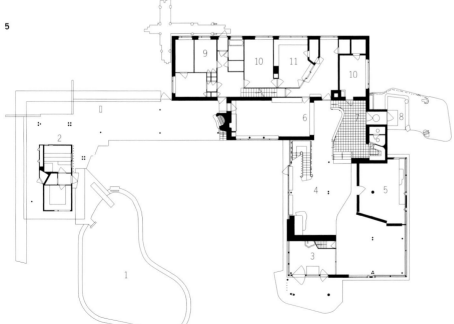

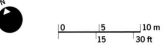

Guggenheim Museum

Frank Lloyd Wright, 1867–1959

New York City, New York, USA; 1943–59

Solomon R. Guggenheim, one of the richest men in America, was a serious art collector with predictably conventional tastes — until he met the artist Hilla Rebay, a German baroness and confidante of leading Modernists. Her closest links were to Rudolf Bauer, who claimed his brand of abstract painting represented a cosmic 'realm of the spirit'; together they christened it 'Non-objectivity'. Rebay moved to New York in 1927, where she met the Guggenheims and then, two years later, escorted them to Europe. Solomon returned with the first pieces — by Kandinsky, Mondrian, Moholy-Nagy and Bauer, among others — in what was destined to become a major collection of Non-objective art. He placed money at Rebay's disposal and talked about building a museum as a 'Temple of Non-objectivity'. To Rebay, Non-objectivity was a pure art of space, form and line that went beyond the formalized abstractions from nature that had become basic to much of Wright's architecture. It was deemed capable, in the sensitive observer, of effecting spiritual transformation, and Guggenheim's museum was to be, in Rebay's words, 'a quiet, peaceful, elevating sanctuary for those who need a cultural life'.

Although Wright's organic approach was broadly sympathetic to Rebay's ideas, in other respects he was an unlikely choice to design the museum, never having been slow to hide his disdain for most Modern art. Wright initially favoured a horizontal, spreading building on a hilltop site overlooking the Hudson River, but a location on Fifth Avenue, close to the Metropolitan Museum and facing Central Park was finally agreed. For this he turned to his 1923–4 project for the Gordon Strong Automobile Objective and Planetarium. Its circular, ziggurat-like form, developed around a double helix of ramps for cars, might appear an improbable addition to New York's grid plan, but in Wright's mind the continuity of surface, light and experience it could afford would be ideal for creating both an imposing unity and the intimate encounters with paintings that Rebay believed vital.

The final circular, inverted ziggurat form was one of several Wright explored, and from the start serious doubts were expressed about how paintings might be displayed along a continuous ramp, and whether or not people would become bored by the almost unchanging experience. As a monument to 'cosmic order' its merits were clear, but its practicality, let alone flexibility, as a working gallery was less obvious. For Wright, Non-objective art demanded a radically new form of display — paintings were freed of frames and glass, angled down towards the viewer and 'liberated' in space by the curved wall. He called it 'an atmosphere' for art and argued that comparisons with conventional galleries could not begin to suggest the power of the total integration of painting and environment he envisaged. The finished building offers the ultimate expression of continuity and plasticity in Wright's work and, more specifically, of the 'fluid nature' of concrete. When it finally opened, the building's public reception was hugely enthusiastic, but professionals were still divided about its suitability for the display of paintings and its appropriateness to the site, some even describing it as an egotistical, attention-grabbing attack on both Modern art and the city.

As a museum, Wright's design was inseparable from the radical aspiration of creating a new kind of 'temple' for art, but what has never been in doubt — and was recognized even by his dissenters from the moment it opened — is its social success. The Guggenheim Museum quickly became one of New York's major tourist attractions and a popular meeting place for residents, yet despite their numbers the interior retains an extraordinary feeling of serenity — a quality no longer apparent in many more traditionally conceived museums.

1 Entrance
2 Main Gallery
3 Ramp
4 Gallery
5 Offices
6 Sculpture Garden

1

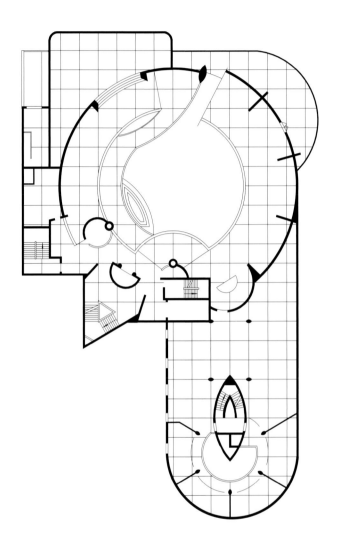

2

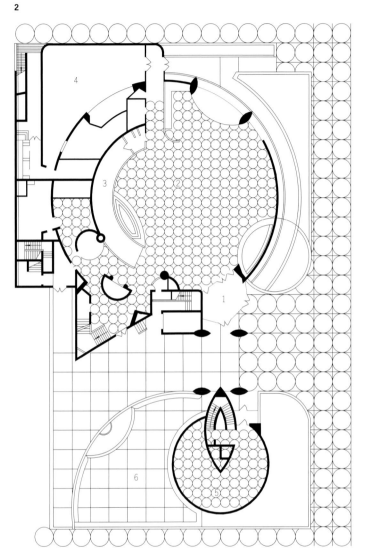

3

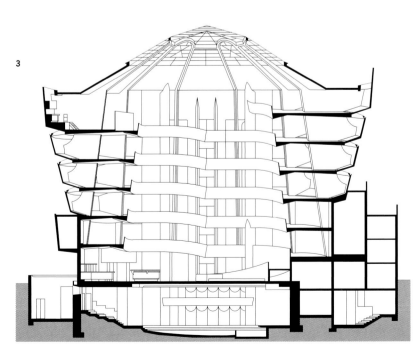

0   5   10 m
15   30 ft

Eames House

Charles, 1907–78, and Ray, 1912–89, Eames

Los Angeles, California, USA; 1945–9

The Eames House is the best known of many developed under the acclaimed 'Case Study House Program' run, until the early 1960s, by John Entenza, editor of the hugely influential Californian magazine *Arts and Architecture*. Commissioning mostly young architects, he encouraged them to be innovative in their use of materials and in planning for the climate of southern California. Although Charles Eames was an architect, he and his wife Ray, a painter, made their reputation as furniture designers. The initial design for their house was prepared in 1945 in collaboration with Eero Saarinen, but when the materials finally arrived on site in late 1948, Charles Eames radically altered his ideas.

The delicate glass and steel design that emerged from Eames's on-site improvisation used standard industrial lattice beams and window sections to create a modular structure assembled from bays 2.25 metres wide by 6 metres deep (7^1/$_2$ x 20 feet). Organized into two two-storey pavilions, the accommodation was ranged between a 60-metre (200-foot) long retaining wall and a screen of mature eucalyptus trees. The larger pavilion, eight bays long, contains the house proper, and this is separated from the five-bay studio

by a courtyard. The end bay is left open on two sides to form a porch, and a first-floor sleeping loft covers part of the volume internally.

Both pavilions are enclosed by slender black steel window sections, horizontally proportioned and variously in-filled with a mixture of different types of glass, from clear to translucent, and solid panels. To avoid an overly insistent repetition of the module, blocks of either white or one of the primary colours are deployed in a wide range of sizes. Internally, the ribbed underside of the profiled steel ceiling is exposed and painted white, as are the steel beams. The mezzanine sleeping loft is reached via a delicate spiral stair with plywood treads and the light can be modified by sliding panels modelled on Japanese *shoji* screens. The interior is made magical by the varied play of light created by the combination of clear and translucent glass, and the play of shadows from the eucalyptus trees that either dapple the floor or flicker across the milky-white translucent panels.

The Eames House was conceived, literally and metaphorically, as a frame for living, and much of its magic resides in the way that the trees, plants, furniture and carefully assembled objects and decorations – many bought on the Eames's

extensive travels – become as much part of the total effect as the building fabric. For many, it came to epitomize the emerging California lifestyle. To his friend Peter Smithson, for example, Charles Eames seemed 'a natural California Man, using his native resources and know-how – of the film-making, the aircraft and the advertising industries – as others drink water; that is almost without thinking'. For magazines such as *Life* and *Vogue* the house offered a perfect emblem for the burgeoning consumer society and was widely used in fashion and advertising photography. And to architects, the house represented, as Entenza put it, 'an attempt to state an idea rather than a fixed architectural pattern'. This struck a chord worldwide and by the mid 1960s the Eames house was established as one of the iconic achievements of post-war architecture.

| 1 | West Elevation | 3 | East Elevation | 5 | First Floor Plan | 6 | Section Through Studio | 7 | Ground Floor Plan | 8 | North Elevation |

5 First Floor Plan

1 Upper Part of Living Room
2 Bedroom
3 Dressing Alcove/Room
4 Hall
5 Bathroom
6 Storage Deck
7 Upper Part of Studio

7 Ground Floor Plan

1 Living Room
2 Dining Room
3 Kitchen
4 Utility Room
5 Courtyard
6 Dark Room
7 Studio

2 Section Through Living Room

4 South Elevation

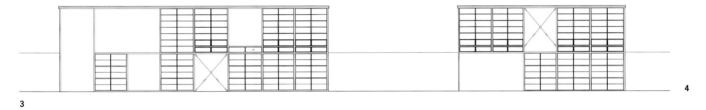

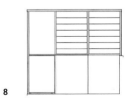

1

2

3

4

5

6

7

8

0   5   10 m
    15   30 ft
N

Farnsworth House

Mies van der Rohe, 1886–1969

Plano, Illinois, USA; 1945–51

Edith Farnsworth, the client for one of the defining projects of post-war architecture, was a successful nephrologist. She met Mies at a party and mentioned that she was thinking of building a weekend house; he naturally offered his services. They became good friends (but probably no more, contrary to popular assumptions), and she was quickly won over to Mies's vision of a 'less is more' architecture. The site she owned was prone to flooding, and in response the single-storey house was elevated by 1.5 metres (5 feet), with rectangular floor and roof planes hovering between eight H-section columns.

A broad flight of steps leads up to a third rectangular plane, intermediate between the ground and living planes and floating above the ground on stubby columns. A further flight of identical steps rises onto a covered terrace at the end of the fully glazed volume. The interior is an open 'universal space' (cp. **Crown Hall**, page 106) sub-divided, but not partitioned, by a free-standing service core containing two bathrooms, a galley kitchen and a fireplace. Privacy was afforded by curtains and, as in the **Tugendhat House** (page 60), Mies's own furniture was laid out in perfect islands on cream-coloured rugs.

The materials are quietly luxurious – travertine floors, primavera wood panelling on the core, and Chinese shantung silk for the curtains – and the detailing minimal and meticulous. The paving is perfectly flat, with open joints for drainage, and the columns are welded to the face of the beams, with all traces of workmanship removed by grinding the welds flat and painting the steel white. When tapped, the structure rings like a tuning fork, and through its taut, minimal forms the house encourages an acute awareness of the environment: waking up to see the curtains alive with the silhouettes cast by the leaves of the adjacent lime tree was, according to a later owner, Lord Palumbo, one of its particular pleasures.

As in all his work, Mies's ideal structure was proportioned by eye, not calculation. Both beams and columns were over-sized according to conventional structural requirements, the former to ensure that the planes remained perfectly level, with no trace of sag, and the columns to suit the size Mies deemed correct visually. Interestingly, the tendency of iron structures to appear uncomfortably slender had been used, in the nineteenth century, as an argument against the acceptance of metal construction.

In the architectural world, the Farnsworth House was widely regarded as the ultimate expression of both the open plan and Mies's aesthetic ideal of *beinahe nichts*, 'almost nothing'. But Edith Farnsworth found its openness intimidating and this, compounded by the fact that it made no concessions to the climate and cost almost double the estimate, led her to sue Mies. He promptly counter-sued for unpaid fees, and eventually won, but the house became the focus of a campaign against the 'self-chosen elite who are trying to tell us what we should like and how we should live', as an article in *House Beautiful* put it.

For Mies the design also marked a turning point. The Farnsworth house retained something of the dynamism and asymmetry that characterized his work of the 1920s, but in retrospect, its frozen perfection and hidden symmetries can be seen to have announced the direction towards the more static, symmetrical and essentially neo-Classical design configurations of later projects, such as Crown Hall and the **Seagram Building** (page 118).

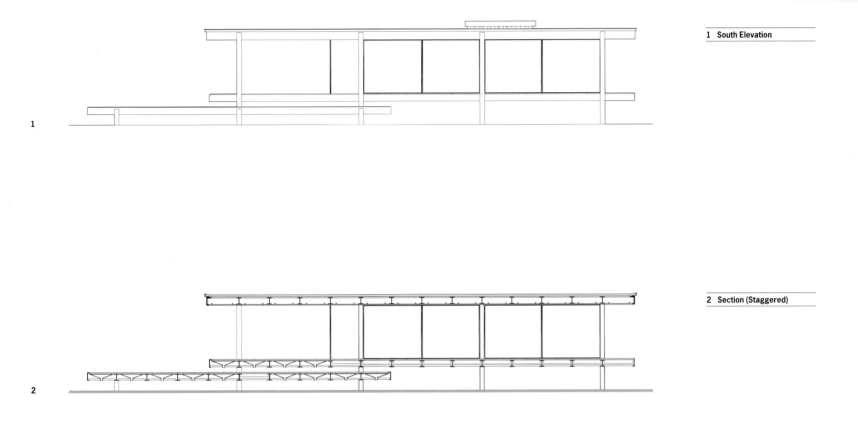

1 South Elevation

2 Section (Staggered)

3 Plan

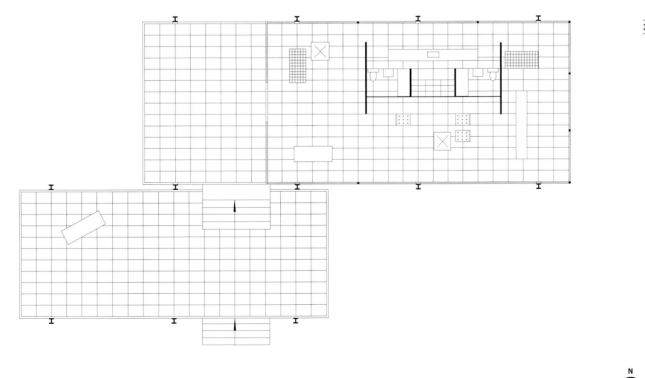

1

2

3

0		5		10 m
	15		30 ft	

N

Kaufmann Desert House

Richard Neutra, 1892–1970

Palm Springs, California, USA; 1946

As the client for Frank Lloyd Wright's **Fallingwater** (page 78), Edgar Kaufmann was already well known as an architectural patron. Having studied with Wright in the Taliesin Fellowship, his son, Edgar Jr., was understandably keen that his father should commission Wright again when he came to build a winter house in Palm Springs, California. Preferring something much lighter in feeling, however, he turned instead to Neutra – and secured from him another classic twentieth-century house.

Although it now forms part of a burgeoning suburb, the 'Desert House' was originally just that, an isolated dwelling sited on a 60 x 90-metre (200 x 300-foot) plot enjoying spectacular views of the surrounding desert and mountains. The main entrance was to the south, and from it a covered path led past a large carport to the living and dining areas, organized around a central fireplace. The servants' quarters were placed to the west and guest accommodation to the north, across a covered patio (later filled in). The master bedroom was to the east, beyond the living room and sharing with it a view of the pool. The overall feel of the house was light and airy, the heaviness of the stone walls being set off by large areas of glass. It was also a model of sophisticated – if not, by today's standards, fully energy-conscious – environmental design: the roof overhangs, adjustable louvres and underfloor heating and cooling systems combined to provide comprehensive and unobtrusive climate control.

The cruciform plan organized around a central fireplace may well have owed a distant debt to some of Wright's early Prairie Houses – and found a more recent echo in the Wingspread House that Wright designed for the Johnson family close to their headquarters in Racine (**Johnson Wax Administration Building**, page 82) – but the attitude to the site that Neutra's house embodied was very different to that espoused by Wright, and intended as a critique of it. Modern technology, Neutra argued, 'enables the architect to extend the habitable area of the world' by taking advantage of prefabrication and air-conditioning, and so a desert house 'cannot ... be "rooted" in a soil to "grow out of it" ... It is frankly an artefact, a construct transported in many shop-fabricated parts over long distance into the midst of rugged aridity.' Unlike Wright, whose own 'desert encampment', Taliesin West, was framed by low, earth-hugging walls whose colour and texture were calculated to echo the surrounding rocks and hills, Neutra preferred an abstract architecture of floating planes and reflective surfaces. Designed to present a complete contrast to the richly textured surroundings, they helped 'to make the rocks more rocky', as he put it.

Around the house Neutra created a 'natural' garden of indigenous rocks and cacti. This was to prove even more influential than the building itself, anticipating ideas promoted in magazines in the 1950s about new approaches to domestic design appropriate to the Californian climate and landscape. It was not, however, a radically 'sustainable' solution because, as generally in southern California before worries about water shortages began to change attitudes, the native planting was contrasted with a verdant oasis of neatly mown lawn around the large, rectangular swimming pool. Neutra's vision, however, echoed in the work of a new generation of architects, helped to define a distinctive southern Californian lifestyle.

1 Living Room   8 Bathroom
2 Dining Room   9 Storage
3 Kitchen   10 Car Shelter
4 Bedroom   11 Swimming Pool
5 Utility Room   12 Gallery
6 Dressing Room   13 Patio
7 Guest Bedroom

1

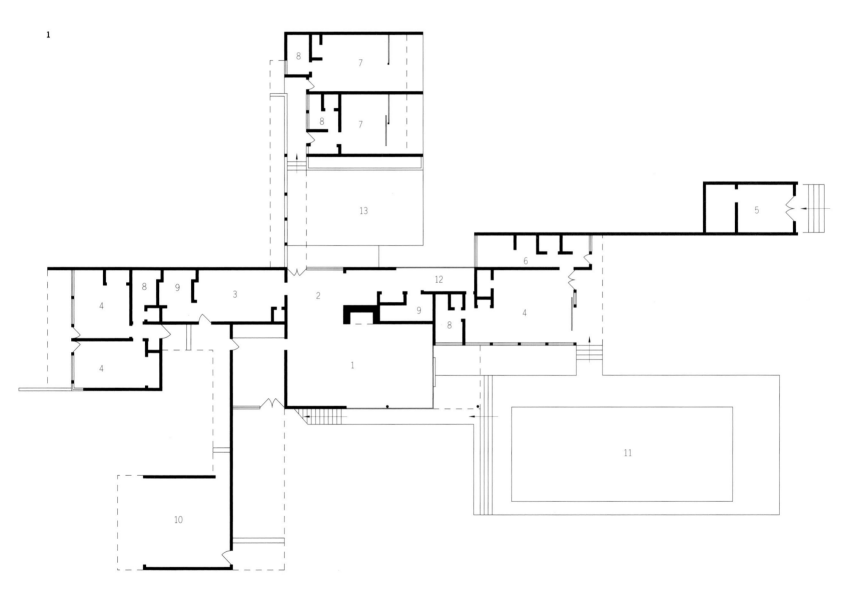

0   5   10 m
15   30 ft

N

Barragán House and Studio

Luis Barragán, 1902–87

Mexico City, Mexico; 1947–8

Born in Guadalajara in 1902, Luis Barragán trained as an engineer before turning to architecture. He travelled to Europe in 1931–2, met Le Corbusier and returned home determined to practise Modern architecture. He established an office in Mexico City, but only eight years later, after completing some 30 International Style projects, announced that he was retiring from commercial practice. He acquired a large estate and worked steadily on it, developing a series of inter-linked walled gardens and one or two houses, the sale of which enabled him to begin work on this house for his own occupation.

Externally, the Barragán House and Studio is stark and unremarkable, an anonymous presence in an unpretentious neighbourhood. But once inside, the ambience is unique. It owes something to Spanish Colonial, more to the vivid colours of traditional Mexican architecture and, in the marked geometric clarity, to the International Style. But the synthesis is uniquely Barragán's: his house is a composition of rooms and, although entirely unrelated stylistically, perhaps the closest comparison is to the *Raumplan* of Adolf Loos's **Müller House** (page 68). The walls are framed in concrete and filled with concrete blocks: most are roughly plas-

tered and brilliantly coloured, their intensity and textures enhanced by indirect lighting. The only other materials visible are pine beams, wide floorboards and volcanic rock paving and steps.

The living room faces the main garden, contained by ivy-clad walls like a captive slice of wild nature. You look into the garden through a vast sheet of glass divided by a thin cruciform mullion: the religious note is deliberate, adding a mystical quality to the boundary between interior and garden. Barragán placed no objects in the garden and, reportedly, never entered it again, allowing free rein to the natural processes of growth and decay.

From the hall a granite staircase supported by a yellow wall connects to the bedrooms, and from the upper floor a small staircase leads to the roof garden. Barragán raised the walls in 1954, six years after moving in, so that this abstract, almost surreal world now opens only to the sky. The idea clearly owed something to Le Corbusier, and the space is contained by coloured walls — cream and terracotta, scarlet and purple — of varied heights, interspersed with tall blocks covered with plain cement. In a light less intense than Mexico's it would be unthinkable and the colours can still appear misleadingly lurid in photographs.

Like Tadao Ando's much later **Koshino House** (page 186), Barragán's home was designed as a defence against an increasingly hectic and unpredictable world. 'The walls create silence', he said, and sheltered by them he could face life. Deeply Catholic, Barragán believed in the redemptive power of beauty and regarded acceptance of solitude as the necessary response to the human condition. His house was also a demonstration of his ideas on time: about the luxury of 'wasting' time in contemplative inaction; about surfaces that register its passage through the development of patina — the antithesis of the pristine, Machine Age finishes of the International Style, intended to appear unchanging and timeless; and finally the ability of the house to change through time in response to his needs and ideas. The cross of redemption in the living room window, for example, was one of his last interventions, its timeless form set against the ever-changing garden that he had long ago abandoned to fate. A bastion against the tumult of modern life, Barragán's house was more like a life lived than a conventional design, and half a century later it remains a compelling critique of the idea that a dwelling place can be reduced to an industrial product or to a frozen work of art.

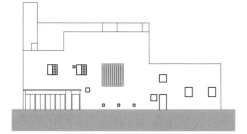

1

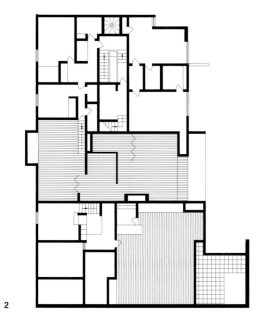

2

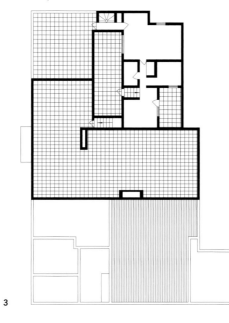

3

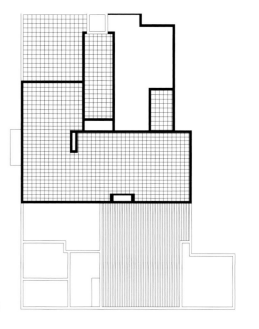

4

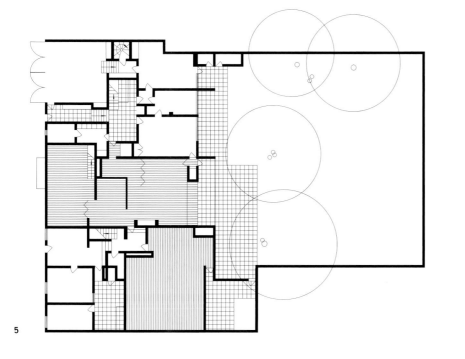

5

0   5   10 m
15   30 ft

N

Unité d'Habitation

Le Corbusier, 1887–1965

Marseilles, France; 1947–52

Promoted as a response to the demands of reconstruction after war, the Marseilles Unité was Le Corbusier's grandest vision of a 'machine for living in'. He called it a 'vertical garden city' – an assemblage of private houses arranged to afford direct access to health-giving nature. The Unité was emphatically not a conventional apartment block and Le Corbusier's conception of the dwelling was at heart thoroughly traditional. It should be centred, he believed, around 'the fire, the hearth', where the family should eat together – although he considered it quite acceptable for modern 'fire' to come down pipes or through wires.

In the absence of servants, he argued, 'the living-room must be a kitchen, the kitchen a living-room': this statement was italicized for emphasis in the book about the project he published in 1953, and he believed it vital that this age-old tradition 'be rehabilitated lest the modern family fall to pieces'. The key to preventing the family's dissolution, he argued, lay in efficiently planned and serviced homes: privacy must be ensured by isolating them from potentially noisy neighbours and a range of support facilities should be close at hand. The Unité was therefore designed as an independent structural framework into which the

individual units could be slotted. In principle, they could have been mass-produced, and a steel-framed prototype was developed by Jean Prouvé; in practice, traditional on-site methods were adopted.

The two-storey units lock together in an ingenious cross-over section, giving each family a frontage and private balcony on both sides of the building, and enabling one broad corridor – Le Corbusier called it an 'interior street' – to serve three storeys. The double-height living room is open to the kitchen, which is placed either under or on the mezzanine floor. The parents have an en suite bathroom, the children their own shower, and light reaches deep into the plan thanks to full-height glazing; which was protected from overheating by a concrete sun-screen or *brise-soleil*.

Twenty-three variants of the basic unit were designed and the 18-storey block contained 337 apartments in all. On the roof were a swimming pool, covered and open gymnasia, and a running track. On the two floors below were a crèche and nursery, and half the seventh and eighth floors were occupied by other communal facilities – a co-operative store, smaller shops, restaurant and hotel.

The first residents preferred to go out for most of their shopping and recreation and the

internal commercial and residential 'streets' became lonely corridors. Gradually, however, the Unité was seen as a desirable place to live by middle-class professionals, and the shops and hotel have now succeeded in serving niche markets. As a fragment of a larger idea for the radical restructuring of the modern city the Unité was flawed. But as an expression of what Le Corbusier described as the 'essential joys' of *soleil, espace et verdure* (sun, space and vegetation), it is almost unrivalled. To Le Corbusier, a roof garden could offer the experience of what he called 'ineffable space', and in his *Œuvre Complète* he set a model of the Unité's sculptured rooftop against a photograph of the Alps: the confrontation with nature, direct and heroic, would be a theme of subsequent work.

Aesthetically, the Unité also marked a radical break. The abstract planes, smooth surfaces and slender columns of his Purist style were abandoned in favour of muscular, sculptural forms and the roughness of raw concrete struck from grainy, timber-boarded shutters. He called this 'new' material *béton brut* and the attitude it suggested was taken up by a younger generation of architects who pioneered a tough new style that English critic Reyner Banham christened the 'New Brutalism'.

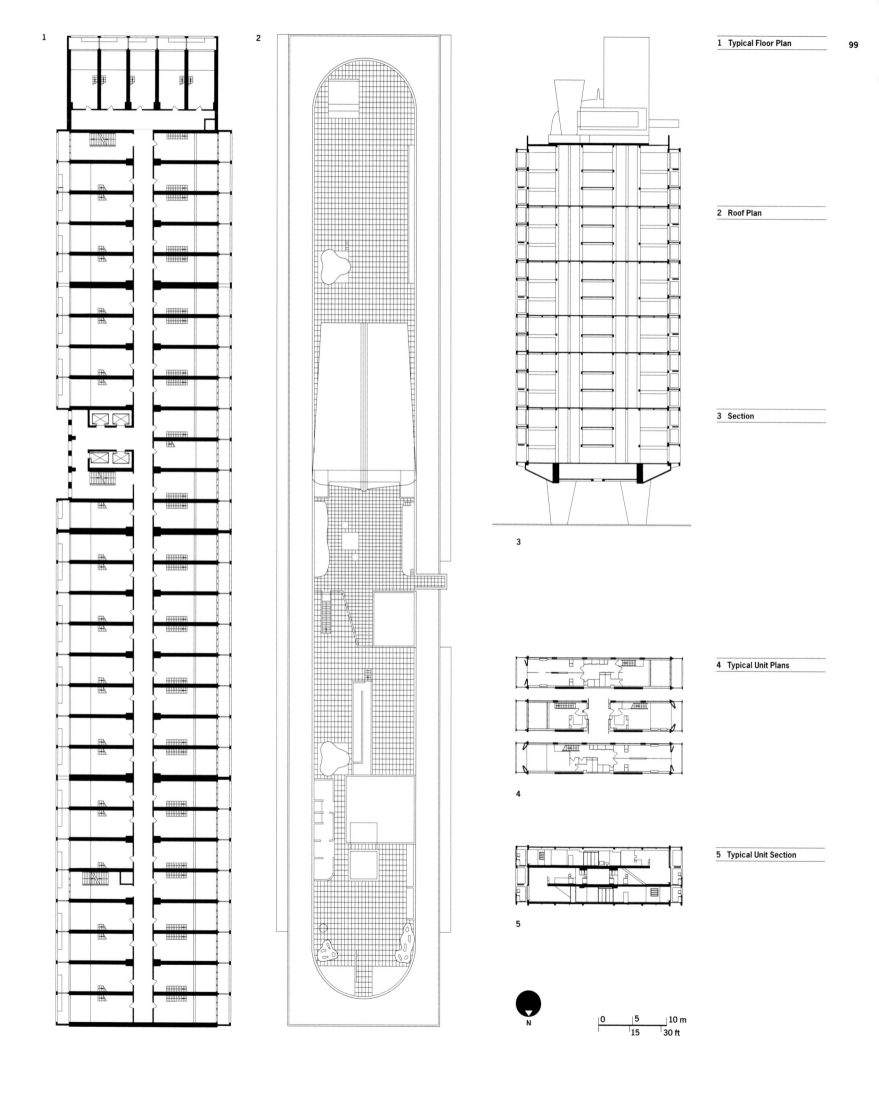

1 Typical Floor Plan

2 Roof Plan

3 Section

3

4 Typical Unit Plans

4

5 Typical Unit Section

5

1

2

| 0 | 5 | 10 m |
| 15 | | 30 ft |

N

Säynätsalo Town Hall

Alvar Aalto, 1898–1976

Säynätsalo, Finland; 1949–52

A small island in Lake Päijänne near Jyväskylä in central Finland, Säynätsalo is dominated by the timber factory of Enso-Gutzeit, for whom Aalto prepared a plan for a company town in 1944; his Town Hall proposal was selected, following a competition, five years later. The design's roots lie in Aalto's love of Italy. He idealized the city-states of the early Renaissance and saw this commission as an opportunity to express a vision of 'the good life' for the recently independent Finnish nation. The courtyard plan can be seen as a direct development from the **Villa Mairea** (page 86), but in place of Finnish farmsteads, Aalto cited Italian *cortili* as an inspiration. The massing and choice of local bricks – unusual for public buildings in Finland – also reflect his fascination with Italian vernacular buildings, and Aalto's initial studies recall sketches of San Gimignano made in the 1920s.

To create a picturesque composition with a relatively modest amount and variety of accommodation, Aalto chose to express the different spaces. This extends from the bold articulation of the council chamber, whose elevated, cubic form and distinctive butterfly roof denote its civic status, to the subtle steps in plan, visible on the west elevation, that mark the individual units. The main entrance and civic spaces are raised one storey above the surroundings and are reached via either a formal flight of stone steps or the timber-retained grass stairs, which were intended to double as an informal gathering place. In practice the latter were little used, but their symbolic role was vital as an expression of the counterpoint between 'nature' and 'culture' that pervades Aalto's mature work. Similarly, the bank and shops below the council chamber and library did not prove viable and are now used by the council.

Envisaged as a fusion of garden and piazza, the courtyard originally had extensive areas of brick and tile as well as grass and the rectangular pool and fountain. The paving was vital in helping to unify building and ground but has gradually been allowed to be submerged by grass, greatly weakening the intended effect. An open colonnade was hardly practical in Finland and in its place Aalto designed a glazed, single-banked corridor. To evoke the feeling of openness, the bricks are carried through and used internally to face the corridor walls, to form a band of paving and to create a continuous bench – reminiscent of the benches around Italian *palazzi*, it also houses the radiators. The hardness of these materials is in marked contrast to the sensuous door handles, which were purpose-made by wrapping leather thongs around a slightly curved bronze frame.

The foyer is also paved in brick and this surface wraps up and around the council chamber between brick walls to form an almost cave-like stair. On reaching the council chamber, brick gives way to smooth, highly polished timber, and raking shafts of sun to daylight softened by Japanese-inspired wooden screens. Unexpectedly tall and dark, the council chamber is attuned as much to the ear as to the eye. The space is presided over by two unique, fan-shaped timber trusses, which Aalto explained pragmatically as means of facilitating the ventilation of the roof space. The unspoken aim was surely to dignify the ceremonial space and to provide a fitting culmination to the composition, which spirals up to this volume.

With Le Corbusier's **Maisons Jaoul** (page 108), Säynätsalo Town Hall demonstrated that brick could be an acceptably 'Modern' material. Hugely influential, especially in northern Europe, Aalto's vision of a setting for local democracy marked his decisive rejection of the pre-war ideals of spatial continuity and universality in favour of an architecture rooted in a particular place and culture.

1 Council Chamber
2 Attic Store

1 Entrance Hall
2 Children's Library
3 Librarian's Desk
4 Adults' Library
5 Newspaper and Magazine
   Reading Room
6 Living Room
7 Study
8 Bedroom
9 Kitchen
10 Guest Room

11 One-room Apartment
12 Staff Coffee Room
13 Welfare Office
14 Local Government/
   Council Meeting Room
15 Municipal Tax Office
16 Municipal Treasurer's Office
17 Municipal Principal's Office
18 Council Offices (Information
   Services)
19 Cloakroom

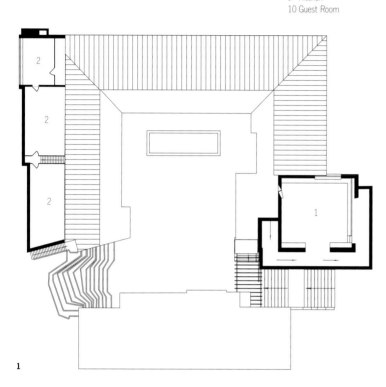

1

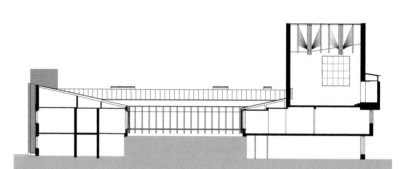

2

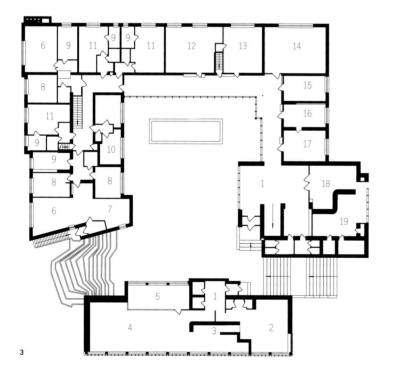

3

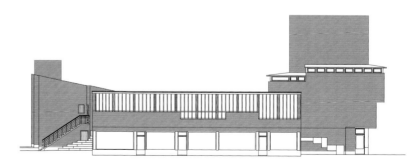

4

|0 |5 |10 m
   |15   30 ft

Lever House

Gordon Bunshaft, 1909–90, of Skidmore, Owings & Merrill

New York City, New York, USA; 1950–2

Founded in Chicago in 1936 by Louis Skidmore and Nathaniel Owings, the firm of Skidmore, Owings and Merrill (SOM) pioneered teamwork principles and introduced many other ideas from American business methods that were to transform the practice of architecture. It would eventually become the largest firm of architects in the world, and a key figure in this irresistible rise was Gordon Bunshaft, who joined the firm as partner in charge of design in 1945. Bunshaft's most influential single project was this, for Lever House on New York's Park Avenue – diagonally across from the site where Mies van der Rohe would later build the **Seagram Building** (page 118).

Lever House consists of two elements, a 21-storey office tower and a two-storey podium building raised on columns and crowned by a roof garden. The podium building was a rectangular donut of offices wrapped around an open court, and both this and the space under the narrow band of elevated accommodation doubled as a protected public open space and a quiet, dignified forecourt for the company's corporate headquarters. Although the columns that support the tower necessarily pass through the podium, visually they appear to spring from the roof garden, as if it

were an elevated ground level. As in Mies van der Rohe's residential towers at 860–880 Lake Shore Drive, Chicago, and at the later Seagram Building, the columns at the base of the tower are exposed, with the glazing to the lobbies set back behind them. A cafeteria and restaurant were also provided at this level.

By setting the structural steel frame of the tower back slightly from the building edge, the whole exterior could be wrapped with a uniform curtain wall of glass. Tinted green to reduce the air-conditioning load due to solar gains, the transparent glass viewing panels and opaque spandrels – which hint at the floor levels – effectively conceal the internal arrangement of the building, maintaining visual and, implicitly, 'corporate' unity while allowing a high degree of flexibility in the subdivision of the floors. The two-storey-high plant-room that crowns the building is subtly differentiated by a change in the glazing pattern, and due to the relatively small footprint of the tower, the service core is kept at one end of the floorplates rather than in the middle, with an additional fire escape positioned to meet the regulations.

The tower-and-podium configuration and light curtain wall deployed for Lever House were emu-

lated worldwide, and eventually such buildings came to epitomize the shortcomings of international corporate architecture – not least its refusal to make any but the most token concessions to local climate, let alone culture. This should not, however, detract from Bunshaft's achievement. The tower-and-podium form had partial antecedents in Le Corbusier's **Swiss Pavilion** (page 70) and in Howe and Lescaze's PSFS building in Philadelphia, but as an urban strategy Lever House was new. Similarly, the feeling of weightlessness and dematerialization Bunshaft achieved – all the more striking then amidst New York's ponderous, stone-clad 'stepback' skyscrapers – was the fulfilment of a century-old dream about a glass architecture for the new age, a carefully calculated result of the combination of wonderfully slender mullions, which appear as no more than lines externally, and the shimmering surface of the semi-reflective glass.

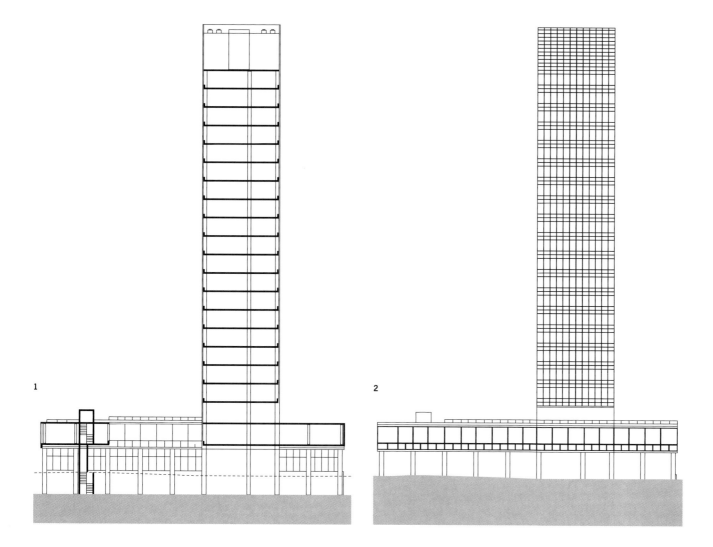

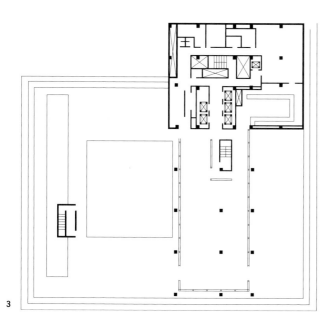

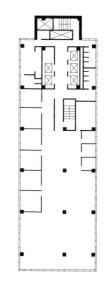

1

2

3

4

0   5   10 m

15   30 ft

Chapel of Notre-Dame-du-Haut

Le Corbusier, 1887–1965

Ronchamp, France; 1950–4

Following the Second World War, the search for universal values in Le Corbusier's work took a new and unexpected turn. The machine no longer provided a presiding metaphor and the 'rational' geometry and smooth finishes of the 1920s gave way to rough, increasingly sculptural forms that reflected his abiding passion for nature and fascination with the architectures of antiquity. The transformation was apparent in the last of his great 'type solutions', the **Unité d'Habitation** at Marseilles (page 98), and with the completion of this hilltop pilgrimage chapel outside the village of Ronchamp in southeastern France, all traces of machine-age modernity were expunged.

The commission arose from the destruction of an old chapel on the site, the rubble of which was incorporated in the new building – a sketch of thick, curving walls was annotated 'how to make stand walls built from the stones of a ruin'. Practical reasons, however, can hardly explain the configuration at which Le Corbusier arrived. He described the curved and battered walls, by turns concave and convex, as a form of 'architectural acoustics', a response to the 'pressure' of the surrounding Vosges mountains and the need to shelter small numbers of pilgrims inside and, on

holy days, vast gatherings outside, when Mass is celebrated at an altar beneath the eastern overhang of the roof.

Despite appearances to the contrary, the building is concrete framed, enabling the curved roof – inspired, according to Le Corbusier, by a crab shell – to float above the walls, allowing a crack of daylight to flash between ceiling and wall. Formally, the composition is anchored by three hooded towers that face in different directions and draw light down mysteriously from above – the top-lighting of the Canopus at Hadrian's Villa, sketched in 1910, seems to have been the inspiration – and the building is locked into the site by allowing the floor to follow the natural slope of the land down towards the altar.

The massive south-facing wall is the primary source of light. It enters through battered openings of varied sizes and shapes, the arrangement of which, despite evolving through numerous iterations and being dimensionally co-ordinated by Le Corbusier's system of proportion, the Modulor, has the inscrutable logic of the punched cards once used to programme computers. Many of the openings are filled with coloured glass, handpainted by Le Corbusier with religious and natural imagery.

Le Corbusier described the chapel as 'a vessel of intense concentration and meditation', and although he had never 'experienced the miracle of faith', it was sufficiently adapted to Catholic liturgy and belief to more than satisfy Christian believers. Despite this, the architecture also strikes an unmistakably pagan tone. Its natural prototype is the cave, while Neolithic standing stones and Cycladic vernacular structures have been cited as possible sources of inspiration, as have certain mud dwellings of North Africa, where similarly random-seeming perforations are encountered. Whatever the precise 'sources', their synthesis is the work of a master architect for whom nature was an abiding stimulus. On its completion in 1954, Ronchamp struck many as an irrational diversion from the evolving mainstream of Modern architecture. Half a century later, it seems almost to have been awaiting release from the teeming organic forms of Le Corbusier's paintings and sculptures, whose architectural implications many of his most fervent admirers preferred to ignore.

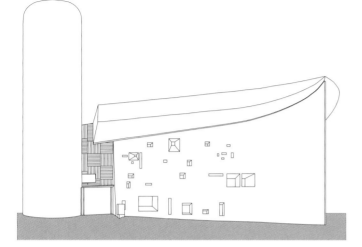

1

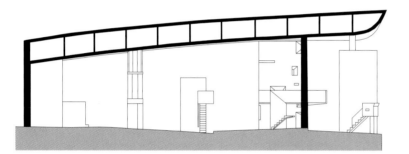

2

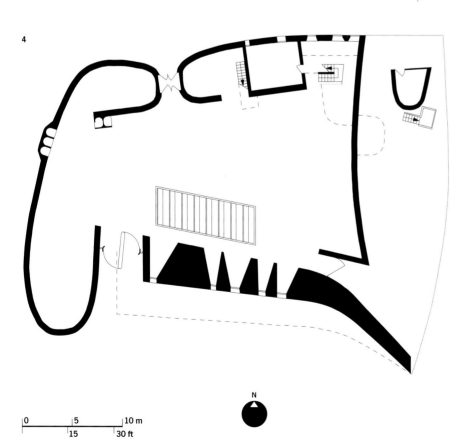

3

4

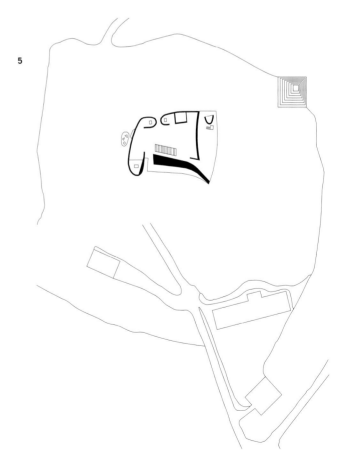

5

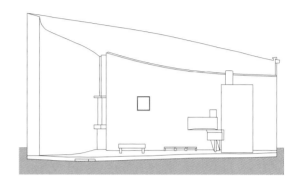

N

0   5   10 m
15   30 ft

Crown Hall

Mies van der Rohe, 1886–1969

Illinois Institute of Technology, Chicago, Illinois, USA; 1950–6

In his celebrated 1938 inaugural address as director of the Armour (later, Illinois) Institute of Technology (IIT), Mies van der Rohe stressed the central role that the 'right use' of materials must play in the search for new forms of architectural expression. The following year he was assigned the task of planning the Institute's new campus, and in 1943, with the completion of the Minerals and Metals Research Building, he revealed — albeit only on the end elevations — what was to become almost the leitmotif of his American work: the use of rolled-steel I-sections as mullions that mediate between skin and structure.

This detail probably owed something to his time working on the long, courtyard wall of Peter Behrens's **Turbine Factory** (page 36), and with the completion of the Alumni Memorial Hall in 1947 it became the basis of Mies's mature 'Classical' expression. There, the steel sections formed part of a continuous brick and glass curtain wall wrapped around the actual steel structure — encased in concrete for fire protection — and the corners were expressed as symmetrical pairs of I-beams joined by a steel angle.

By the time he was commissioned to design Crown Hall, home to IIT's Department of Architecture and Institute of Design, Mies's exploration of steel structures had been clarified through three key projects: the **Farnsworth House** (page 92), the unbuilt Cantor Drive-In Restaurant, and the 50x50 House. In each, the interior was envisaged as a clear-span 'universal space' with external I-section columns. In the Drive-In and the 50x50 House the primary roof beams were also external: a pair of steel lattices in the former and, as in Crown Hall, plate-girders in the latter.

The clear-span 'universal space' at Crown Hall was achieved despite the fact that it was considerably larger than the brief specified (Mies argued that it would allow for expansion) and that the structural solution was inherently expensive. The realized building has a 36 x 66-metre (120 x 220-foot) roof plate and, as in the Farnsworth House, the ground floor is raised and the space wrapped in steel and glass. Large, clear-glazed upper panels give a view of the sky (when not concealed by venetian blinds) and lower translucent panes filter the light and veil the interior from the surrounding campus.

Despite certain similarities to the Farnsworth House, Crown Hall represented a significant shift in Mies's thinking towards a more overtly Classical form of expression. The design of the building as a column-free universal space, elevated above the surroundings and entered centrally by a grand, two-flight marble staircase, was achieved, programmatically, by consigning the Institute of Design to a basement lit only by high-level perimeter glazing — some were not slow to see it as a manifestation of Mies's views on the relative importance of architecture and design!

The building's symmetrical organization was also at odds with Mies's own plan for the IIT campus. Not only was that a free, albeit meticulously studied, composition of volumes in space, but Crown Hall itself occupied a peripheral site for which something altogether less imposing was originally envisaged. Faced with a design of such manifest visual refinement, however, it is difficult not to succumb to one of Mies's most compelling demonstrations of his 'less is more' aesthetic based on the refinement of architecture to its essential structure.

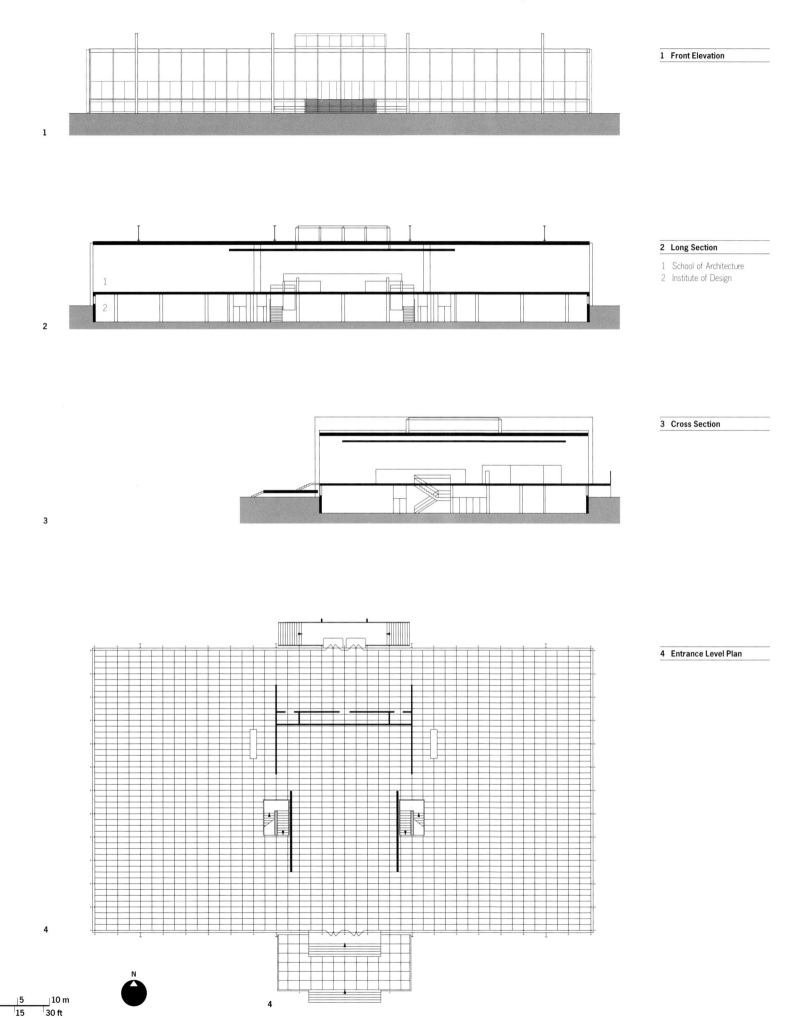

1 Front Elevation

2 Long Section

1 School of Architecture
2 Institute of Design

3 Cross Section

4 Entrance Level Plan

1

2

3

4

0   5   10 m
  15   30 ft

N

4

Maisons Jaoul

Le Corbusier, 1887–1965

Neuilly-sur-Seine, Paris, France; 1951–4

Designed at the same time as the **Monastery of La Tourette** (page 114) and built within easy reach of two of his early masterpieces, the Maison Cook and Villa at Garches, the Maisons Jaoul provided conclusive evidence of Le Corbusier's determination to leave behind the machine-age aesthetic of his early works. Introducing the houses in the fifth volume of his *Œuvre Complète*, Le Corbusier declared this 'one of the most difficult postwar problems' he had to solve. The site was small for two detached properties and constrained by the setbacks required by the planning regulations. Furthermore, the cost of private building was, he said, 'outrageous'! He solved the planning problem by placing two linear volumes at right angles to each other, providing a shared common entrance from a basement garage and giving each house two private gardens.

Partly in response to the building costs, Le Corbusier opted for a traditional form of construction – shallow 'Catalan' vaults – and determinedly crude finishes: roughly pointed brickwork, tiles, board-marked concrete. The spaces were planned using two widths of vault and rendered enticingly habitable by a revetment of plaster and timber. Le Corbusier had always been drawn to the cave-like sense of enclosure of early megaron dwellings, with their deep, narrow spaces and single open ends, and in the Maisons Jaoul this spatial quality is both exploited and exploded by opening up diagonal vistas between the two vaulted zones and by creating double-height volumes above the living areas.

Although the determinedly rough expression is new, the structural and spatial themes have deep roots in Le Corbusier's work. The 'Monol' houses, designed in 1919 as a response to the post-war housing shortages, had shallow, barrel-vaulted roofs, albeit of a less overtly 'peasant' character. Their swelling forms were to be made of a thin layer of concrete poured over a permanent shuttering of corrugated asbestos-cement sheeting: he described the voluptuous geometry as a 'subjective', 'female architecture'.

Le Corbusier returned to the vaulted theme in 1935 in the Little Weekend House, built, like the Maisons Jaoul, in a Paris suburb. This, more than any other project, marked his rejection of what had by then been christened the 'International Style', whose 'objective' forms Le Corbusier now regarded as a 'male architecture'. With its vaulted, grass-covered roofs and rough brickwork, albeit confined to the interior, it might almost have been a prototype for the Maisons Jaoul. One bay of the structure was placed in the garden as a free-standing aedicule, reinforcing the feeling that in this house Le Corbusier had conflated two archetypal dwellings, the 'primitive hut' and the cave – and to reinforce the latter he turned the garage into a decidedly cave-, even womb-like, enclosure.

The Maisons Jaoul divided even the most fervent admirers of Le Corbusier. To Peter Smithson (**Economist Building**, page 140), one of the so-called 'New Brutalists', they were artfully poised 'on the knife edge of peasantism', but to James Stirling (**Leicester Engineering Building**, page 116), who wrote an influential article for *The Architectural Review* entitled 'From Garches to Jaoul', they represented a retreat from the vigour of what Alison and Peter Smithson later christened 'The Heroic Period' of the 1920s. For Le Corbusier, however, there would be no turning back: in almost everything else he designed in the following decade (see the **Chandigarh Parliament Building**, page 110), the primitive and the archaic would co-exist with constantly renewed means of expression.

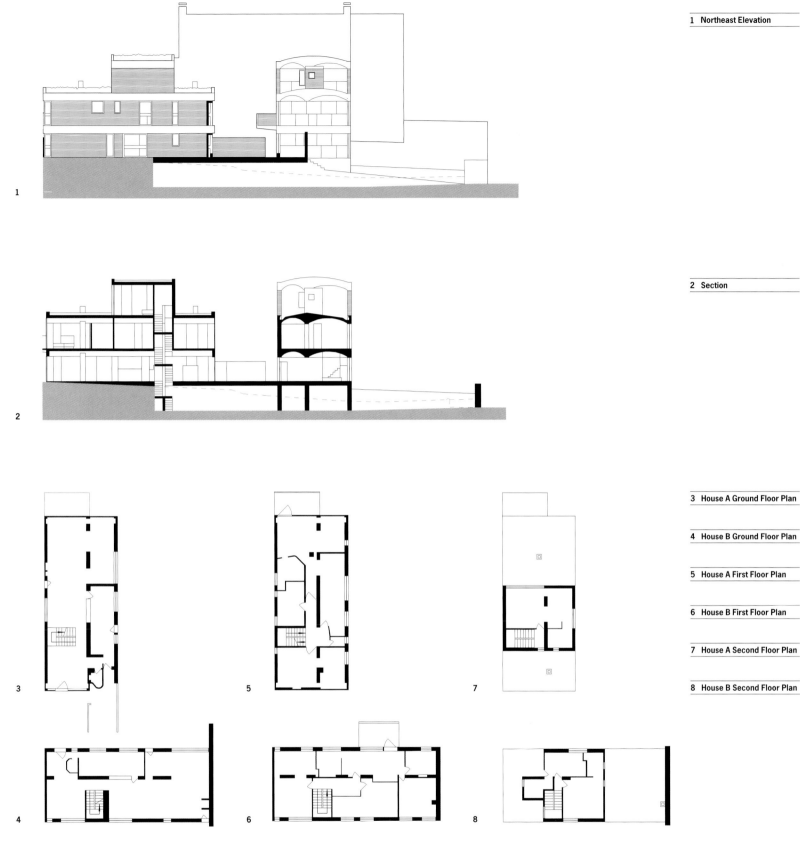

1 Northeast Elevation

2 Section

3 House A Ground Floor Plan

4 House B Ground Floor Plan

5 House A First Floor Plan

6 House B First Floor Plan

7 House A Second Floor Plan

8 House B Second Floor Plan

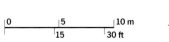

0   5   10 m
    15   30 ft

Parliament Building

Le Corbusier, 1887–1965

Chandigarh, India; 1951–63

In 1948, Western Punjab and its capital, Lahore, were ceded by India to the newly created Islamic state of Pakistan, leaving the eastern, Hindu part of the Punjab bereft of a capital. Le Corbusier was appointed in 1951 to prepare a plan, and in response he offered a variant of the *Ville Radieuse* – 'Radiant City' – developed in the early 1930s. Placed symbolically at its head was a 'Capitol' of government buildings: the Governor's Palace, the Parliament (or Assembly) Building, the High Court and the Secretariat.

While preparing to design these representative buildings, Le Corbusier studied the verandahs, exotic roofscapes and use of water found in Mogul architecture. These local traditions were then fused with ideas drawn from Western Classicism and from his own, intensely personal fascination with such potentially universal themes as the hydrologic and solar cycles that govern the planet. A key motif to emerge from the conflation of these ideas took the form of an upturned, crescent-shaped parasol, part sunshade, part water collector and part inversion of that most familiar symbol of authority, the centralized dome. It crowns the Governor's Palace and was greatly enlarged to become the roof of the High Court, while on the

Parliament Building, the form is extruded and tilted to cover the vast portico that ranges across the main front.

In plan, the Parliament both echoes and subverts the familiar neo-Classical type of the domed circular space at the centre of an orthogonal plan. The main chamber is housed in a cooling-tower-like funnel, displaced to one side of the plan by the square Senate Chamber, which is expressed externally as a lop-sided pyramid, like a giant version of the oratory at the **Monastery of La Tourette** (page 114). Some of Le Corbusier's sketches show sunlight entering the funnel in a way that recalls the feeling of a miniature cosmos evoked by the Pantheon in Rome, and externally it is enriched by a mysterious collection of curved planes: designed to represent the passage of the sun, they may well have been inspired by the celebrated Jantar Mantar observatory at Delhi. The solar symbolism is pervasive: it dictated the rotation of the chamber to align with the zenith of the sun's path, was represented decoratively on the great enamelled doors, and is made almost tangible by a roof opening that ensures that a shaft of sun falls on the Speaker's Chair each year on the day of the official Opening of Parliament.

Built entirely of *béton brut*, rendered all the more rugged by the handwork involved in realizing it in India, the Chandigarh Capitol buildings had, almost from their moment of completion, something of the quality of ruins, majestic and timeless. The roughness of the Parliament's exterior was emphasized by the unrelenting black and white rhythm of the *brises-soleil* that line its flanks, but once inside you discover an unexpectedly cool, calm world. Slender concrete columns, smooth and dense like stone, rise to flared capitals that receive the load of the vast horizontal ceiling plane: painted black and wrapped all around by a narrow slot of light, it appears to float overhead. Animated by the closed forms of the two chambers and threaded through with ramps, stairs and lifts, the public interior has the dignity of a hypostyle hall. At once circulation space and political forum, it is one of the great interiors of the twentieth century.

1 Second Floor Plan

1 Assembly Chamber
2 Office
3 Senate Chamber
4 Journalists' Lounge
5 Balcony

2 Southeast Elevation

3 Ground Floor Plan

1 Main Entrance
2 Concourse
3 Assembly Chamber
4 Vestibule
5 Office
6 Pool

4 Section through Assembly Chamber

1 Assembly Chamber
2 Gallery
3 Journalists' Lounge

1

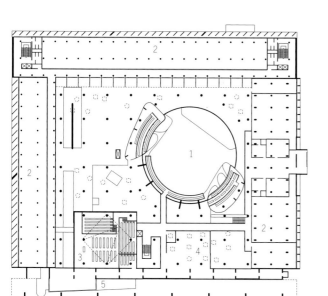

2

3

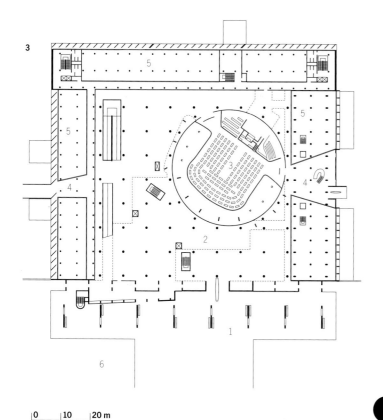

4

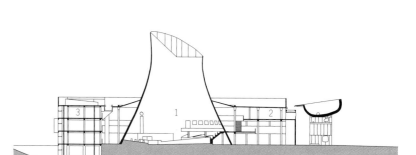

0   10   20 m
30   60 ft

Niemeyer House

Oscar Niemeyer, 1907–

Canoas, Brazil; 1953

The most gifted of a group of young Brazilian architects who collaborated with Le Corbusier on the design of the Ministry of Education and Health Building (1936–43), Oscar Niemeyer is best known as the architect of the new capital Brasilia. He came to international attention early, with the design of the Brazilian Pavilion at the New York World's Fair of 1939, and in a group of leisure buildings — casino, yacht club and restaurant — at the resort of Pampulha, completed four years later, achieved a fluidity that anticipated developments in Le Corbusier's own work.

Niemeyer's own house — the second and finest he built for himself — occupies a dramatic site between two towering hills, with spectacular views down-slope. Niemeyer decided to preserve the views by ensuring almost total visual continuity through the interior. This demanded large areas of glass shaded by an overhanging roof to ensure transparency, and minimal internal divisions. The four bedrooms and a sitting space were duly consigned to a lower level, cut into the hill, and their roof treated as new ground, across which the living spaces and an open terrace were disposed like a freeform transformation of Mies van der Rohe's **Barcelona Pavilion** (page 58).

At first sight the plan of the main floor resembles an abstract painting by Hans Arp or Joan Miró more than a building. A continuous broken line, signifying the roof, meanders apparently at random around freely arranged curved and straight planes. A shallow arc makes a place for the dining table — memories, perhaps, of Mies's **Tugendhat House** (page 60) — and then breaks free to zig-zag into the landscape, like a mysterious petroglyph. An irregular pentagon drawn with a thick black line represents a massive, immovable boulder, which juts into the freeform swimming pool, supports a column and, as in a Japanese house, stands as a miniature of the adjacent landforms. Beyond the house, more wriggling lines describe tropical plants, of which the roof, suddenly, appears like a massive enlargement. 'The canopy', Niemeyer said, 'bears a closer relationship to the shape of the surrounding natural forms than to the floor plan which it shelters.'

Some early visitors from Europe found the relationship between the two floors incoherent and the intensely personal quality of the forms arbitrary. But by rejecting the formal consistency of orthodox Modern architecture and responding directly to the forms of nature — mediated by

abstract art — Niemeyer achieved an unsurpassed integration with the setting. House and garden were inseparable — the latter was designed by his friend Roberto Burle Marx, one of the major modern masters of the art.

To Niemeyer, the biomorphic forms that found their most compelling expression in this house had national as well as natural connotations. 'It is not the right angle that attracts me,' he later explained, 'nor the straight line, hard and inflexible, created by man. What attracts me is the free and sensual curve — the curve that I find in the mountains of my country, in the sinuous course of its rivers, in the body of the beloved woman.' In this house, he pushed the *plan libre* to new extremes of freedom, but for all its suave sophistication it also conjures up the atmosphere of a primitive shelter: as a vision of an earthly paradise lived close to nature it has few rivals.

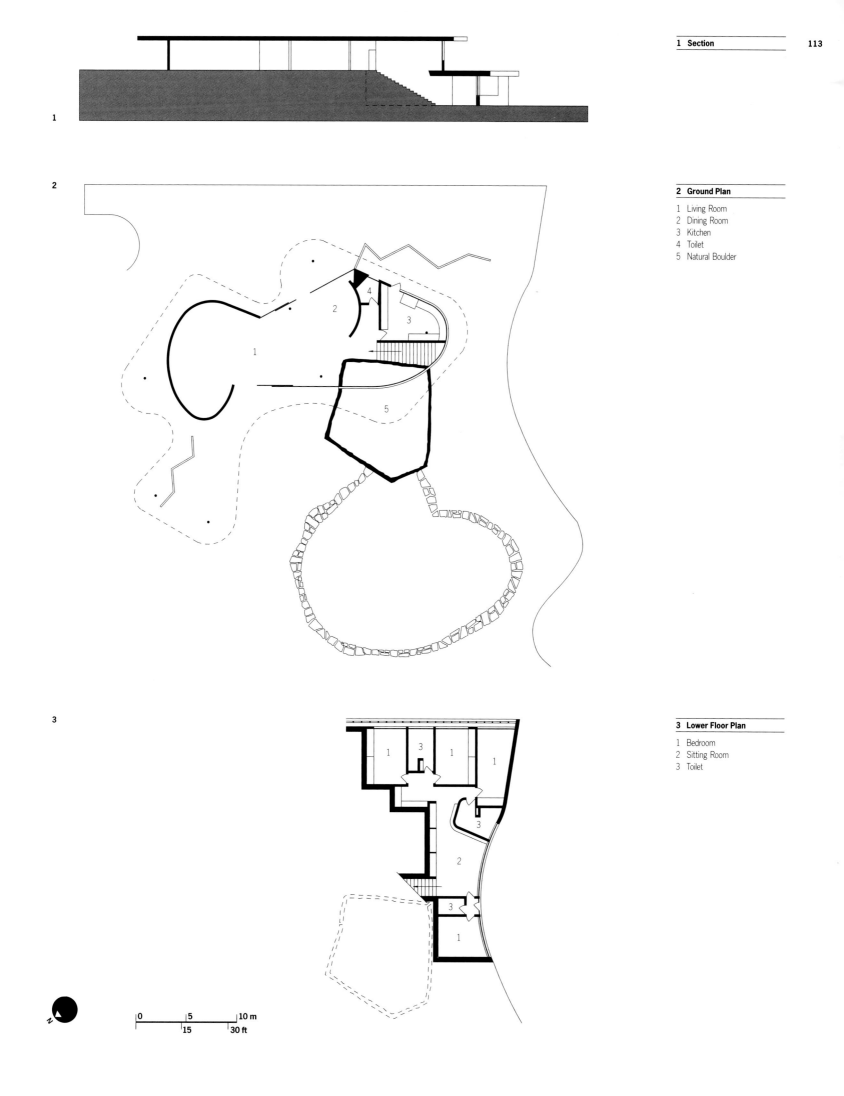

2 Ground Plan

1 Living Room
2 Dining Room
3 Kitchen
4 Toilet
5 Natural Boulder

3 Lower Floor Plan

1 Bedroom
2 Sitting Room
3 Toilet

```
0        5        10 m
  15         30 ft
```

Monastery of La Tourette

Le Corbusier, 1887–1965

Eveux-sur-Arbresle, near Lyons, France; 1953–7

A Dominican Father, Alain Couturier, was instrumental in securing for Le Corbusier the commissions for both the **Chapel of Notre-Dame-du-Haut** at Ronchamp (page 104) and the Monastery of La Tourette. As editor of the magazine *L'Art Sacré*, Couturier was one of several influential Dominicans who advocated a 'back to basics' reform of their order, for which they saw rural Romanesque churches as an architectural model. Ever since visiting the Charterhouse at Ema in Tuscany at the age of 20, Le Corbusier had been fascinated by the monastic way of life. Its strict spatial and temporal order, and balance between communal and private life, held a natural appeal for him, while the boldly framed views of nature enjoyed by the monks' cells were to find repeated echoes in his work.

As preparation for designing the monastery, Couturier recommended a visit to the Cistercian establishment of Le Thoronet in Provence to see how elemental architectural means could be marshalled to evoke a feeling of sacred space. Le Corbusier responded with characteristic enthusiasm, later writing a brief introduction to a book of photographs, published by his friend Lucien Hervé in 1957. Noting the 'utter plenitude' to be derived from the utmost economy of means, he extolled 'light and shade' as the 'loudspeakers of this architecture of truth, tranquillity and strength': he might almost have been describing La Tourette. The perennial monastic spatial form, the cloistered court, finds an obvious echo in plan; *béton brut* enabled a similar 'clarity of outline and roughness of surface' to stone; and the high-walled roof garden, where the monks could stroll and meditate undisturbed beneath the sky, was almost certainly inspired directly by Le Thoronet.

But as always in Le Corbusier's work, the relationship to traditional forms was transformed by the development of a radically new tectonic and spatial language. Thus the three-sided 'cloister' of cells is elevated above the communal facilities, and these in turn are served not by the conventional perimeter circulation but by a cruciform of inclined walkways, which, like all the accommodation save for the long, enclosed volume of the chapel that closes the western side, float above the steeply sloping site.

As befits its monastic role, the chapel – one of Le Corbusier's sublime creations – is altogether more austere than that at Ronchamp. The main rectangular volume is lit by a narrow gap between the ceiling and south-facing end wall, while lower, broader slots with coloured reveals are cut through the flank walls above the rows of pews. This severity is played out against a cave-like side chapel enclosed by a battered, double-curved wall. Placed at the lowest level of the entire composition, the chapel is the culmination of a journey, downwards and inwards – literally and metaphorically – that begins almost directly above, where the curved wall helps to guide visitors around towards the entrance.

Internally, the wall's inward lean serves to press the monks towards the seven altars that step up the hillside. To reinforce this subterranean feeling, natural light enters only from above, through three splayed cylindrical skylights, painted red, yellow and blue on their interior surfaces. These 'light cannons', as Le Corbusier christened them, were but one of several elements – thin directional piers, *brises-soleil*, the rhythmically arrayed mullions he called *ondulatoires*, and wooden ventilating panels ('*aérateurs*') inserted into the fenestration – that expanded the Corbusian formal repertoire and were widely emulated by his followers.

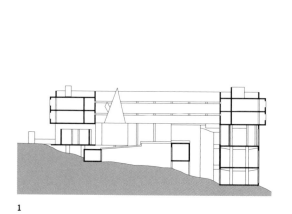

1

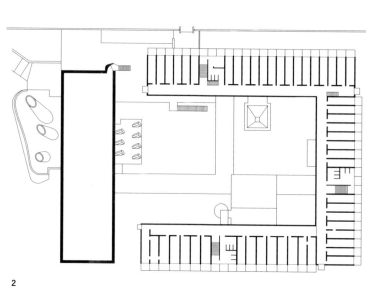

2

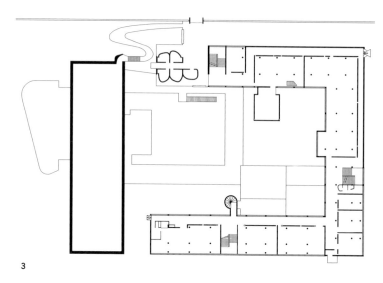

3

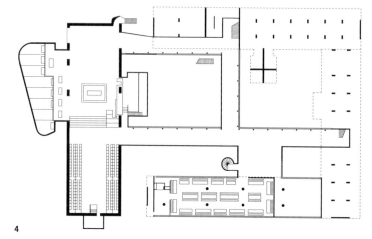

4

0   10   20 m
  30   60 ft

N

Leicester Engineering Building

James Stirling, 1926–92, and James Gowan, 1923–

Leicester University, Leicester, England; 1953–63

Designed in partnership with James Gowan, this building marked the emergence of the most original British architect of the late twentieth century, James Stirling. Like his contemporaries Alison and Peter Smithson (**Economist Building**, page 140), he was determined to reinvigorate Modern architecture in Britain by re-connecting it to the so-called 'Heroic Period' of the 1920s, and by exploring neglected national traditions such as the industrial vernacular architecture of his native Liverpool.

The brief for the Leicester building called for large, north-lit workshops and a 30-metre (100-foot) head of water for hydraulic experiments. In the architects' typically laconic, strictly functional account of the design, these two requirements, combined with the organizational limitations imposed by a cramped site, were said to dictate both the distinctive 45-degree geometry of the industrial roof-lighting system and the decision to house the staff offices in a slender tower of sufficient height for the water tank.

In reality, of course, these necessities provided convenient practical justifications for a design predicated on an almost unprecedentedly vigorous, sculptural articulation of each element of the required accommodation. Hence the laboratories

are assigned a squat tower of their own, the sloping undersides of the lecture theatres are boldly projected, the tall flue is dramatically expressed as a free-standing element, and the stair and lift towers are designed as slender 'servant' towers in a manner reminiscent of Louis Kahn's contemporaneous **Richards Medical Research Building** (page 128). But unlike in Kahn's building, the main stair here diminishes in size as it rises as a direct, 'functional' expression of the reduced number of people using it.

The articulation extends down to such secondary elements as the projecting splayed windows of the laboratory and the spiral escape stair from the rear of the main theatre that doubles as a discreet entry for students arriving late for lectures. Formally, the autonomy of each element is emphasized by treating the solid volumes in hard red engineering bricks, and by glazing and linking them using a relatively newly invented system of aluminium patent glazing (it proved seriously prone to leaks and has been over-clad with new glazing, greatly to its detriment visually). The glazing is at its most dramatic in the cascade between the two towers, where the complex faceted forms had to be detailed on site.

Although governed by a rigorous formal language, the building offers a self-conscious commentary on the 'Heroic Period'. The lecture theatres, for example, recall Melnikov's Rusakov Club of 1927; an external Corbusian ramp initiates a vertical *promenade architecturale* that begins beneath the watchful gaze of a 'battleship' flue; and the overall design recalls both Hannes Meyer's rhetorically functional 1926 'factory' project for the League of Nations Building and Wright's **Johnson Wax Administration Building** (page 82).

This play on the language of Modern architecture led one critic to describe the design ironically as an example of 'Futurist revival'. In retrospect, for all its originality, the Leicester Engineering Building appears less like an innovative enrichment of the Modern tradition than a knowing commentary on it. And in this sense it can be linked to the emergence of post-Modernism epitomized by Robert Venturi's similarly knowing **Vanna Venturi House** (page 142), to the self-conscious use of the Purist style of Le Corbusier by Richard Meier a decade later (see his **Atheneum**, page 180), and to Stirling's own deployment of more eclectic historical references at the **Staatsgalerie** in Stuttgart (page 182).

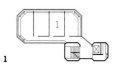

1

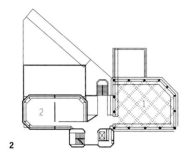

2

2 Sixth Floor PLan

1 Metallurgy Laboratory
2 Head of Department's Office

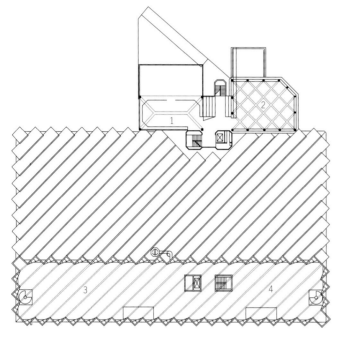

3

3 Fourth Floor Plan

1 Library
2 Machines Laboratory
3 Upper Part of
   Electrical Laboratories
4 Upper Part of
   Aerodynamics Laboratory

4 Northeast Elevation

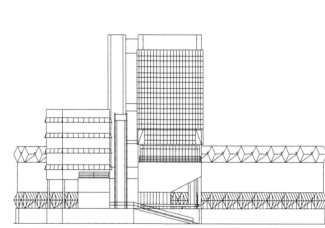

4

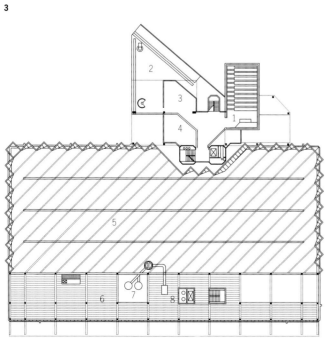

5

5 First Floor Plan

1 Small Lecture Theatre
2 Terrace
3 Lobby
4 Upper Part of Entrance Hall
5 Upper Part of Workshops/
   Laboratories
6 Paint Shop/Store
7 Upper Part of Boiler Room
8 Instruction Boiler

6 Section

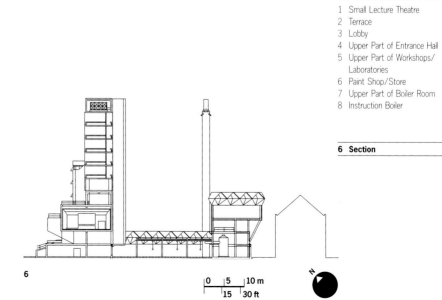

6

0 5   10 m
15   30 ft

Seagram Building

Mies van der Rohe, 1886–1960

New York City, New York, USA; 1954–8

Mies van der Rohe first gave expression to the tall building as a steel- or concrete-framed architecture of 'skin and bones' in his projects for glass sky-scrapers of 1919 and 1923. In the Lake Shore Drive Apartments, completed in Chicago in 1950, he finally achieved the first definitive expression of the tower as a rectangular prism. Raising the accommodation on columns above a recessed ground floor, he used exposed steel I-beams to give rhythms to the façades and to act as 'signs' of the actual structure, which fire regulations required to be encased in concrete. With the Seagram Building, realized in collaboration with Philip Johnson, Mies deployed essentially the same system in defining an image for the prestige office building: it influenced architecture worldwide.

The client was the whisky manufacturer Joseph E. Seagram and Sons, whose president, Samuel Bronfman, had become concerned about the need for architecture to contribute to the lives of both the occupants and the city. The site, on New York's Park Avenue between 52nd and 53rd streets, was prestigious: McKim, Mead and White's neo-Renaissance Racquet and Tennis Club was directly across the avenue, and **Lever House** (page 102) on the adjacent block to the north.

The New York City building regulations allowed a tower to occupy only 25 per cent of its site, so to set the building apart from its likely future neighbours – Park Avenue was undergoing a rapid transformation from residential to predominantly commercial uses – Mies decided to set the shaft back on all sides from the site boundaries. The tower rising sheer from an open plaza was unprecedented in New York and established a pattern that many would emulate elsewhere.

In response to the symmetrical Tennis and Racquet Club opposite, five-storey wings were added and, to meet the required area of accommodation, additional volumes were included to the rear, making the tower altogether more complex volumetrically than it first appears. The symmetry is echoed in the design of the travertine-covered plinth, with its paired rectangular pools flanked by marble sitting-ledges – a moment of cool and calm in New York that retains an extraordinary feeling of generosity.

In place of his previous palette of steel and clear glass, Mies chose bronze and amber-grey glass. As in the Lake Shore Drive apartments, the projecting I-beams emphasize the shaft's verticality and, by meeting on the corner column, visually

wrap the planes around the corner. They also give the façade a density and, especially in oblique views, an opacity quite different to the far slicker skin of the curtain wall that Gordon Bunshaft used on the nearby Lever House.

Although Mies frequently cited Augustine's aphoristic assertion that 'beauty is the splendour of truth', and believed in architecture as 'the art of building', the 'truths' he tells in the Seagram – as in all his work – are architectural rather than strictly constructional. The rectangular curtain wall has nothing to say about the diagonal wind bracing concealed within, just as its perfect, abstract form, rising sheer through 37 storeys, ignores the vastly higher loads experienced by the columns at its base. To Mies, the anonymity and abstraction achieved by the endless repetition of an identical module were apt expressions of the modern city. In the Seagram Building he pushed repetition to its limits, and achieved with it something bordering on the sublime.

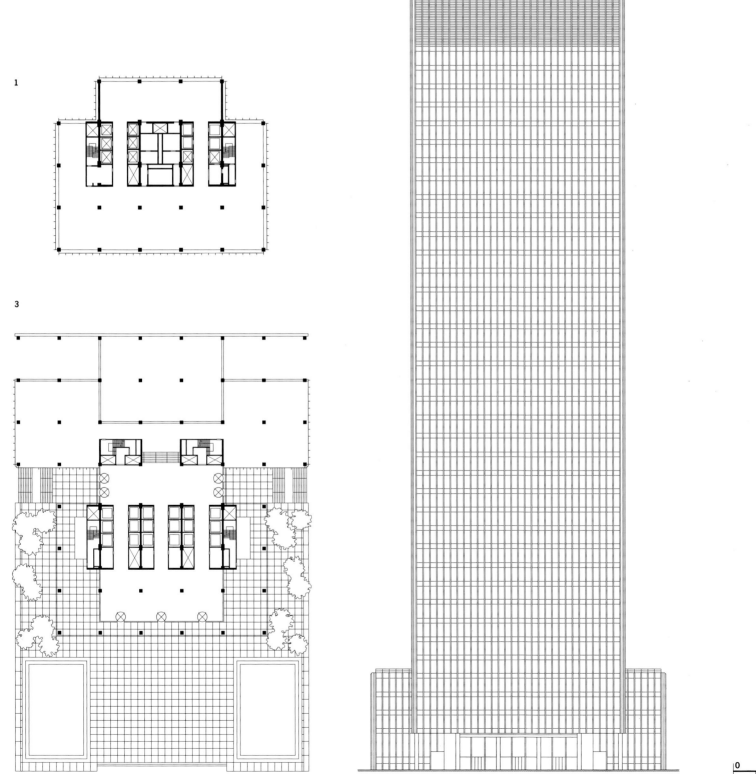

Amsterdam Municipal Orphanage

Aldo van Eyck, 1918–99

Amsterdam, The Netherlands; 1955–60

Born in 1918, Aldo van Eyck came to attention as a critic of pre-war Functionalism. Imagination, he argued, should be embraced as 'the only common-denominator of man and nature', and in articulating his ideas he developed a distinctive, poetic language. Instead of abstractions like space and time, he spoke of place and occasion, of doorsteps and in-between realms. Rejecting the gross simplifications of function and zoning, he advocated reciprocity and ambiguity and called for designs of 'labyrinthian clarity'. He illustrated his ideas with the best examples of early Modern architecture and the settlements of the distant and ancient cultures encountered on visits to Africa and further afield.

In van Eyck's vision, the static harmony of a Greek temple and taut asymmetry of a Mondrian painting could happily coexist, and increasingly his interest focused on articulating the interval between different objects or spaces, on setting what he called 'the mild gears of reciprocity' into motion. His first opportunities to implement these ideas came in 1947 as an architect in the Amsterdam City Architect's office, when he designed a series of playgrounds. Crisply geometric, his plans combined the Classical calm of 'local symmetries winking at you' with the dynamism of De Stijl.

Playgrounds, however inventive, do not make major architectural reputations and it was with the design of this orphanage that van Eyck confirmed that he could match ideas with compelling form. As in an Islamic town, the design is assembled from a multiplicity of small cells. The basic unit is square, covered by a shallow, squashed dome and framed by circular columns and distinctive pre-cast concrete beams with rectangular slots that create an horizon of light. These units are variously aggregated to form 'houses' for different age groups and these in turn are strung along a meandering internal 'street', off which can be discovered a succession of outdoor rooms. The repetitive order is broken by the eight larger domes that mark the different departments: they house play spaces for the younger children and, at first floor, the bedrooms for the older residents.

Having established the basic, essentially repetitive framework of the architecture – an approach that later critics would refer to as 'structuralist' – van Eyck set about transforming it into a network of particular places, using low walls, changes of level, bright but marvellously subtle colours and, most distinctively, a liberal sprinkling of circles – restful, centred counterpoints to the

diffuse order of the whole. Circular sand-pits appear in many of the courtyards, while small circular doorsteps, a human pace in diameter and placed half in the building, half out, articulate tiny 'in-between realms'. For the young children, a circular play pool unfolds around a column, and is half surrounded by a semi-circular seat with eight concrete 'backs' that might, almost, evoke memories of standing stone circles.

Van Eyck loved circles, but said they should be treated as 'gentle squares' to ensure that the centre was not allowed to dominate. In the play spaces, therefore, he mitigated the centrality implied by the large dome by placing a small circular 'play house' at the centre of a rectangular composition of walls, steps and sunken floor, and then shifting the whole ensemble diagonally off centre.

As a demonstration of van Eyck's ideas, the Amsterdam orphanage was a triumph, but it was five years in the making and by the time it opened in 1960 the city authorities' approach to housing orphans had moved against such large institutions and it fell into disuse. In 1990 it re-opened as the home to the Berlage Institute, a private school of architecture directed by van Eyck's most distinguished student, Herman Hertzberger.

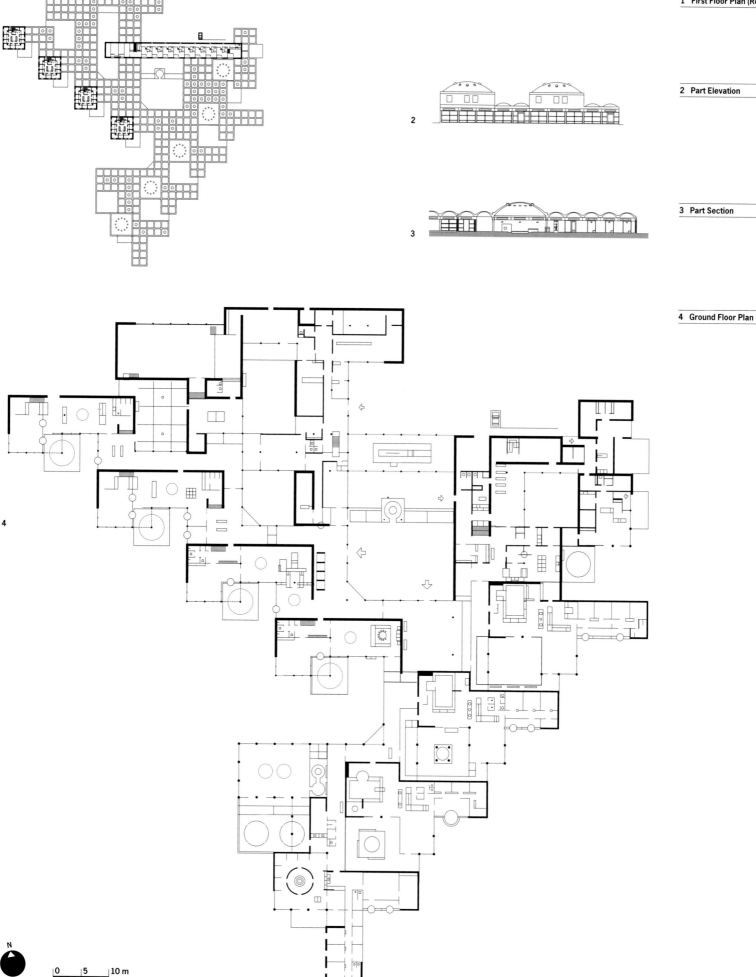

1 First Floor Plan (Reduced)

2 Part Elevation

3 Part Section

4 Ground Floor Plan

1

2

3

4

N

| 0 | 5 | 10 m |
| 15 | 30 ft | |

Halen Housing Estate

Atelier 5 (1955–)

Herrenschwanden, near Berne, Switzerland; 1955–61

Although, in the wake of two world wars, the 'housing problem' had been seen as a central challenge by successive generations of Modernist architects, Modern architectural thought had almost no impact on the housing market in liberal democracies. Along with Jørn Utzon's contemporaneous **Fredensborg Courtyard Houses** (page 144), the housing estate at Halen was one of only a handful of privately funded developments to make a major international impact. Designed by Atelier 5, a group practice founded in Berne in 1955 by Erwin Fritz, Samuel Gerber, Rolf Hesterberg and Alfredo Pini, its organization was indebted to two unbuilt projects by Le Corbusier: the so-called 'Roq and Rob' housing proposed for the French Riviera in 1949 and a similarly dense 'mat' of accommodation envisaged for the Sainte Baume project a year earlier.

Realized on a wooded, south-facing slope outside Berne, Halen consists of 81 privately owned houses organized into three stepped terraces. Both the planning and construction of the narrow- and medium-frontage house types, with their deep plans and sheltered, south-facing private balconies, recall the apartments in Le Corbusier's **Unité d'Habitation** at Marseilles (page 98).

Although their systematic, repetitive forms would have been ideal for prefabrication, no available system was considered suitable and they were built using traditional, on-site techniques. The structural party-walls are made of two leaves of concrete block, 120mm (5in) thick, with an 80mm (3in) cavity between; no pipes run through the cavities and each house is connected to a large, central service duct via sound-insulating joints, ensuring – as in the Unité – an exceptionally high level of acoustic privacy within the dwelling.

This determination to ensure the individual family's privacy – the lack of which was a common source of complaint in much cheaply produced social housing – was matched by a commitment to remedy the widely perceived failings of private housing to address communal needs and responsibilities. Not only are the building services centralized, but the residents also share ownership of a range of other facilities, including roads, paths, open spaces, sports equipment, swimming pool, laundry, garage with service station, the caretaker's house and parts of the surrounding woodland. The densely packed spatial organization also means that the roofs of the lower houses become the gardens of those higher up the slope.

Administered through an Owners' Association, the provision and maintenance of these facilities required innovative legal as well as architectural arrangements. Although comparable to practices that were becoming common in many apartment blocks at the time, the architects' aspiration to use them to help forge a feeling of belonging to a particular place was exceptional, and links the Halen housing project to broader efforts to renew Modern architecture by reinterpreting traditional settlement patterns such as streets, courtyards and the compacted forms of Mediterranean hill towns – and their near-relative, the casbah, beloved of so many third-generation Modern architects.

With its campanile-like boiler flue and central piazza and street, the Halen estate is structured like a settlement, and as such takes its place in a distinguished lineage that includes Aldo van Eyck's **Amsterdam Municipal Orphanage** (page 120) and Candilis, Josic and Woods' Free University in Berlin. It also remains, arguably, the most persuasive of several attempts to reinterpret, in horizontal, ground-hugging form, the ideal of collective housing for which the ultimate prototype was the 'vertical community' of Le Corbusier's Unité.

1

2

3

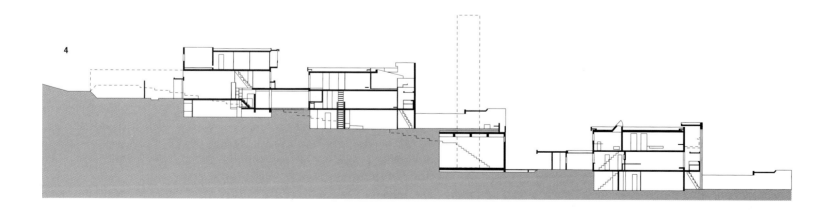

4

| 0 | 5 | 10 m |
| 15 | 30 ft | |

Philharmonie Hall

Hans Scharoun, 1893–1972

Berlin, Germany; 1956–63

Hans Scharoun was the only entrant to the 1956 competition to design a new home for the Berlin Philharmonic Orchestra who proposed a plan that offered 'music in the round'. Adapted from the world of theatre, it was an unprecedented idea for a classical orchestra but met with the immediate approval of the Philharmonic's magisterial conductor, Herbert von Karajan, who considered 'the complete concentration of the listener on the musical event' ideal for their needs.

Scharoun likened the building's organization to a terraced valley, with the orchestra in the bottom and 'a sprawling vineyard climbing the sides of its neighbouring hills'. Its practical advantages were obvious, and Karajan thought that the resulting acoustic qualities would be ideal for the Philharmonic's distinctive style of playing, with what he called its 'long outswing' and 'special breath in beginning and ending a musical phrase'. The arrangement also ensured that no one in an audience of 2,200 people need be further than 32 metres (107 feet) from the podium.

By breaking the audience up into blocks of 100–300 people, Scharoun created what he calls a 'community of listeners' gathered around a similarly sized group of performers — much as people gather informally in a circle around improvised music in a square. To reinforce this feeling, he arranged the banks of seats at angles to each other and to the orchestra, suggesting a multiplicity of viewpoints and making the focus of attention manifestly, rather than strictly geometrically, in the centre. Each terrace has an exit at its own level, turning the foyers below the auditorium, with their multiple stairs and raking columns, into one of the most dynamic spaces in modern architecture. The engineer Frei Otto called it 'the room of a thousand angles' and despite being, in principle, logically organized around the entry sequence from car park to seat via the cloakrooms, its labyrinthine circulation patterns can prove confusing for the uninitiated.

Acoustically, the resolution of Scharoun's idea was demanding: orchestral sound is directional and that of singers far more so. In response, the plan has a frontal bias and the interior was developed as a complex ensemble of reflecting planes, with a convex, tent-like ceiling and hanging reflectors to prevent any undesirable focussing of the sound. Scharoun's love of freely 'organic' arrangements was ideally suited to responding to his acoustician's demands, and the resulting lack of normal perspective clues about the size and shape of the space lends it an endlessly shifting quality. It appears much smaller when seen from the centre than is suggested by wide-angle photographs, which rarely manage to capture the intimacy Scharoun achieved.

The Philharmonie was not built on the site chosen for the competition but was moved to a devastated area at the corner of Tiergarten on what had been Kemperplatz — as close to the centre of Berlin as possible, but still in the West. A Chamber Music Hall, designed by Edgar Wisniewski based on a sketch by Scharoun, was added in 1984–7, and the intention was always to create a Kulturforum. Despite such additions as Mies van der Rohe's National Gallery and Scharoun's own design for the State Library, the ensemble still defies efforts to make it cohere into a convincing urban place. Spatially and acoustically, however, Scharoun's superb interior remains, arguably, the finest performance space of the twentieth century.

1

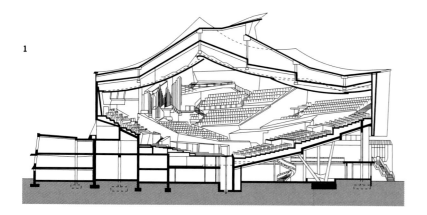

2

3

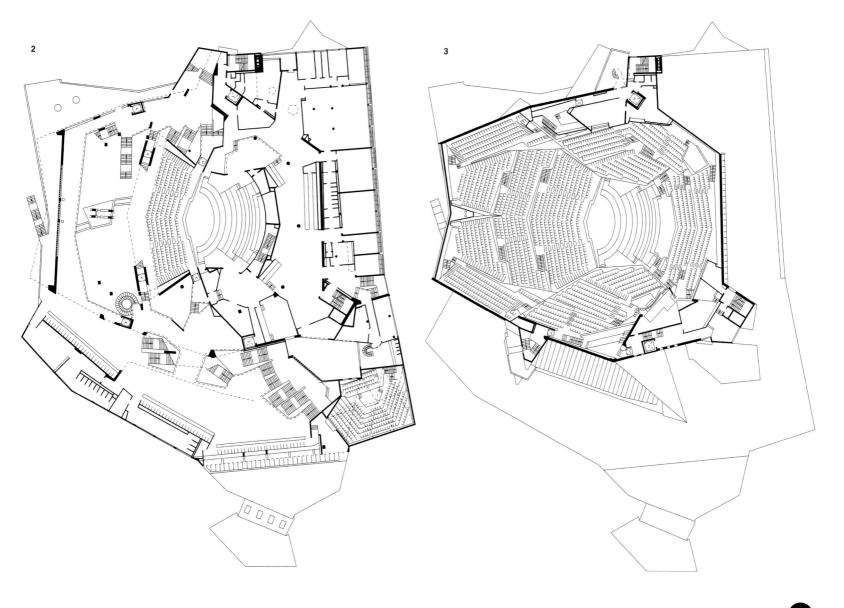

Sydney Opera House

Jørn Utzon, 1918–

Sydney, New South Wales, Australia; 1956–73

The aftermath of the Second World War saw a radical revaluation of the 'Machine Age' ideals that had inspired the mainstream of Modern architecture. Many sought to combine the technical possibilities of modern construction with ideas drawn from nature and from diverse ancient cultures. Nowhere was this more true than in what was destined to become the most famous building of the twentieth century, Sydney Opera House – a commission won in 1958 by a young, and then almost unknown, Danish architect, Jørn Utzon.

Organizationally, the key to Utzon's scheme was the decision to place the two main auditoria side by side on a stepped platform that filled the narrow, peninsula site. This necessitated placing the side- and back-stage areas in the platform below, and servicing them with massive lifts, and it freed the upper surface to become a continuous public realm. It was an idea of startling clarity and the great steps – an almost uninterrupted run nearly 90 metres (300 feet) wide – became arguably the century's greatest public space.

The inspiration behind the platform lay in a 1949 visit to the remains of the Mayan temples in the Yucatan in Mexico, but in his competition report Utzon likened the design to an artificial acropolis, from which the amphitheatres were carved and on which – like monumental temples – he placed the shells that enclose them. The sculptural forms were calculated to shift constantly as you move around, and to be seen from above from the Harbour Bridge, and the decision to tile them was inspired by the domes of mosques scintillating above the low mud-brick fabric of Islamic towns. The tiles themselves took three years to develop and yielded surfaces uniquely responsive to the harbour's ever-changing light.

The realization of Utzon's design became a political and architectural *cause célèbre*: there was no budget (a State Lottery was eventually set up to fund it); political considerations demanded a premature start on site; and Utzon's idea of building the 'sails' as thin concrete shells proved technically impossible. After three years of work by the engineers, Ove Arup and Partners, to match Utzon's 'shells' with a structurally viable and geometrically regulated form, Utzon came up with the idea of cutting them from the surface of a single sphere. Sharing the same geometry, they could be split into tapering ribs, and these in turn could be subdivided into pre-cast units and post-tensioned into vast pointed arches, making the project a remarkable demonstration of the potential of prefabricated construction to create varied forms. The tiles were also laid up in pre-cast 'tile lids', and the result accorded perfectly with Utzon's vision of nature as a model for 'flexible standardization'. He matched the shells with similarly inventive ideas for the acoustic ceilings and glass walls that were to be hung from them. Inspired by watching the waves breaking outside his studio, the ceilings were to have been generated by traces of a rolling cylinder and fabricated using 15-metre (50-foot) long sheets of plywood made in a factory that was accessible by barge from the site. The glass walls, their geometry derived from the wing feathers of a skua in flight, would also have exploited the world's longest sheets of plywood.

Following a change of government in 1966, and Utzon's forced departure the following year, all his ideas for the interior were to remain unrealized by the local architects appointed to complete the building. Despite the relative mediocrity of their work, the Opera House's unforgettable forms and superlative setting secured it world renown, setting a standard for would-be city icons that only Frank Gehry's **Bilbao Guggenheim Museum** (page 222) has come close to rivalling.

1 Concert Hall Auditorium
2 Orchestra Platform
3 Foyer
4 Duct Space
5 Lounge
6 Opera Theatre Auditorium
7 Orchestra Pit
8 Stage
9 Lifts
10 Light Control Room

1

2

3

4

5

0   10   20 m
30   60 ft

Richards Medical Research Building

Louis Kahn, 1901–74

University of Pennsylvania, Philadelphia, USA; 1957–61

Although born in 1901, Louis Kahn did not come to international attention until the 1950s. His Russian parents emigrated to the USA in 1905 and he was educated at the University of Pennsylvania, the finest of America's Beaux-Arts academies. He became aware of the Modern Movement in 1928, thanks to the exiled Oscar Stonorov, who introduced him to the writings of Le Corbusier – 'I came to live', he later said, 'in a beautiful city called Le Corbusier.' The decisive phase in Kahn's development came in 1950–1 during his time at the American Academy in Rome. Travelling around the Mediterranean, he came face to face with the origins of Western architecture. Kahn was a superb draughtsman, and in his sketches the pyramids, the hypostyle hall at Karnak, Hadrian's Villa and the classic Greek sites assumed an intensity and vitality they had not had for generations of Classically trained architects.

The rediscovery of mass and volume, originally learnt from the Beaux-Arts, received welcome reinforcement from the new directions in Le Corbusier's work, exemplified by the **Unité d'Habitation** in Marseilles (page 98), but it was not until 1955 that Kahn was ready to re-think architecture from scratch. Never again could any-

thing be taken for granted, every aspect of a building must be interrogated from first principles. Such moments are inevitably rare, and the building in which some of the central questions were first asked and answered was almost as modest as the Abbé Laugier's Primitive Hut: a bath-house, part of an otherwise unrealized plan for Trenton Community Center, New Jersey.

At Trenton, four pyramid-roofed buildings were arranged symmetrically around a central space, their roofs supported by square 'columns' built of concrete blocks and left hollow to contain entrances or house services. Despite its small size, the building had an archaic power, and it crystallized the principles of all Kahn's later work. These can be summed up as a radical division between 'servant' and 'served' spaces, and a thoroughgoing integration of space and structure into what he spoke of, reverentially, as 'Order'.

The Richards Medical Research Building was the first major fruit of this new vision. The laboratory towers are again square, and served by brick shafts at the centres of their free sides. These contain lifts, stairs and service ducts, but they do not support the structure. This is made of pre-cast concrete elements, with columns placed at

the third points on each side supporting cantilevered beams that step in response to the diminishing load. Above the brick spandrels, everything that is not structure is glazed: at this stage in his development, Kahn was still struggling to find an appropriate Order for the building's skin.

The wonderful clarity of Kahn's plan yielded a picturesque massing reminiscent of, but certainly not modelled on, the towers of an Italian hill town such as San Gimignano. It also had the town-like quality of enabling its occupants to look across into each other's laboratories. Unfortunately the design was less able to accommodate the messy demands of laboratory life. Pipes and ducts proliferated outside their assigned voids, spaces were difficult to subdivide flexibly, and they tended to overheat, leading to an unsightly array of remedial measures taped to the glass.

These shortcomings were clearly disappointing for the building's occupants, but they did nothing to diminish the architecture's iconic power. Although many of its key features were anticipated by Wright's **Larkin Building** (page 26), Kahn's design was an original and highly expressive resolution of many of the central challenges, practical and aesthetic, confronting architecture.

1

2

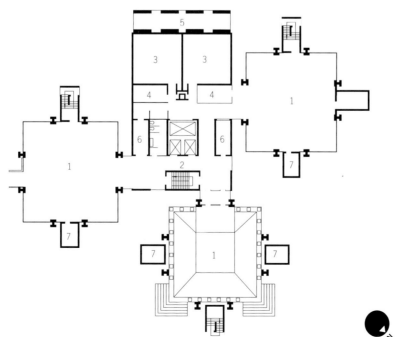

2 Upper Floor Plan

1 Studio Towers
2 Elevators and Stairways
3 Animal Quarters
4 Animal Service Rooms
5 Fresh Air Intake Stacks
6 Air Distribution Shafts
7 Fume and Exhaust Stacks

3

3 Ground Floor Plan

1 Studio Towers
2 Elevators and Stairways
3 Animal Quarters
4 Animal Service Rooms
5 Fresh Air Intake Stacks
6 Air Distribution Shafts
7 Fume and Exhaust Stacks

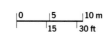

|0   5   10 m
    15   30 ft

Palazzo dello Sport

Pier Luigi Nervi, 1891–1979

Rome, Italy; 1958–9

Thrilled by the sight of the Eiffel Tower and Machine Hall at the Paris Centennial Exhibition of 1889, Anatole de Baudot, a pupil of Viollet-le-Duc, declared that 'a long time ago the influence of the architect declined and the engineer, *l'homme moderne par excellence*, is beginning to replace him'. Among progressive architects, engineers were the new heroes – Adolf Loos went so far as to pronounce them 'our Greeks'. The reasons are not hard to find.

For more than two millennia, stone had been the basis of Western architecture. Its constructional properties were understood through evolving building practices, but in the nineteenth century architects were suddenly faced with a crop of new building materials – iron, steel, reinforced concrete – for which there were few, if any, precedents. Engineers, on the other hand, had the knowledge to work with these materials empirically, to calculate appropriate sizes of structural members. And when they did so without reference to past architectural forms, the results frequently exhibited the 'efficiency' and 'fitness for purpose' that had become key aspects of the functionalist theories of beauty that began to develop in the eighteenth century. In time, it was inevitable that works of

'pure' engineering – such as the bridges of the Swiss engineer Maillart – would be admired as works of art.

Only a few engineers have built major architectural reputations for their independent work and among those none has achieved more acclaim than Pier Luigi Nervi. To Nervi, the split between the 'art' of architecture and the 'technique' of engineering was artificial and damaging: 'to build correctly', he believed, is the essence of architecture. He specialized in reinforced concrete and became architect, engineer and – finding no one willing to build his ideas – contractor. He developed construction techniques undreamt of by conventional builders and demanded a standard of workmanship in the finest Italian traditions.

Nervi attracted international attention early, following the completion of the Municipal Stadium in Florence in 1932. He won the competition on grounds of cost, but the grandstand – with its stiffened shell roof supported by dramatically cantilevered beams that fork at their base – had a startling grace and clarity, while the statically indeterminate helicoidal spiral stairs were like abstract sculptures. For the vast dome of the Palazzo dello Sport, one of three buildings Nervi designed for

the 1960 Rome Olympics, he returned to a roof system developed in 1948–9 for an exhibition hall in Turin. The ribbed sections are all prefabricated, joined by in-situ poured concrete at their tops and bottoms and gathered at their ends so that the loads are transmitted through prefabricated triangular sections into 48 joints that rest on the ring formed by the upper section of seating. This in turn is supported by in-situ columns with angular, warped surfaces: their complex geometry combines with the reticulated surface below the seating to striking visual effect.

Externally, the Palazzo dello Sport is disappointing compared with the smaller Palazzetto, its primary structure obscured by a glass-enclosed gallery that renders it static and ponderous. Internally, however, the drama of the vast concrete dome that appears to hover above a band of light is compelling: its forms may, as Nervi always claimed, be derived from strict structural logic, but the choice of structure was always informed by his equally impeccable feeling for form.

1

2

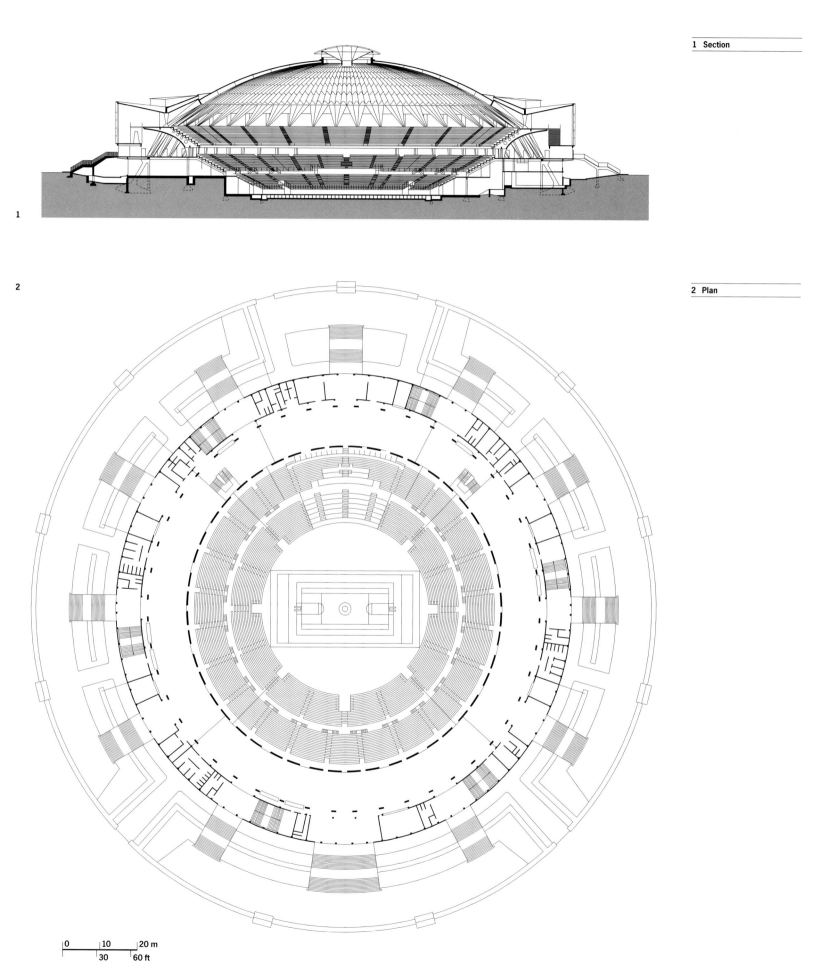

|0 |10 |20 m
|30 |60 ft

Dulles International Airport

Eero Saarinen, 1910–61

Chantilly, Virginia, USA; 1958–62

The son of the distinguished Finnish architect Eliel Saarinen, Eero was born in Hvitträsk – a masterpiece of National Romanticism – and emigrated to the USA in 1923 following his father's success in winning the $20,000 second prize in the Chicago Tribune competition. With the patronage of a millionaire car-maker, Eliel established a progressive art and design school at Cranbrook, north of Detroit, but despite this, Eero elected to pursue a conventional Beaux-Arts education at Yale. After graduating in 1934 he worked with Norman Bel Geddes, and three years later, through Geddes, met Charles Eames. At Eero's suggestion, Eames was invited to become Head of the Department of Experimental Design at Cranbrook, where he worked alongside Florence Knoll, Harry Weese, Ralph Rapson and Harry Bertoia. This was almost a roll-call of the designers who were to transform American post-war furniture, and in 1940 Eames and Eero Saarinen won first prize in the two main categories of a competition for 'organic' furniture run by the New York Museum of Modern Art.

From 1941 until Eliel's death in 1950, father and son worked in partnership. The commission that brought Eero to international attention was a vast, 900-acre Technical Centre for General Motors. Its essentially Miesian style gave no indication of the exuberant, plastic forms for which he would become famous, but his description of some of its innovative features – notably the neoprene gasket system used to seal the glass and enamelled metal panels into the aluminium frames – suggested that he aspired to revolutionizing the building industry through mass-production.

Saarinen's approach, but not his level of ambition, were to change dramatically, and his new, 'organic' attitude to architectural form was seen at its most exuberant in the 1956 commission for the TWA terminal at New York's Idlewild (now Kennedy) Airport. Probably only Utzon's **Sydney Opera House** (page 126) achieved a higher public profile than Saarinen's curvilinear 'great bird', but the built reality was disappointing. Much smaller than it appeared in photographs, the TWA building was almost lost among its neighbours and dogged by technical problems with its moving pavements and other advanced features.

With the commission to design a complete airport system to serve Washington D.C., Saarinen set about replacing the time-consuming 'finger' system of circulation. After exhaustive studies, he concluded that a version of the supposedly 'primi-

tive' shuttle-bus system still used in Europe would work best. The key to this was, in Saarinen's words, 'a departure lounge on stilts and wheels, a part of the terminal which detaches itself from the building and travels out to where the plane is conveniently parked or serviced'. Here, fully working, was the kind of mobile architecture of which, in the 1960s, the avant-garde could only dream.

The terminal building formed a linear threshold between the land side and the air side, through which passengers could move as directly as possible. Freely extendible, its form was conceived in section as a plane 'hovering between earth and sky'. Structurally, Saarinen used catenary cables to carry the concrete roof, with outward leaning columns to resist the lateral forces. The resulting sag-curve ceiling is hugely impressive, and made visible from outside by concave glazing that avoids the tendency of flat sheets to appear opaque. Completed following Saarinen's tragically premature death from cancer, it proved to be his masterpiece.

1 Entrance
2 Ticket Offices
3 Customs
4 Departure Gates for Mobile
   Lounges
5 Administration and Control
   Tower

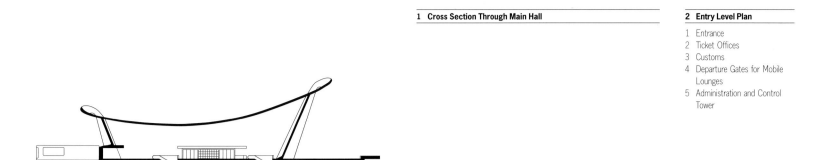

1

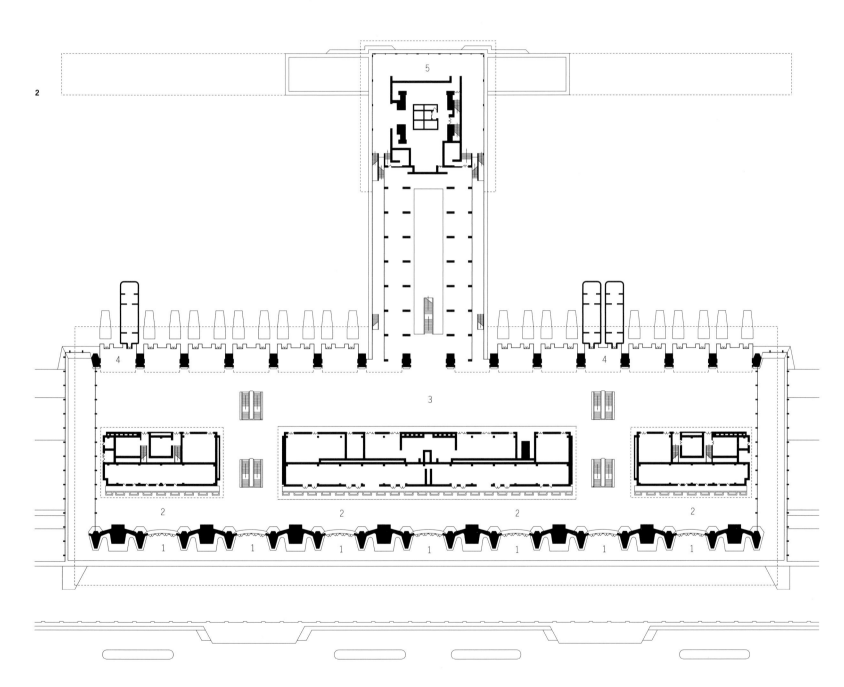

2

Milam Residence

Paul Rudolph, 1918–97

Ponte Vedra, Florida, USA; 1959–61

Although best known for his monumental public projects, such as the Art and Architecture Building at Yale University and the State Service Center in Boston, Massachusetts, Paul Rudolph came to attention as the architect of a series of outstanding houses in Florida, among which the Milam Residence remains the most distinctive. After graduating from Walter Gropius's elite master's class at Harvard University's Graduate School of Design, Rudolph moved to Florida to work with Ralph Twitchell, an architect almost 20 years his senior. He was offered a partnership in 1949 and together they built a succession of houses that, while adapted to the local climate, would not have looked out of place among the California Case Study Houses promoted by John Entenza (e.g. the **Eames House**, page 90).

Determined to pursue his own ideas, Rudolph broke with Twitchell in 1952, and in the inaugural edition of *Perspecta*, the journal of Yale University's School of Architecture, was identified as a leading heir to the mantle of European Modernism. His interest in Mies and Le Corbusier and in the search for more monumental forms of expression was complemented by a fascination with the idea of the primitive hut. In part this was stimulated by the challenge of building on pristine coastal sites, but it was also encouraged by renewed concern for the neo-Classical theory associated with the Abbé Laugier and by exhibitions on the anthropology of architecture staged by the Museum of Modern Art in New York, beginning with 'Arts of the South Seas' in 1946.

By the time Rudolph came to build the Milam house he had assimilated a broad range of influences and felt free to cast off the controlling discipline of a rigid modular system that informed his previous work. Here, the only dimensional control was the size – 20 x 20 x 40 centimetres (8 x 8 x 16 inches) – of the standard concrete blocks that were used, fair-faced, for structural and partition walls alike. The key to the house's organization lies in the sections rather than plans. Articulated into several levels, the 'floors' are transformed into a series of platforms disposed around an off-centre fireplace. Their height and placement are calculated to create a series of different 'moods' in the interior, attuned to the varied needs of sitting in groups or alone or of retiring to read. As a complex spatial resolution of a box-like volume, the project's most obvious affinities are with European Modernism, but it equally clearly reflects Rudolph's early admiration for the houses of Frank Lloyd Wright: the use of exposed blockwork to give a dimensional 'grain' to the composition might well owe a debt to Wright's experiments with textile blocks in the 1920s.

The Milam house's most striking feature is the three-dimensional screen that dominates its eastern side. Although the plans suggest that this developed as a transformation of the classically inspired systems of piers deployed on earlier houses, it was clearly also indebted to Le Corbusier's increasingly expressive use of *brises-soleil*. But the house was air-conditioned so that, freed from the environmental constraints that lent rigour to Le Corbusier's forms, Rudolph was free to develop his in purely spatial/sculptural terms. The playfulness that enters in here would soon develop into the full-blown Mannerism, with its aggressive articulation of form and space, that became characteristic of his public buildings.

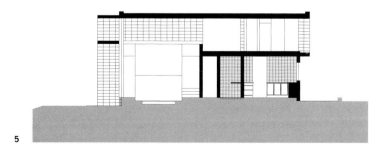
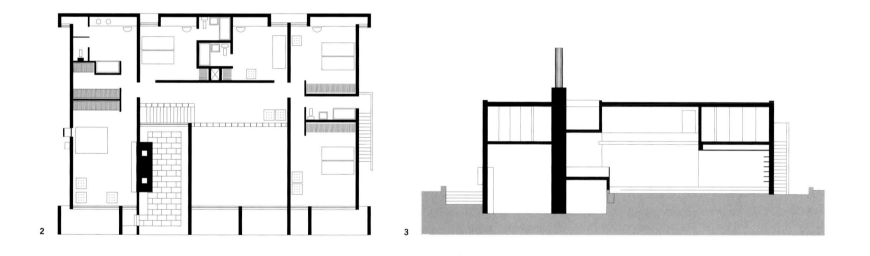
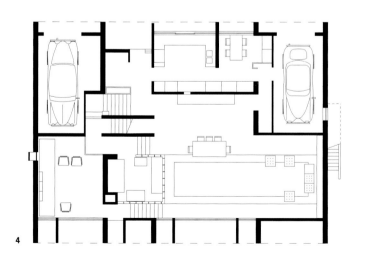
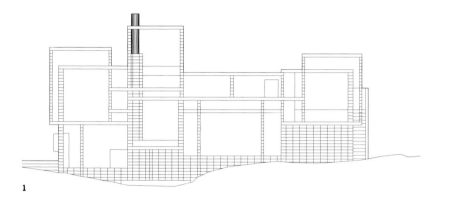

1

2

3

4

5

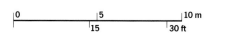

Querini Stampalia Foundation

Carlo Scarpa, 1906–78

Venice, Italy; 1959–63

Carlo Scarpa elevated the often humdrum task of converting old buildings to new uses to high art. He worked in and around Venice, where he was born, and came to attention in the 1950s, first as a designer of exhibitions, then for what would now be called 'interventions' in existing buildings – most famously at the Castelvecchio in Verona (1958–64) and, equally successfully, at the more compact Querini Stampalia Foundation in Venice. The Querini family's palazzo began life in 1510 – such buildings are rarely 'finished' – and on his death in 1869 Count Giovanni Querini Stampalia left the building and its collection to 'promote study'. Giuseppe Mazzariol was appointed director of the Foundation in 1958 and the following year began work with Scarpa on its transformation.

The brief evolved with the work, and the first – controversial – move was the new bridge from Campiello S. Maria Formosa that enters through a former window. The bridge itself provides in miniature a perfect introduction to Scarpa's approach. It is based on making a clear distinction between primary and secondary elements. The primary structure consists of two parallel arches welded from eight steel plates, off which the solid oak steps are lifted apart and supported by complex steel brackets. The same logic is applied to the handrails – a lower, 'structural' tubular steel one supports oval sections of teak joined by brass connectors.

From the bridge you pass between a pair of steel and glass doors, which remain open during the day and neatly line the reveal of the former window, and then through a frameless glass door into an entrance room in which Scarpa declares all the key moves of the interior. The new floor is of the brilliant white Istrian stone found throughout Venice and is edged with high concrete kerbs – a response to the *acqua alta* that regularly floods Venice. Arranged in orthogonal panels, the floor is separated from the irregular old fabric by a narrow 'moat' and exactly the same logic is applied to the walls and ceilings. The latter are made from panels of that iridescent Venetian speciality, *stucco lucido*, while the stucco on the walls is framed in steel in irregularly sized panels, like a giant Mondrian.

Water enters the interior through the former watergate, originally the main (gondola) entrance. Scarpa lined the opening with steel and brass-hinged grilles, reminiscent of Islamic windows, and from the water a 'ladder stair', cast in concrete and capped with polished Istrian stone, rises symbolically to the new floor level. The magical play of

reflections through the screen is a preparation for the elaborate limestone columns, indented with grooves lined with gold leaf, that partially screen the main exhibition room – beyond which lies an exquisite garden.

The exhibition room (above), like the entrance, is a meditation on the *acqua alta*: its pre-cast concrete floor panels have a washed aggregate finish and turn up the lower part of the walls to protect the polished slabs of travertine above. The concrete is irregularly divided by strips of Istrian stone, making the floor a 'local' product, whereas the travertine, a celebrated Roman stone, is divided by strips of brass: this unashamedly luxurious combination recalls the fronts of traditional Venetian palazzi which were often lined with exotic stones in a conspicuous display of the resources available to a maritime empire.

1 Campiello S, Maria Formosa
2 Entrance Bridge
3 Entrance Room
4 Watergate
5 Northeast Room
6 Main Exhibition Room
7 Staircase to Library
8 Lift
9 Washroom
10 Southwest Room
11 Garden Terrace
12 Lawn
13 Minor Court
14 Entrance Doors
15 Switch Cupboard
16 Passageway Door
17 Travertine Door
18 Radiator 'Column'
19 Watergate Grilled Gate
20 Dry Well
21 Water Source
22 Pond
23 Rio S.Maria Canal
24 Ladder Stair
25 Garden Door
26 Former Entrance
27 'Moat'

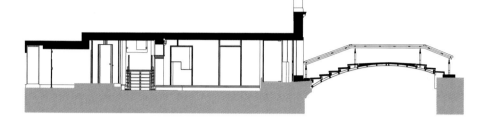

1

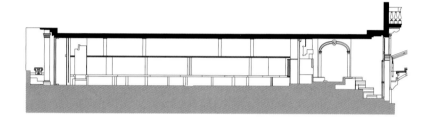

2

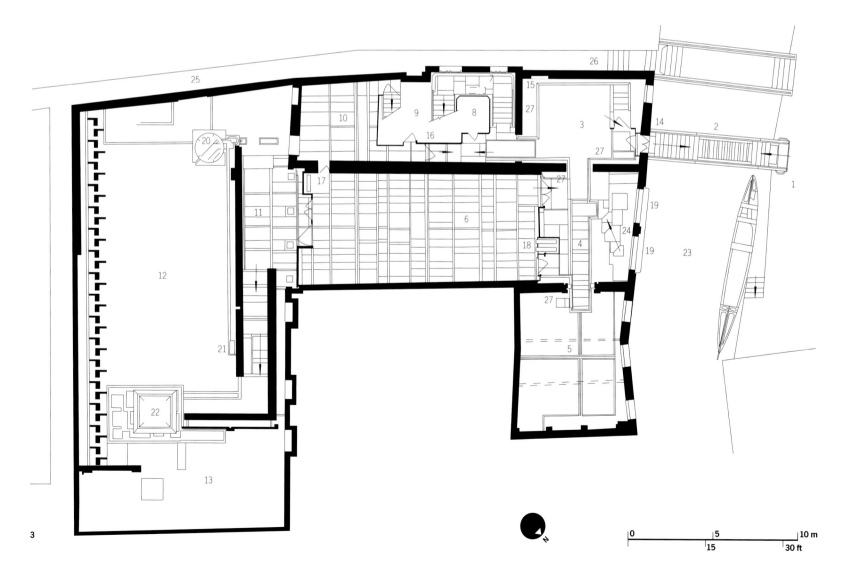

3

Salk Institute

Louis Kahn, 1901–74

La Jolla, California, USA; 1959–65

Founded and directed by Dr Jonas Salk, the discoverer of the first vaccine against polio, the Salk Institute is a centre for biological research intended to promote an holistic approach to health in which the humanities, as well as the 'hard' sciences of physics and chemistry, have a part to play. Salk visited Kahn's office in Philadelphia in 1959 with the idea of asking for recommendations for suitable architects for his project, but after seeing the **Richards Medical Research Building** (page 128) under construction, he offered Kahn the commission.

The city of La Jolla donated a vast coastal site and the completed Institute was intended to include residences for the Fellows and a large Meeting House. The latter was sadly destined to remain one of his finest unrealized designs. In the first plans for the entire Institute, made in 1960, the laboratories were organized as pairs of towers around courts – a response, almost certainly, to Dr Salk's mentioning to him his love of the monastery of St Francis of Assisi. The towers were then converted into linear, ground-hugging blocks, which Kahn at first visualized as a deliberately non-hierarchical series of units ranged across the site.

In the built project, a single pair of larger laboratory buildings frames a central garden that became a paved court articulated only by a central water channel. Raised two stories above the ground to either side, the court is framed by cloisters running the length of each block – a response to the local climate as well as an echo of the monastic order of Assisi. Above the cloisters the scientists' studies are detached from the heavily serviced laboratories behind. On the drawings Kahn referred to the arrangement as 'porticoes of studies', and his adoption of a 45-degree geometry, angled to direct the view towards the Pacific Ocean, gives the court its distinctive, serrated edges.

Having seen the pipes and ducts at the Richard Laboratories escape their assigned 'servant spaces', Kahn decided to allocate a full storey-height service zone to each laboratory. To facilitate the passage of ducts, the voids are framed by reinforced concrete Vierendeel trusses supported by post-tensioned columns. The authorities were initially sceptical that this arrangement would be able to cope with earthquakes but, in a *tour de force* of structural design, the engineer, August Kommendant, was able to achieve twice the controlled ductility that steelwork would have offered.

Preoccupied with the search for an all-embracing system of spatial and constructed order, Kahn frequently had difficulty dealing with such ordinary matters as making an entrance or window: violating the integrity of a wall by arbitrarily cutting openings into it could never, for him, be part of architecture. The unbuilt project for the Salk Institute contained one of Kahn's most potent ways of addressing this issue, which he referred to as 'wrapping ruins around buildings'. To control the sun reaching the windows he placed freestanding screens around the building, with large frameless openings that gave it a monumental scale reminiscent of ancient Roman remains.

The feeling of ruins is almost omnipresent in Kahn's mature work, and an encounter with these laboratories can feel like discovering some ancient Greek site. Rising through a small wood, you are greeted by a procession of blank walls, symmetrically arrayed either side of a void. Dead centre, framed by a tiny square enclosure, a spring of water rises to begin its progress towards a small pool at the far end of the empty plaza. But the pool is lowered sufficiently to be hidden from view and the water appears destined to return to its source, the ocean. Linking wall to wall, the travertine-paved surface rises to the sky, making the entire space feel as if it might have been carved from a solid block, an immutable frame holding sky and ocean in a timeless embrace.

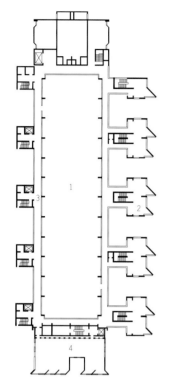

2 Upper Floor Plan at Laboratory Level

1 Laboratory
2 Portico of Studies
3 Service Tower
4 Mechanical Wing

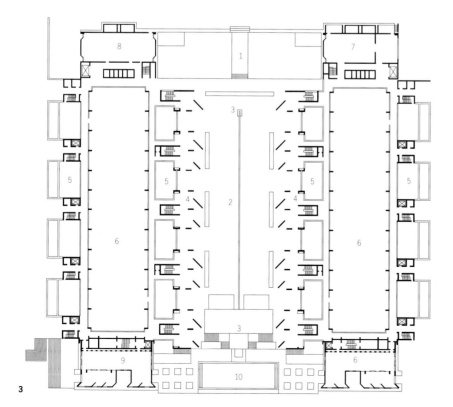

3 Ground Floor Plan at Laboratory Level

1 Entry from Torrey Pines Road
2 Central Court
3 Fountain
4 Portico of Studies
5 Light Well
6 Laboratory
7 Mechanical Services
8 Photo Laboratory
9 Library
10 Terrace

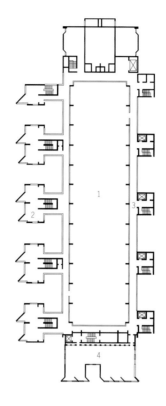

0	10	20 m
	30	60 ft

Economist Building

Alison, 1928–93, and Peter, 1923–2002, Smithson

London, England; 1962–4

Alison and Peter Smithson married in 1949 and the same year won the competition to design a secondary school in Hunstanton, Norfolk, England, which was an early landmark of New Brutalism. They formalized their architectural partnership the following year and, although they built relatively little, their writings made them among the most influential architectural thinkers in Britain. By the end of the century, their pioneering interest in the ordinary and everyday had ensured renewed interest in their ideas.

The commission for the Economist Building – headquarters for the influential magazine of the same name – was in many respects comparable to that for **Lever House** (page 102). But whereas Skidmore, Owings & Merrill were designing in the context of tall buildings and a rapidly changing Park Avenue, the Smithsons' site was in St James's Street, a venerable part of London's West End. Although many of St James's eighteenth-century buildings had been replaced, it retained a scale that posed a major challenge given the amount of accommodation The Economist needed as part of a complex mixed-use development. The Smithsons' response was to create three buildings linked by a two-level basement and

a raised public plaza that rises from the St James's frontage up to the level of Bury Street at the rear of the site. The bank building on St James's, the lowest of the three, was designed to match the height and echo the proportions of the adjacent building – home to Boodles' Club and one of the most notable buildings in the street. The tall ground floor housing shops, and the even loftier *piano nobile* containing the banking floor, relate to the adjacent building, while the rhythm of the columns responds to the neo-Classical façade of Brooks Club opposite.

To the rear of the site are two towers, similar in form and construction but different in size, proportions and use. The larger is a 16-storey tower housing the editorial offices of *The Economist*, while the smaller, comprising 11 lower-height storeys, houses the ladies' residential annex of Boodles' Club. All three buildings are constructed using the same system, consisting of a structural in-situ concrete core and a perimeter of pre-cast columns. For the bank and the office tower, the module is 3.2 metres (10 feet 6 inches), while for the residential tower this is halved to 1.6 metres (5 feet 3 inches). Externally, the columns and spandrel panels are all clad in roach

bed Portland Stone – the limestone traditionally used on many of London's major buildings. To control the weathering of the façades, and potential staining by water-borne dirt, a system of vertical gutters and horizontal sills was developed to channel rainwater down to plaza level. Although visually understated here, the 'registration' of weather through the elaboration of secondary elements such as gutters became a significant element in the Smithsons' later work, such as that at Bath University.

To reinforce the unity of the group, the corners of each building were chamfered. And to integrate Boodles' Club into the composition, a diminutive version of the bank building was added, like a giant oriel window, to its blank, previously unseen, side elevation to create a new card-playing room. Like Lever House and the **Seagram Building** (page 118), the Economist complex was an exemplary demonstration of how commercial redevelopment could yield worthwhile public space, and at the time was almost unique in achieving this while integrating unashamedly modern buildings into an historic context.

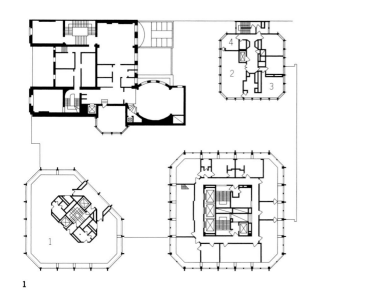

1

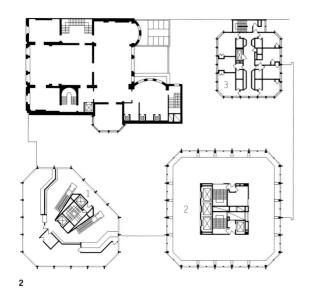

2

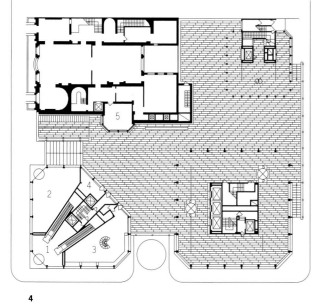

4

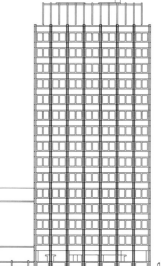

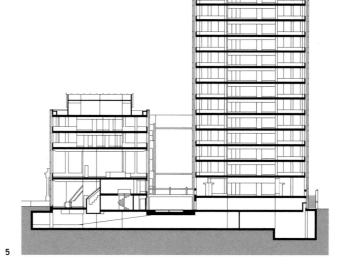

3

5

1 Top Floor Plan

1 Office Space
2 Living Room of Flat
3 Bedroom
4 Kitchen

2 Typical Floor Plan

1 Banking Hall on First Floor
2 'Economist' Office Floors
3 Boodles Chambers (Floors 1–3)

3 South Elevation

4 Plaza Level Plan

1 Upper Part of Bank Entrance
2 Upper Part of Shop One
3 First Floor of Shop Two
4 Kiosk
5 Card Room of Boodles Club

5 West-East Section

0   5   10 m
15   30 ft

Vanna Venturi House

Robert Venturi, 1925–

Philadelphia, Pennsylvania, USA; 1962–4

Designed for his mother, Vanna Venturi, this small house was a built demonstration of the ideas Robert Venturi published in 1966 in the short but hugely influential book, *Complexity and Contradiction in Architecture*. In part this was a witty and polemical attack on what Venturi called 'orthodox modern architecture' of the Miesian less-is-more kind. 'Less is a bore', Venturi declared, and in arguing the case for complexity, perceptual ambiguity and the inclusiveness of 'both-and' rather than 'either-or', he drew eclectically on architectural history. Favouring the impure over the pure – Mannerism over the High Renaissance, Hawksmoor over Wren – he was widely seen as rejecting Modern architecture. However, Le Corbusier and Aalto loomed large in his architectural pantheon, and Louis Kahn, for whom he worked, was a decisive influence.

Gabled and symmetrical, with a big central chimney, a door in the middle and windows to either side, the design is almost as house-like as a child's drawing – and about as far from a Modernist machine-for-living as could be imagined. It is also determinedly complex and contradictory. The gable is split down the middle and the fissure rests on a lintel through which Venturi has drawn the line – the 'sign' – of an arch. No two windows are alike: to the left are square holes in the wall, while to the right a Corbusian ribbon-window slides into the corner, furthering the destabilization instigated by the central split. The latter is a thoroughly Mannerist move but, one suspects, was derived from Luigi Moretti's apartments on the Via Parioli in Rome, rather than from more ancient sources: they are illustrated on page 29 of *Complexity and Contradiction*.

On the garden elevation, symmetry is again asserted and denied. Here, the three self-consciously different openings are a direct response to differing internal requirements – 'functional' in a way that many International Style buildings rarely were. The external complexities reflect a plan of considerable, if at times slightly contrived, subtlety. Again, symmetry is affirmed then undermined – Venturi used the term 'accommodation' to denote the adaptation to functional requirements that provided the justification for many of the moves.

As in a house by Wright (e.g. **Robie House**, page 34) or Lutyens (e.g. **Deanery Garden**, page 24), the plan is organized around a focal fireplace. To the front, the kitchen balances a bedroom, but not exactly, and the fireplace and stair do battle for supremacy at the centre of the composition. The stair is wider at its bottom than at the top, as befits the transition from 'public' downstairs to 'private' upstairs, and sliced by an angled wall that eases open the entrance porch to make room for double doors. At three of the four corners, recesses and a verandah expose the thinness of the cardboard-like timber-framed walls, turning the front and rear elevations into screens – an effect Venturi reinforces by terminating them with parapets to emphasize their nature as layered 'fronts'.

From its four-paned squarish windows, use of 'forbidden' ornament, such as dados and non-structural arches, to the distorted symmetries, fascination with symbolism and elemental reinterpretation of Classicism, Vanna Venturi House anticipated many of the motifs and interests that were to appear in architecture over the next two decades. Although small, it was destined to become, arguably, the most potent icon of architectural post-Modernism.

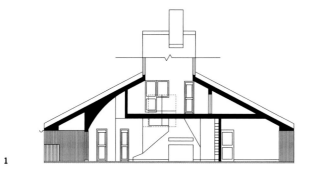

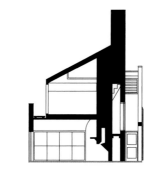

1

2

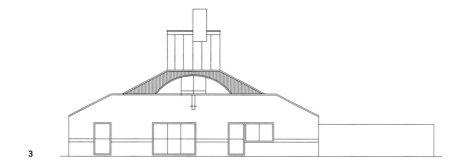

3 Rear Elevation

3

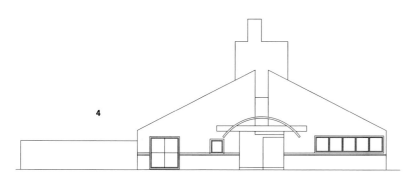

4 Front Elevation

4

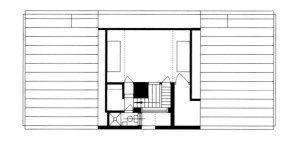

5 First Floor Plan

5

6 Ground Floor Plan

6

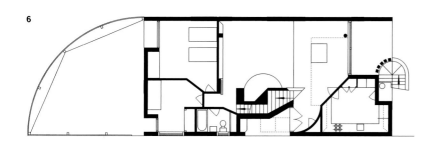

N

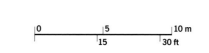

Fredensborg Courtyard Houses

Jørn Utzon, 1918–

Fredensborg, Denmark; 1962–5

In 1944, while living out the German occupation of Denmark in Stockholm, Jørn Utzon heard a lecture by Alvar Aalto in which the Finnish master proposed a branch of flowering cherry as a model for housing: all the flowers were essentially the same, but no two exactly alike, due to their individual history and position in relation to adjacent flowers, the sun, wind and so on. The image haunted Utzon and in 1954, when the region of Skåne in southern Sweden organized a competition for low-cost housing, he entered with a proposal for a courtyard form designed to accommodate the changing needs of a growing family.

Utzon's idea won the competition, but it proved problematic to realize: the cost of the enclosing walls was considerable and banks were reluctant to finance them. Three years later, Utzon persuaded the mayor of Helsingør in Denmark to make land available for what became known as the Kingo Houses. They proved widely influential and in 1962 came to the attention of the organization Danes Worldwide. It was contemplating building a small community for members returning after years of work abroad and Utzon was asked to find a suitable site. He identified land on the edge of Fredensborg, home to a famous Royal Castle.

The site slopes southwest towards farmland and a golf course, and the final plan has an apparently continuous chain of 49 courtyard houses in three fingers, served by short culs-de-sac and framing a greensward of common land. At the head of two of the chains Utzon placed the communal facilities on a low brick plinth – dining, lounge and party rooms, offices and a small 'hotel' – while to the northeast a further 30 units were accommodated in two-storey terraced houses.

As in much of Utzon's work, Islamic architecture played a decisive part. Not only was the introverted, courtyard form typical of the Middle East, but Utzon's choice of details and materials – a buff brick and similarly coloured rooftiles – were calculated to unify the individual units into a cohesive whole. The houses feel almost as if they have been carved from a solid block of material, and in this their chimneys play a vital role. Not only are they – with their mono-pitch, tiled caps – like miniatures of the houses, but they are made to rise sturdily as a continuation of the walls, not to perch precariously on the tiles. En masse, the houses have a quite extraordinary unity, for which Roland Rainer's description of an Islamic mud-brick town as 'made in one casting' seems entirely apt.

Although, as retirement homes, the capacity to grow and change envisaged for the Skåne houses was not needed, Utzon nonetheless sought to give the scheme the organic variety expressed in Aalto's image of cherry blossom. Rather than design all the courtyard walls, he made allowance in the cost estimates for the materials and work involved, and then determined their configuration individually on site. As the work was to be done after he moved his office to the Opera House site in Sydney he instructed an assistant, who remained behind, to sit on the patio of each house in turn, and decide what arrangement of walls would allow the sun in, protect from wind, prevent overlooking by neighbours, etc. This work could not be done with the required degree of responsiveness on a drawing-broad, and it yielded a subtlety of variation that evokes memories of settlements that have evolved over many years.

As the multiple dwelling was steadily incorporated into the domain of formal architecture, or handed over to developers whose only interest was financial gain, housing was to prove one of the twentieth century's most challenging tasks. Few, if any, developments were to match the seemingly effortless grace Utzon achieved here.

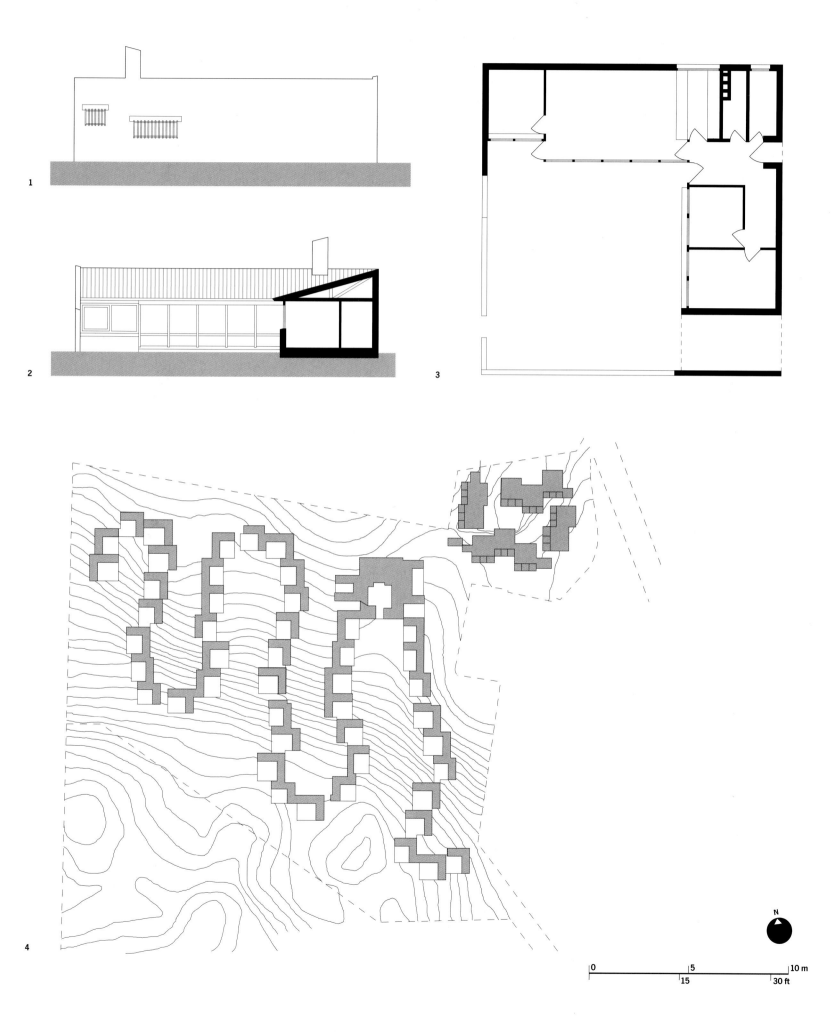

1

2

3

4

N

|0 |5 |10 m
       |15 |30 ft

St Peter's Church

Sigurd Lewerentz, 1885–1975

Klippan, Sweden; 1962–6

In 1915 Sigurd Lewerentz began a protracted collaboration with Gunnar Asplund on the design of the Woodland Cemetery south of Stockholm. His contributions to the landscape design – arguably the century's finest – were decisive, while the Resurrection Chapel of 1922 is an unsurpassed example of modern Classicism. Lewerentz went on to design a Classical cemetery in Malmö and then, like Asplund, made the transition to Functionalism. When the break with Asplund came it was acrimonious. Wounded and perplexed by his treatment, Lewerentz devoted less time to architecture, working for years for a manufacturer of metal windows.

Invited to design two chapels in Malmö during the war, Lewerentz rejected both Functionalism and Classicism, developing an austere, pared down language that culminated in two brick churches – St Mark's at Björkhagen and St Peter's at Klippan. Not widely known at the time of their completion, they later acquired cult status as works of startling authenticity.

The starting point for St Peter's was the redefinition of the Lutheran Mass described by Rudolf Schwartz in his 1938 book, *Vom Bau der Kirche* (How to Build a Church). The basilican plan, with the altar at the end of a 'sacred path', was

rejected in favour of 'the open circle', with the priest at the centre of the congregation. Lewerentz used the Latin term *circumstantes* to denote a similar arrangement and in Klippan the altar is surrounded by the bishop's seat, pulpit, organ, choir, font, congregation and lay-clergy, while the more secular meeting rooms and other parish facilities are placed in a separate, L-shaped block to form an outdoor 'street-court'.

As at St Mark's, Lewerentz opted to roof the space with brick vaults supported by steel beams. To reduce the spans to manageable dimensions he placed a column centrally in the square plan. Its paired steel sections support two short cross-beams and these in turn support beams that span to the walls. The evocation of Christ's Cross is as inevitable as it is unforced, making what might have been an intrusive, expedient column the symbolic focus – almost the *raison d'être* – of the space.

The entire building and its principal fittings are made of brick, and Lewerentz refused to use any special sizes or shapes or to allow the standard ones to be cut. To build in this way, the mortar joints had to expand and contract freely, so that in places the bricks appear to float in a

matrix of mortar. He cited ancient precedents, notably in Persia, but the result feels at once primitive and radically Modern.

The sense of containment by bricks is overwhelming. You walk between walls of brick, beneath brick vaults, which swell gently like ocean waves, and on a floor of brick – not being level, it seems to move beneath your feet and in one place swells and cracks open to create the baptismal font, as if water had burst through rock. No frames mediate the openings, which are cut abruptly into the walls and sealed by glass or doors placed over the openings externally, evoking memories of Louis Kahn's 'ruins without frames' (**Salk Institute**, page 138). Photographs cannot convey the almost preternatural darkness that binds the fabric of Klippan into an all-enveloping unity, and perhaps only Le Corbusier's **Monastery of La Tourette** (page 114) matches the feeling it evokes of an austere, passionate intensity wrought with the noblest poverty of means.

1 East Elevation

2 Section

3 Ground Floor Plan

1

2

3

N

0   5   10 m

15   30 ft

Seinäjoki Library

Alvar Aalto, 1898–1976

Seinäjoki, Finland; 1963–5

Following the series of picturesque brick buildings typified by **Baker House** and **Säynätsalo Town Hall** (pages 84 and 100), Alvar Aalto returned to the use of white rendered surfaces in developing an architecture characterized by a Baroque plasticity of form and space, richly modelled by light. Among these late projects, the Church of the Three Crosses in Imatra, completed in 1959, and this library in Seinäjoki, part of a complete civic centre, were outstanding.

The library's spatial form is generated by the juxtaposition of a free, undulating line with a straight one. In section, a richly modelled ceiling is played against the horizontal ground plane, while in plan, orthogonal secondary spaces are juxtaposed with a fan-shaped arrangement of shelving. The latter was a direct response to the necessity of visual supervision in the days before magnetic tagging (the librarian also commands views into the sunken reading area – a feature of all Aalto's libraries), while the ceiling was designed to reflect natural and artificial light throughout the interior. Both the curving profiles are, therefore, eminently 'functional' – but they also contribute to a long-standing narrative in Aalto's work that develops out of his interest in 'naturalizing' architecture.

In the **Villa Mairea** (page 86), the references to nature revolved around the idea of the interior as a metaphorical 'forest space' and were sustained by surprisingly direct analogies between columns and trees, as well as by the general articulation and lighting of the space. In Seinäjoki, the links to nature are less literal but no less pervasive. In part they depend upon a reading, well established in Aalto's work and more widely in Modernist art, of the freely curving line – or of biomorphic forms in general, as in the work of Aalto's friend Hans Arp – as representative of nature and the body, as opposed to the straight lines and right angles conventionally associated with rationality and the machine.

The undulating line made its first appearance in Aalto's work in the 1930s as a rippling wooden ceiling deployed to improve the acoustics of the auditorium of the Viipuri Library and, more tentatively, as a projecting balcony in an unrealized project for the Finnish Pavilion at the 1937 Paris World's Fair. It blossomed two years later as the leitmotif of the pavilion at the 1939 fair in New York, where it could be read as both an abstraction of the characteristic contours of the Finnish landscape, which was liberally displayed in giant photographs, and of the aurora borealis – an interpretation reinforced by the coloured lights that played across its billowing surfaces.

In Utzon's **Bagsværd Church** (page 158), the connection between clouds and ceiling – memorialized in the word's derivation from the Latin (*coelus*) and French (*ciel*) words for sky – is more literal than in Aalto's library, but it is nonetheless present here. Similarly, although the screen of closely spaced, vertical, white-painted metal bars along the straight elevation find functional justification as security devices, they also reinforce the nature-culture discourse in Aalto's work, in which horizontally stratified building masses are contrasted with vertically striated surfaces, echoing a pervasive quality of the Finnish landscape. If the dome can be read as the architectural equivalent of the unbroken vault of the southern sky, what Aalto offers us in Seinäjoki is its northern counterpart: an architectural image of a landscape of shifting clouds and broken sun.

1 Young People's Library
2 Driveway for Library Van
3 Circulation Desk
4 Reading Room
5 Main Library
6 Study Room
7 Administration
8 Conference Room

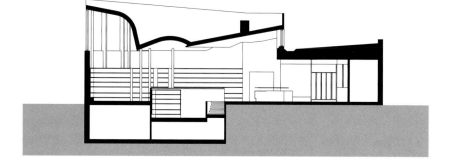

1

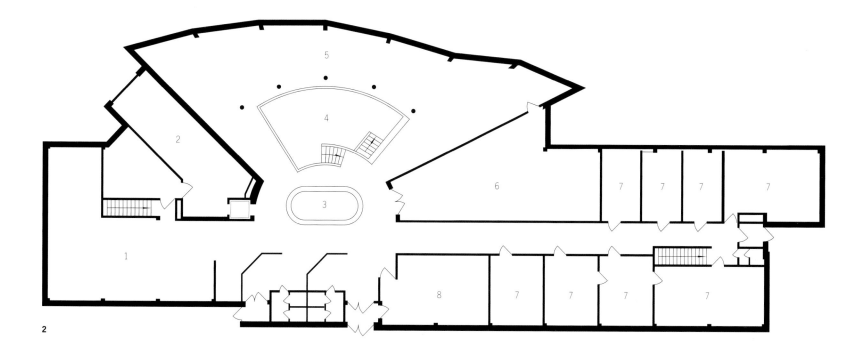

2

Ford Foundation Building

Kevin Roche, 1922–, and John Dinkeloo, 1918–81

New York City, New York, USA; 1963–8

Buildings organized around a central courtyard or atrium are almost as old as architecture. But it was only in the nineteenth century, with the industrialization of glass and iron production, that they could be covered to create protected spaces, sheltered from the weather but still allowing in ample daylight and preserving the view of the sky. Despite its conspicuous advantages, exploited in such outstanding early examples as the Bradbury Building in Los Angeles, designed by George Wyman in 1893, and Frank Lloyd Wright's **Larkin Building** (page 26), the glazed atrium only came back into favour in the 1960s. Its return was heralded by two buildings: the Hyatt Regency Hotel in Atlanta, completed in 1967 to designs by Edwards and Portman, and the Ford Foundation Building, finished in New York the following year by Roche and Dinkeloo.

Roche and Dinkeloo worked with Eero Saarinen (**Dulles International Airport**, page 132) before establishing their partnership in 1961, following Saarinen's premature death. Like Saarinen they were keenly interested in the ideas of a 'new monumentality' that began to be talked about in the USA during the 1940s. (It was only following the death of Dinkeloo that Roche began

to follow where the search for monumentality so easily led – as with Mies van der Rohe's **Seagram Building** and **Crown Hall**, pages 118 and 106 – towards the use of symmetry and, in Roche's case, overtly Classical references.)

Home to 350 employees, the Ford Foundation Building occupies a site on 42nd Street, near to Second Avenue and adjacent to a small park. To exploit the site conditions, the atrium is not placed centrally, but forms a transition between the city and the workspaces, which are accommodated mostly in two 12-storey wings that form an 'L' of accommodation framing the atrium. Additional rooms – dining facilities for all the staff, plus the office suites of the president and chairman of the board – occupy the two upper floors. Surrounding the atrium on all four sides, they give greater definition to the atrium as an enclosed volume, and act as a giant cornice externally – scaled to match the massive granite-clad piers, two of which house escape stairs.

The atrium is crowned by a distinctive rooflight, formed of alternating sections of ridge-and-furrow glazing supported by Cor-ten (weathering) steel, and all the offices have sliding windows that open into the atrium. Socially, by providing a

shared communal space, the atrium helps promote a sense of cohesion, while practically, it acts as a return-air plenum for the air conditioning system. By the 1980s, in less demanding locations both climatically and in terms of pollution, the atrium would be widely adopted as part of passive environmental control systems.

Externally, the atrium linked in to the adjacent city play park, while internally it was transformed into a vision of earthly paradise by the landscape architect Dan Kiley. From the pool at its base, planting – including substantial trees – extends up the stepped lower floor, and then surmounts three projecting floors on the north side. Although visible from the city, the space remained private, and while it would be churlish to criticize the Ford Foundation for the sins of its successors, it can be seen as anticipating the proliferation of pseudo-public spaces that came with the widespread privatization of urban space in the late twentieth century.

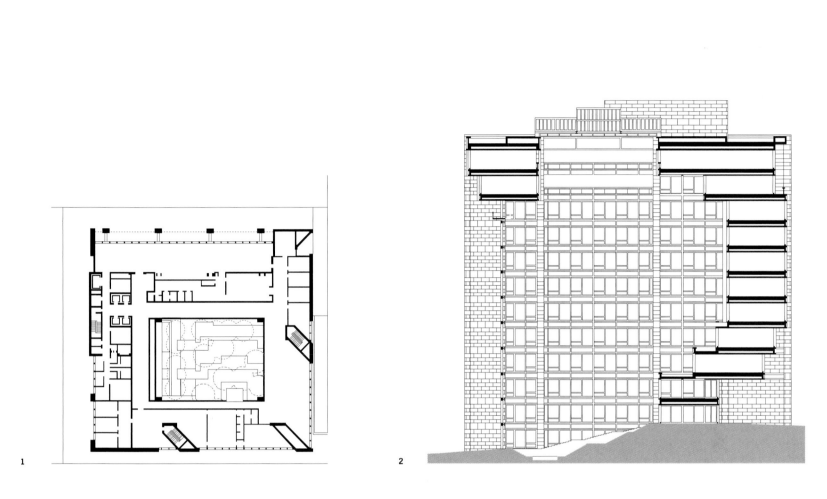

1

2

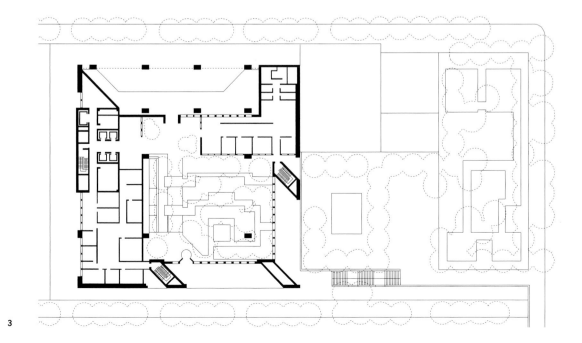

3

Roman Catholic Church

Aldo van Eyck, 1918–99

The Hague, The Netherlands; 1964–9

Faced with a cramped site in a characterless suburb of The Hague, Aldo van Eyck turned the design of this church into an exercise in the transformation of a box. The main entrance, approached down a broad flight of steps, is marked by a protruding half-cylinder. There is no canopy, and for an architect renowned for his 'articulation of the in-between' in his **Amsterdam Municipal Orphanage** (page 120) it seems a rudimentary affair. In fact, van Eyck has compressed the celebration of entry into a notably subtle treatment of the doors: you enter, singly or in family groups, through a normal-size door that opens inwards; but you leave, as a congregation, through a much wider, outward swinging one. And where the doors overlap he inserted tiny square panes of glass to allow light to slide in sideways and to give a glimpse of the world beyond.

Once inside, the real entrance sequence begins. The half-cylinder turns out to be a small chapel, the first of a family of identically sized cylindrical volumes that house additional chapels, the font and confessionals. The lobby is low and dark, but ahead, in front of a second cylinder that screens one of two larger side-chapels, the light descends invitingly from above. As you approach,

the space opens up unexpectedly: the rooflight and the two broad steps below it mark the start of a tall, nave-like space that runs the full width of the plan and steps gently up, in four easy stages, towards a large cross at its far end.

Despite the presence of the cross, the tall space has no equivalent in traditional church architecture. Neither nave nor narthex, it is defined by broad, split piers and forms the circulation and processional spine of the church, not a gathering space. Four chapels and secondary altars are placed along it, while to either side it gives access to the congregation space, where Mass is celebrated, and to a general use hall that, when required, can provide additional space for worshippers.

In a complete inversion of expectations, the 'church' proper is low and square, more crypt than nave, lit from above not the sides, and sloping laterally, not towards the centrally placed altar — a familiar anchor in its expected place. The rooflights are housed in concrete drums, the same diameter as the cylindrical chapels and, like them, placed so as to straddle the structural beams, not sit conventionally in the centres of the bays. By allowing the beams to split the drums without touching them, van Eyck not only makes the light richer

and more mysterious, but he also destroys the traditional hierarchy between centre and periphery.

The beams themselves are beautifully emphasized by being lit, but the two semi-circles that face away from each other insist on being read as just as much a 'form' as the two that reunite above the beam to form a complete cylinder. As in a Cézanne still-life, where spaces between objects are as spatially significant as the objects themselves, van Eyck manages to transform the entire ceiling, as Herman Hertzberger has pointed out, into 'a single whole', as unifying as a dome, yet de-centred and thoroughly Modern.

In a provocative interpretation of the church, the Finnish architect Reima Pietilä has suggested that 'the skylights materialize light in a way that keeps people in touch with their own real world', and thereby renders the ritual enacted before them an unmistakably historical event belonging to the past. But for its believing clients, van Eyck's design is better understood in the context of the radical reforms of the Roman Catholic church's liturgy initiated by the Second Vatican Council of 1962–5: as a setting for the 'devout togetherness' that was supposed to replace 'otherworldliness', its spatial poetry could hardly be bettered.

1 Congregation Space
2 Extension and Space of
  General Use
3 Altar
4 Chapel
5 Font
6 Confessionals
7 Kitchen
8 Sacristy
9 Toilets
10 Meeting Room
11 Office
12 Bicycles
13 Heating

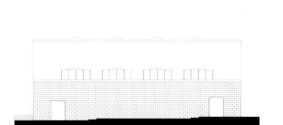

1

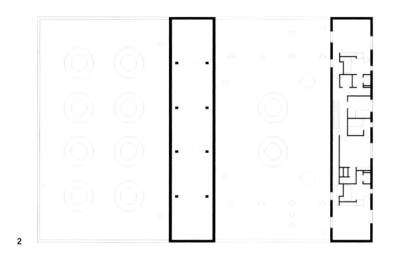

2

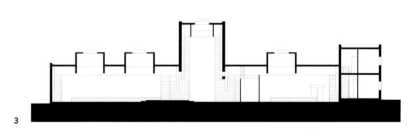

3

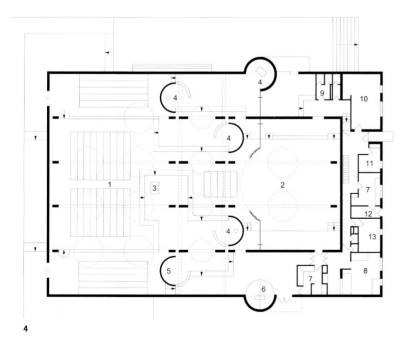

4

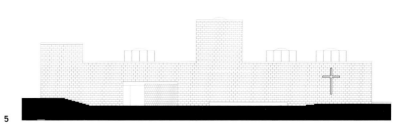

5

| 0 | 5 | 10 m |
| 15 | | 30 ft |

Condominium at Sea Ranch

MLTW (Moore, Lyndon, Turnbull, Whitaker), 1962–70

Sonoma County, California; 1965–6

Built as a second-home community on a windswept Pacific shoreline 100 miles north of San Francisco, Sea Ranch was intended as an early model of ecologically sound architecture. The 5,000-acre property occupied ten miles of coastline where the only man-made features were regularly spaced belts of Monterey Cypress trees planted at right angles to the coast to provide protection from the wind. Lawrence Halprin, one of the most distinguished landscape architects of his generation, was commissioned to prepare a masterplan, Joseph Esherick to design clustered houses, and MLTW to make proposals for the building that was to become synonymous with Sea Ranch, the first of several planned condominiums, completed in 1966.

When MLTW began work on Sea Ranch, they were known as designers of individual houses. These were vigorously opposed to the vision of the dwelling represented by Mies van der Rohe's **Farnsworth House** (page 92). In place of 'universal space' MLTW aimed to create 'particular places', and in doing so deployed similar devices to Aldo van Eyck in the **Amsterdam Municipal Orphanage** (page 120). They were also concerned with the idea that the architecture is governed by

a controlling image that gives people a feeling of knowing where they are. A building is not simply a demarcation within a continuous 'field of space', but a container, something to be in, with a recognizable image and a definite inside – or rather, and this was something of an MLTW speciality, several degrees of 'inside' that begin with the making of a place in the landscape and culminate in the heightened intimacy of fireside or bedroom.

A landscape of such overwhelming power polarizes the options open to the architect: stand out, or blend in. With ten units of accommodation to organize, MLTW had sufficient volume to match the scale of the cliffs. They opted to group them around two shared courtyards, with most of the roofs forming a single slope down towards the sea. An occasional projection runs against the grain, and bay windows poke out beyond the envelope, bracingly close to the windy outdoors. The shed-like roofs have no overhangs for the wind to grab, and windows are few and large – sufficient in area to give ample light, but far enough apart so as not to destroy the sense of enclosure.

Each dwelling varies according to its position in the whole, but all consist of one barn-like volume, boldly wind-braced and made of rough tim-

ber. Most contain what Charles Moore called two 'little houses', made of smooth wood and painted to give them the feel of being between toy houses and giant pieces of furniture: a 'four-poster' sheltering a fireplace and sunken 'conversation pit' below and supporting a bed-space on top; and a more complex unit, with a kitchen below, and bath and dressing room above, and sometimes a sleeping loft above that.

MLTW's condominium was widely acclaimed and imitated, and several of their and Esherick's houses were also highly successful. But Sea Ranch as a whole quickly succumbed to overdevelopment and less sensitive design. Forms became fussy, lawns spread out in vain efforts to colonize the landscape, and all-too-visible and individualistic buildings appeared on sections of land where Halprin's masterplan said there should be no development. It was a valiant attempt to fight the trend towards homogenization, but in the end 'market forces' won out.

1 Entrance
2 Parking
3 Condominium
4 Laundry
5 Electric
6 Deck

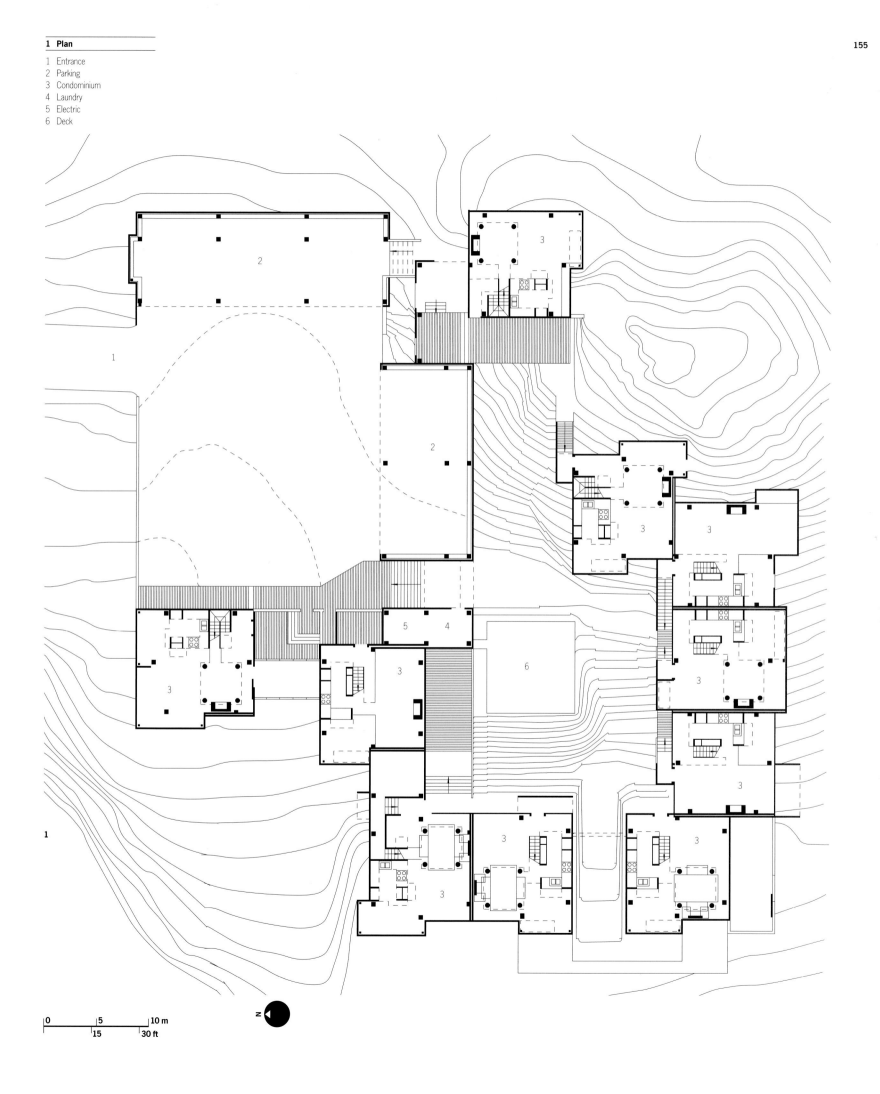

0   5   10 m
  15   30 ft

Kimbell Art Museum

Louis Kahn, 1901–74

Fort Worth, Texas, USA; 1966–72

Louis Kahn was preoccupied with the play of light and shade on elemental masonry forms and with finding ways to admit light into buildings that grew out of the essential 'nature' of the construction: 'structure', he declared, 'is the maker of light'. In designing any art gallery, the control of natural light, both to illuminate the works and to ensure that no damaging ultraviolet rays reach them, is a key challenge. In Texas, with its high, intense sun, the easiest solution would have been to admit only north light, but for Kahn an interior must be in contact with passing clouds and the movement of the sun. From the outset, therefore, he explored a vaulted roofing system in which light would be admitted from above and variously baffled and reflected before reaching the art works.

The chosen section uses a curved vault, split by a central slot that allows light down to a reflector. Although it makes sense to speak of the structure as 'vaults', they are more like curved beams and span lengthwise between columns. The structurally determined curve is a cycloid, the path traced by a point on a rolling circle, and the bays are 30.5 x 6.7 metres (100 x 22 feet). At their ends the vaults are stiffened by a shallow downstand beam, and the junction between this and

the walls is a tapering slot made by juxtaposing the 'logical' circular geometry of the wall with the cycloid above: the unusual geometry of the structure is thereby revealed.

The museum sits in a corner of the Will Rogers Memorial Park and the galleries are placed on a platform containing the service spaces. To preserve its solidity as a support for the 'temple' above (cp. **Sydney Opera House**, page 126), the offices are lit from long, narrow light wells. The entrance from the car park is placed at this lower level, while that from the park is at the upper level, reached via a gentle flight of steps up to a porch that stands like a 'ruin' of the galleries. The gallery level plan is bipolar with a central entrance hall and galleries to either side. These are articulated by two light courts and the upper volumes of the conservators' rooms below, and partly occupied by the cafeteria. The spatial quality resulting from this simplest of plans is extraordinary. Looking down the vaults, the interior seems to be composed of a succession of adjacent rooms, while looking across them, the alternation of flat and vaulted spaces, and subtle changes of light, make for an extended and exquisitely differentiated volume.

From the beginning, Kahn aimed at 'rooms structured in concrete that will have the luminosity of silver', and the design of the reflector was crucial to the galleries' success. Developed by Richard Kelly, the lighting consultant, it went through several iterations before the final version, made of solid and perforated aluminium, emerged. To clad the non-structural walls Kahn chose a pale-coloured travertine, and the silvery quality was reinforced by blasting the stainless steel surfaces of fixtures and fittings with the shells of pecan nuts to eliminate shiny highlights. The resulting quality of light, responsive to every nuance of changing conditions outside, is enchanting. Completed two years before his death, the Kimbell Art Museum is, arguably, Kahn's masterpiece and one of the major achievements of twentieth-century architecture.

1 Entrance Gallery	9 Gallery
2 Bookshop	10 Portico
3 Lower Level of Library	11 Light Court
4 Slide Room	12 Upper Part of
5 Librarian	Conservators' Court
6 Work Room	13 Upper Part of
7 Auditorium	Conservators' Studio
8 Cafeteria	14 Upper Part of Light Well

1

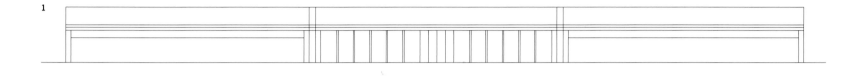

2

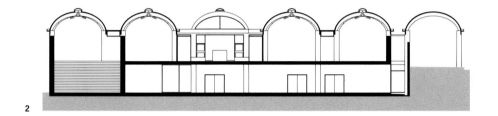

3

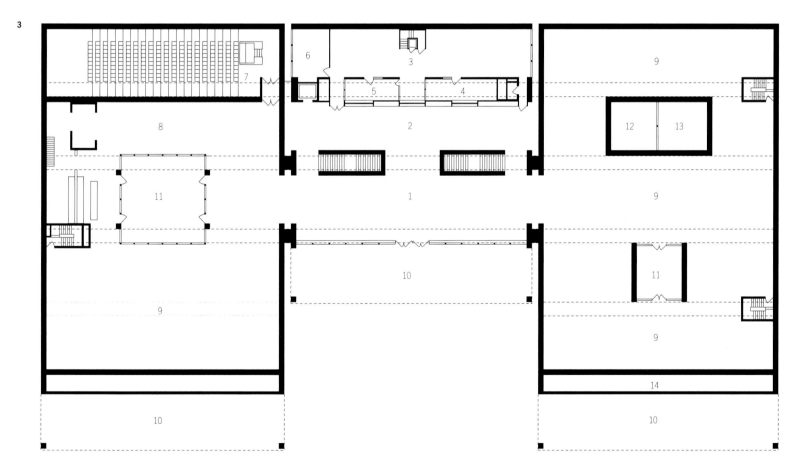

0	5	10 m
	15	30 ft

Bagsværd Church

Jørn Utzon, 1918–

Bagsværd, near Copenhagen, Denmark; 1967–76

Despite the fact that its exterior feels unmistakably 'Danish' in its simplicity and modesty – it is said to remind many of the traditional agricultural buildings of the area – the decisive moment in the design of Bagsværd Church came far away on Hawaii, where Jørn Utzon was teaching following his premature departure from **Sydney Opera House** (page 126). Lying on a beach, he noticed a regular succession of cylindrical clouds passing overhead: they struck him as perfect for the ceiling of his new commission. It was, as so often in such moments of 'inspiration', a case of fortune favouring the prepared mind. The top-lit interior of the Melli Bank that Utzon had designed in Tehran a decade before had a folded-plate roof structure, the effect of which he likened to sunlight breaking through banks of clouds. Following his failure to realize his idea for thin-shell structures in Sydney, he was determined to demonstrate their potential here: the surfaces suggested by the billowing clouds were ideal, and – as with the unrealized acoustic ceilings in the Opera House – they were rationalized into cylindrical sections of varying radii.

For the plan, Utzon turned not to Christian churches for inspiration, but to the Buddhist temples of China. As the site was bounded on its long sides by a major road and a car park, a sequence of introverted rooms and intimate courtyards framed by cloister-like corridors seemed ideal to secure the necessary quiet and detachment. In contrast to the apparently free form of the voluptuous ceilings, Utzon developed an orthogonal construction system that had the simplicity of a child's toy. Pairs of columns, joined at their tops by beams of variable depth, frame the uniform-width corridors and are in-filled with pre-cast concrete planks and sealed with diminutive pitched roofs of glass.

Some found the result too barn-like, too industrial, but for Utzon it seemed entirely appropriate that, as in Gothic Europe, a church should be built by refining the latest forms of construction, not anachronistically by reverting to craft traditions. The concrete panels were made using crushed marble as an aggregate and the result, most conspicuously on the interior, is intensely, yet almost ethereally, white. The lines of the vaults within are subtly marked externally by glazed tiles similar to those used at Sydney: reflecting the sky, they hint at the celestial origins of what lies in store.

The church is entered through shallow, glazed porches, and once inside the only light entering the corridors comes from above: there are no windows, not even into the courtyards. The transition from the perimeter colonnade to the main space is dramatic, far more so than the relatively modest size of the church might suggest. The beauty and strength of the space lie not only in the exquisite play of light across the white surfaces, made all the more vivid by the visually stable matt finish of the wooden furnishings, but also in the fact that the ceiling is not merely an artful play of form but the building's actual structure – the lightweight roof is propped off the ceiling. Utzon summed this up perfectly: 'You have the reassurance of something above your head which is built, not just designed.'

An interior designer might have produced similar forms by spraying acoustic plaster onto mesh frames and then hanging them from a concealed steel structure – and this might, conceivably, have been done without tell-tale joints. But it would have remained interior design, not architecture; a visual effect, not a constructed space. Just how we sense that these voluptuous, board-marked surfaces are actually doing the structural job of spanning the width of the church is not easily explained, but we sense it as surely as we thrill to the gravity-defying ribs of a Gothic vault.

1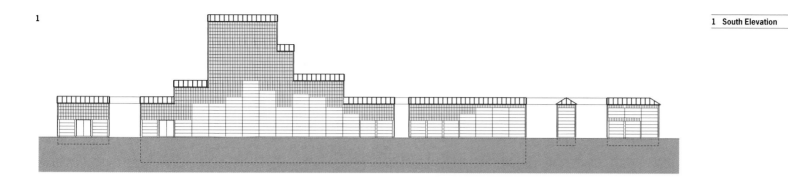

2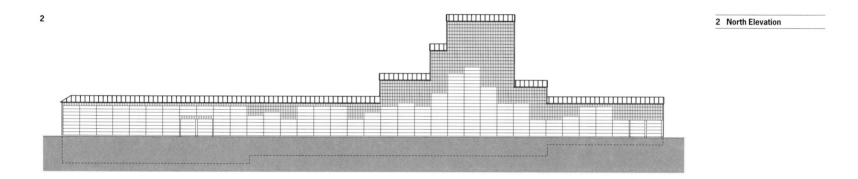

3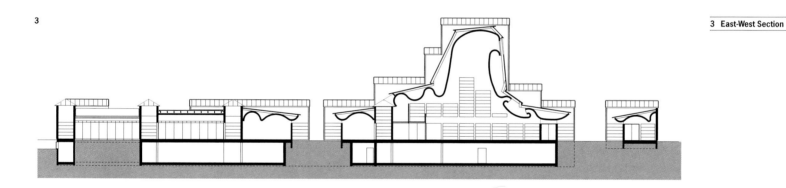

4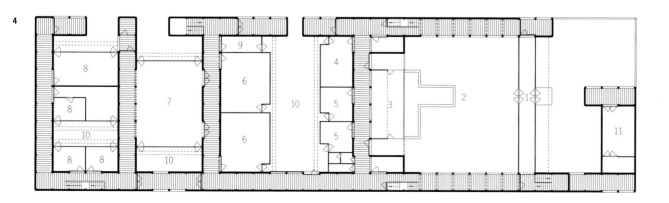

4 Ground Floor Plan

1 Entrance
2 Church
3 Sacristy
4 Waiting Room
5 Office
6 Candidates' Room
7 Parish Hall
8 Meeting Rooms
9 Kitchen
10 Atrium Garden
11 Chapel

N

0 5 10 m
15 30 ft

Archbishopric Museum of Hamar

Sverre Fehn, 1924–

Hamar, Norway; 1967–79

After studying with the leading Norwegian Modernist, Arne Korsmo, Sverre Fehn joined the Norwegian division of CIAM. Known as PAGON (Progressive Architects' Group of Norway), the members included Korsmo, Geir Grung and Christian Norberg-Schulz, who was to become one of the most influential historians and theorists of his generation. Like Utzon, van Eyck and several other architects who came to prominence in the 1950s, Fehn travelled to Morocco, where he spent a year studying North African vernacular buildings.

Fehn made a major international impact in 1962, with the completion of the Pavilion of the Nordic Nations in the Gardens of the Venice Biennale. Arguably the most impressive structure on the site, it consists of a tightly knit, double-layered grid of deep concrete beams that create a shaded island of 'Nordic light' under the southern sun. Three large trees were not only preserved, but also allowed to interrupt the structure: a close relationship with nature is a fundamental aspect of Nordic aesthetics, and in the Hamar Museum – as it is generally known – Fehn accords similar respect to the traces of the past.

The museum re-occupies the U-shaped remains of a nineteenth-century farm building,

which in turn sits over traces of a medieval fortress demolished in the sixteenth century. The site was rich with archaeological remains, and historically gained added importance because it lies on the Kaupang trail, along which the Bishop of Hamar set off for Rome in 1302.

Fehn's brief was to create a museum in which the work of excavating could continue as a living exhibit, and his response was to interfere as little as possible with the existing ground. New roofs, supported by laminated timber columns and trusses, sail above the walls of the former barns, and the rhythm of the new structure – varied but everywhere present – serves to unify the complex. Light enters through bands of glass tiles, or through large sheets of glass that master the gaps between the new roof and old stone walls. Elsewhere, most extensively in the side wings, the gap is filled with red-stained timber boarding. Inside, close to the entrance where the excavations were still proceeding, square concrete 'treasuries' for special exhibits stand on single circular columns, and elevated concrete walkways – their balustrades acting as beams – fly through the space, enabling visitors to look down on the excavated ground.

In one wing of the 'U', a partial concrete floor was introduced, while in the other, an auditorium, in the form of a giant concrete staircase, was inserted. From its foyer, a boomerang-shaped ramp shoots out across the site to link interior to exterior: like the other new interventions, it is allowed to make only minimal contact with the existing ground or fabric.

In designing the displays of excavated material, which were added after 1974, Fehn drew on Carlo Scarpa's work in the Castelvecchio in Verona. Many of the exhibits are displayed on rudimentary steel supports that not only add drama and presence to relatively mundane objects, but also integrate them into the orchestration of routes through the interior. This dialogue between old and new informs every aspect of Fehn's design, marking it out as one of the most successful attempts to learn from Scarpa by juxtaposing a radically new architectural language with a precious historic context.

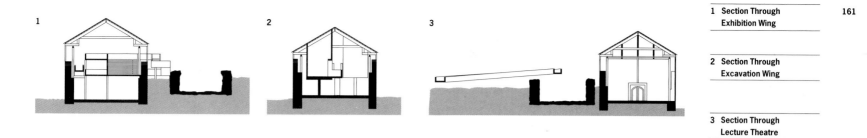

1 Section Through
  Exhibition Wing

2 Section Through
  Excavation Wing

3 Section Through
  Lecture Theatre

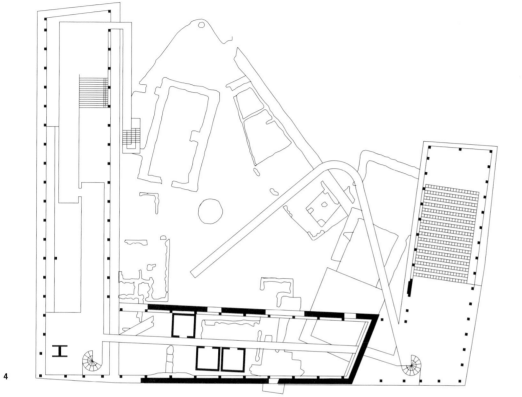

4 Upper Level Plan

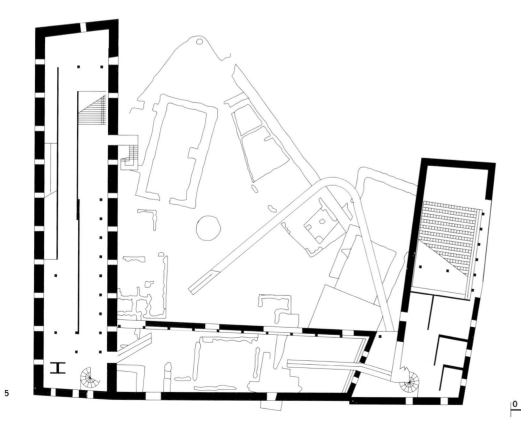

5 Ground Floor Plan

Gallaratese Housing Block

Aldo Rossi, 1931–97

Milan, Italy; 1969–76

Aldo Rossi was the leading member of a revisionist Italian movement known as the Tendenza. Their work was characterized by a radical reduction of architecture to primary geometries, a return to traditional building typologies, and a preference for elevations marked by the dead-pan repetition of square windows that was indebted to the work of Italian Rationalists of the 1930s such as Giuseppe Terragni (**Casa del Fascio**, page 74) — hence, in part, their popular description as 'neo-Rationalists'. Underpinning Rossi's thinking, in particular, was an abiding concern with the essence and continuity of the Classical tradition, epitomized for him by the work of Adolf Loos and of Louis-Etienne Boullée.

Rossi's view of architecture was grounded in a theory of the city expounded in 1966 in the influential book *L'Architettura della città* (The Architecture of the City). Despairing at the destruction that came in the wake of industrialization and 'functional' design, he argued that architects should return to time-honoured urban patterns and building types and reduce them to their essential geometric forms. Whereas a functionalist sought the greatest correspondence between a specific purpose and the proposed form, as a rationalist Rossi advocated generic

forms — 'types' — that were capable of adaptation to the widest range of needs.

The obsession with closed, complete forms was complemented by a fascination with disintegration and by an extraordinary ability to discover a unique poetry in the simplest buildings. His celebrated sketches of beach huts (with their triangular roofs like diminutive pediments), of barns, lighthouses and other vernacular structures have a mesmeric power, and by combining ancient and contemporary fragments many of his projects have the surreal air of those paintings of imaginary *piazze* by Giorgio de Chirico.

The Gallaratese Housing Block forms part of a new residential quarter, close to an autostrada on the outskirts of Milan. Although it appears continuous, it consists of two blocks separated by a narrow gap. The ground floors of both are occupied by open galleries, defined by piers on the northwest side and by 3-metre (10-foot) deep fins to the southeast; at intervals, the fins are replaced by the structures housing the access stairs and lifts to the housing units above. Close to the gap between the two buildings, the fins and piers are replaced by four giant 1.8-metre (6-foot) diameter columns. The gallery of the shorter building is at a

higher level, linked to the lower by a large stair, and serviced by shops and stalls.

The housing units are traditionally planned, and arranged along an external corridor — or *ballatoi* — that alludes to both the Corbusian model of the raised street (**Unité d'Habitation**, page 98) and to a common housing type in Lombardy. For Rossi, the relentless repetition of the piers and square openings created a framework receptive to the incidents of everyday life. Observing the development in 1974, as the residents moved in, he welcomed 'the first open windows, clothes hanging out to dry in the loggias — the first timid signs of life'. 'I am confident', he went on, 'that the spaces reserved for this daily life — the big colonnade, the *ballatoi* — will bring a sharp focus to the dense flow of daily life and the deep popular roots of this residential architecture, of this "big house" which would be at home anywhere along the Milanese waterway or any other Lombardian canal.'

1

2

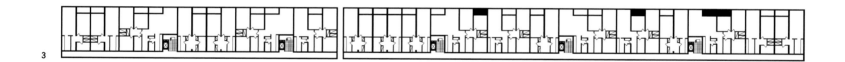

3

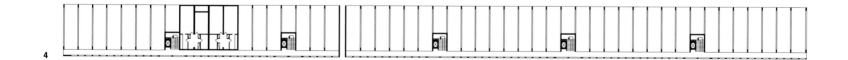

4

5

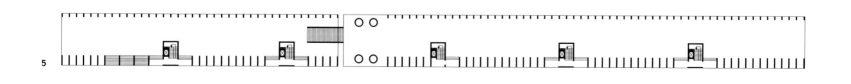

|0 |10 |20 m
|30 |60 ft

Centraal Beheer Insurance Offices

Herman Hertzberger, 1932–

Appeldoorn, The Netherlands; 1967, 1970–2

While at Delft University, Herman Hertzberger came under the influence of Aldo van Eyck. Sharing van Eyck's fascination with additive structures, epitomized by the **Amsterdam Municipal Orphanage** (page 120), and his belief that human beings and cultures exhibit archetypal patterns of behaviour, Hertzberger developed a theory of 'polyvalent form' that laid great stress on the users' role in 'completing' the architecture. Although he aspired to universality, his ideas were a response to the situation in The Netherlands in the 1960s, where the issue of user participation had become a central concern. The most radical proposals were advanced by John Habraken in his 1961 book, *Supports: an Alternative to Mass Housing*, in which he advocated the reduction of architecture to a serviced framework, on which people could build as they wish.

Hertzberger did not envisage reducing the architect's role as comprehensively as Habraken, but his ideas ran along related lines. Rather than providing a fully resolved response to a given programme, he believed the architect should create a strong, but, in terms of use, relatively neutral framework to be variously interpreted and completed by its users. 'What matters', he argued, 'is the interaction of form and users, what they convey to each

other and bring about in each other, and how they mutually take possession of each other.'

Hertzberger's first opportunity to test his ideas on a large scale came from an unlikely client, a major insurance company that required a new headquarters for its 1,000 staff. As in van Eyck's Orphanage, the model was a casbah-like settlement assembled by repetition from a basic spatial unit. The unit was also square, sized to yield four workspaces when divided by a cross of circulation and linked to its neighbours by narrow bridges, thereby generating a vast 'tartan' plan through which light percolated courtesy of rooflights along the narrow bands. The configuration is surprisingly reminiscent of Louis Kahn's **Richards Medical Research Building** (page 128) and the columns were similarly set in from the corners. Stacked up to four storeys high, not including the car park, the repetition of the basic units generates a structure of bewildering complexity. It is made legible, and richly habitable, by a generous communal realm at the heart of each floor that effectively divides the building into four independent blocks defined by arcade-like circulation spaces that reach up to the rooflights. The staff personalized their workspaces by bringing in plants, posters and other material.

Unlike traditional corporate headquarters, Centraal Beheer had no imposing entrance or obvious spatial hierarchy. To many critics, the conspicuous failure of additive structures to create a legible form and organization was a serious weakness. But to Hertzberger it was part of the architecture's resistance to the exercise of corporate power, allowing the employees to slip in and out unnoticed, and precluding any panopticon-like control of their work. For similar reasons, the building was mostly made of that most despised of modern materials, concrete blocks. In Hertzberger's mind, they positively demanded that the users humanize them – unlike more prestigious, do-not-touch materials.

In retrospect, it all seems very Dutch and very '60s, and a decade later, as corporate power grew throughout the Western world, the more extreme forms of personalization were predictably discouraged. But however improbable Centraal Beheer may now seem as a model, and however unfashionable its rejection of some of the traditional disciplines of architectural form, it remains – with Wright's **Larkin Building** (page 26) and Foster's **Willis, Faber & Dumas Headquarters** (page 166) – one of the few radical and humane attempts to re-think that ubiquitous twentieth century type, the office building.

1

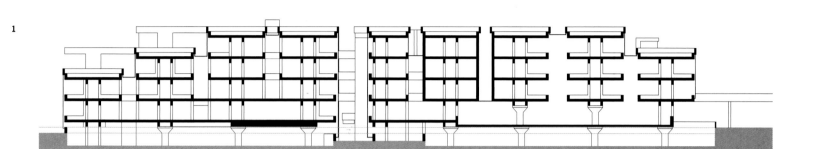

2

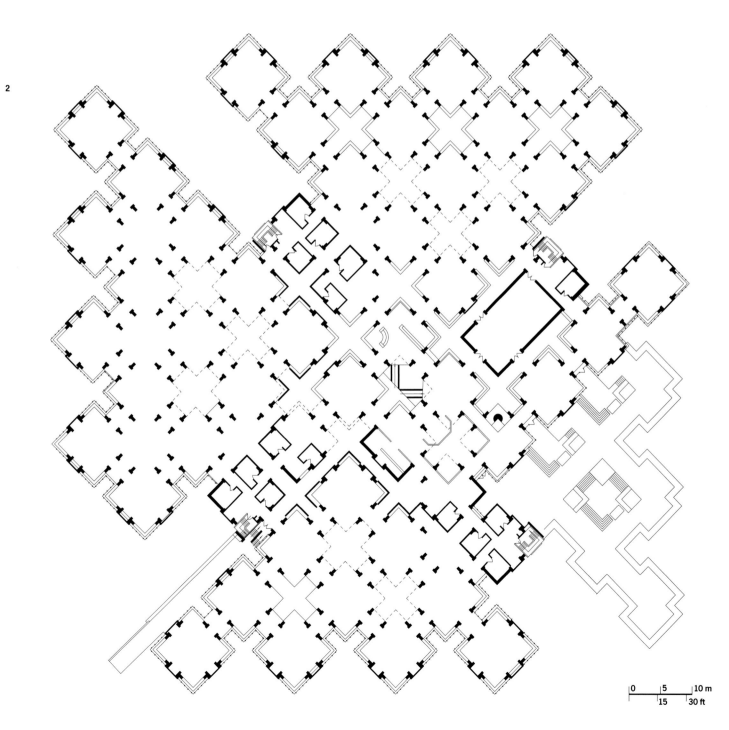

Willis, Faber & Dumas Headquarters

Norman Foster, 1935–

Ipswich, England; 1971–5

The emergence of skeletal constructions of iron and glass has long been seen as one of the key technical factors in the development of Modern architecture. Transparent to the point of invisibility in certain lighting conditions, or offering mirror-like reflections in others, the 'nature' of glass is elusive, and the search for appropriate expressions of glass architecture became a central concern of many early Modern architects, from Bruno Taut (**Glass Pavilion**, page 40) to Mies van der Rohe (**Barcelona Pavilion**, page 58).

An exceptionally prescient article published in Paris in 1849 predicted that buildings with 'wide openings of thick, single- or double-glazed glass panes, either frosted or translucent' would allow 'a magical splendour to stream in during the day-time, stream out at night'. More than 70 years later, in 1922, Mies published his now celebrated projects for Glass Skyscrapers. These included one with a strange, amoeba-like plan that was designed, he explained, to make the most of 'the play of reflections' on the complex curved surfaces. These visions were finally combined with the completion, in 1975, of Norman Foster's headquarters for the insurance brokers Willis, Faber & Dumas in Ipswich, England.

The site, in a Conservation Area close to the centre of Ipswich, was formed by the piecemeal acquisition of properties defined by the city's medieval street pattern. In response, Norman Foster opted to allow the building to flow to the site boundaries, like a pancake in a pan, enabling the required accommodation to be provided within a three-storey height that respected the scale of the surrounding buildings. The resulting deep-plan has – like Wright's **Larkin Building** (page 26) – a spacious atrium at its heart and, in a manner more reminiscent of a department store than a three-storey office building, the floors are linked by banks of escalators that rise dramatically from the entrance hall. The central atrium provided a social heart for the organization, and the effort to democratize the workplace by promoting the feeling of a work-community was equally evident in the provision of a ground floor swimming pool, a roof garden and a restaurant.

Structurally, the building was planned on a 14-metre (47-foot) square grid, with a necklace of perimeter columns that track the site boundary, set well back from the building edge to allow the solar-tinted glass wall to run uninterrupted around the perimeter. Developed with the manufacturer

Pilkington, the glazing system pushed the available technology to the limits. There are no mullions, and the wall is suspended from an edge beam rather than supported from below in the conventional way – in that sense, it is a literal 'curtain' wall. The storey-height panes are connected by corner 'patch' fixings and sealed using silicon, while internal glass fins, at right angles to the surface, provide wind bracing. By day the building becomes – as Mies anticipated – a kaleidoscopic collage of reflections of the surroundings, while at night it offers the 'magical splendour' of golden light streaming out.

Although conceived just before the oil crisis of the 1970s made energy conservation a key issue in building design, the deep plan and insulating quilt of its turf roof made the project energy efficient ahead of its time. It was also pioneering in its use of raised floors, anticipating the IT revolution that was still some years ahead. Innovative on almost every front, the Willis, Faber & Dumas building remains one of the seminal contributions to office design.

1

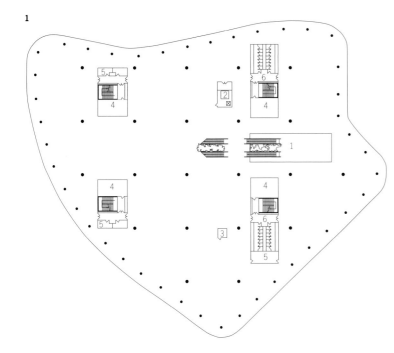

2

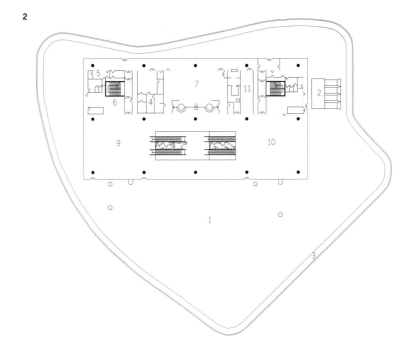

3

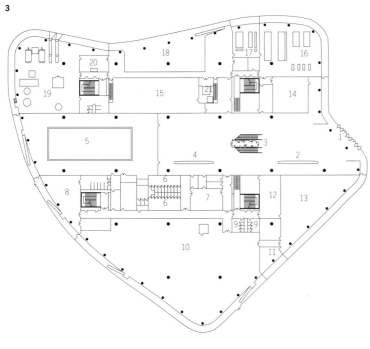

4

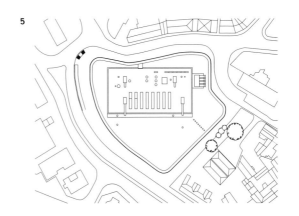

5

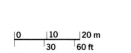

0   10   20 m
30   60 ft

Pompidou Centre

Renzo Piano, 1937–, and Richard Rogers, 1933–

Paris, France; 1971–7

Formulated in the wake of the riots of 1968, the project that was to become the Pompidou Centre began life as a major public library. With the election of Georges Pompidou as President, the brief expanded to embrace a museum of modern art, a centre for industrial design, and a facility – tailored to the needs of the avant-garde composer and conductor Pierre Boulez – for research into music and acoustics. This formed the basis of an international competition, launched in 1970 and won by a team led by Renzo Piano and Richard Rogers.

The chosen site had been cleared in the 1930s and formed a strategic link between a major redevelopment area, formerly occupied by the vast markets of Les Halles, and the then run-down Marais district to the east. Piano and Rogers opted to build on – or, strictly, above – less than half the site, developing the entire ground area as a public space. In the freewheeling, all-embracing spirit of the brief, they envisaged the building as a flexible, highly serviced shed, with its two long façades – addressing motorists on the busy Rue de Renard and pedestrians in the new piazza – treated as giant information screens.

The immediate precedents for the proposal were to be found in the work of the British Archigram group and of Cedric Price, most obviously his flexible Fun Palace project, developed for the avant-garde theatrical director Joan Littlewood. The lineage of these projects could, in turn, be traced back via Oscar Nitschké's unbuilt Maison de la Publicité of 1932 – a steel-framed façade supporting advertisements and projected images – to the work of the Russian avant-garde of the '20s.

Not surprisingly, the radical intent of the competition project was somewhat compromised in execution. The moving floors disappeared, as did the interactive information façades – that to the road is now dominated by exposed, brightly coloured service ducts and the frontage to the piazza by the escalators in glazed tubes that 'process' visitors. The height also had to be reduced, necessitating the filling-in of the open ground floor.

As realized, the building consists of six above-ground floors, 48 metres (160 feet) in width and clear-spanned by vast lattice trusses made of steel tubes – the scale is more like that of civil engineering than building. The design also required two movement zones, beyond the main enclosure, and the structural resolution of this led to the distinctive cast-steel gerberettes. These form collars around the circular columns and cantilever a short distance inwards, to pick up the main beams, and outwards, where they are tied by vertical rods (the system is named after the nineteenth-century German engineer, Heinrich Gerber, who invented it for bridges).

The Pompidou Centre proved a huge popular success from the moment it opened, rapidly outdoing Paris's many other attractions in terms of visitor numbers. Practically and critically, however, it has fared less well. The much-vaunted 'flexibility' of the open floors proved intimidating for many art exhibitions, and Gae Aulenti was eventually commissioned to subdivide the interior into more conventionally scaled and defined spaces. Similarly, as issues of language came to the fore in architectural thinking, the exaggerated expression of structure and services seemed less than satisfactory as a representation of the building's cultural role.

1

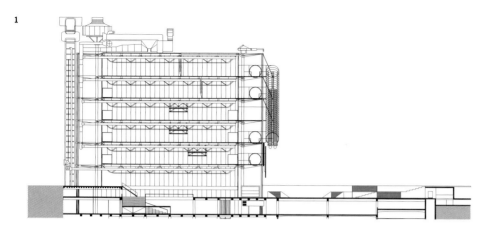

2

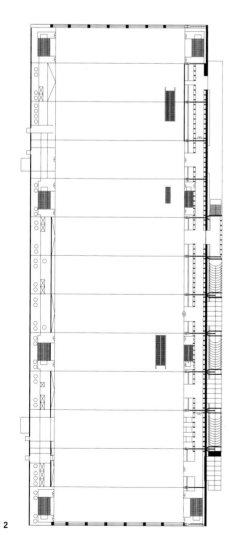

3

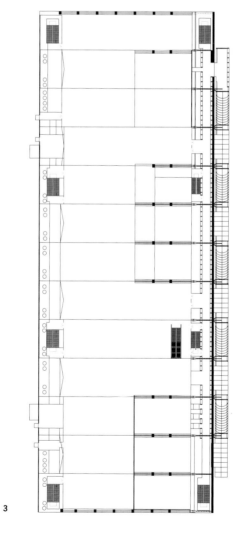

4

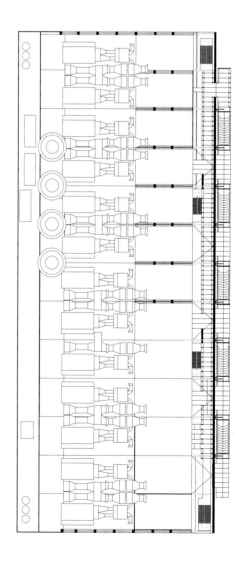

0   10   20 m
  30   60 ft

N

House at Riva San Vitale

Mario Botta, 1943–

Ticino, Switzerland; 1972–3

Mario Botta came to architecture young, completing an apprenticeship and his first independent buildings before entering the Venice School of Architecture at the age of 21. While pursuing his studies he came under the influence of Carlo Scarpa and had the opportunity to work for both Le Corbusier and Louis Kahn. By the time he came to build the house at Riva San Vitale, Botta had managed to assimilate an exceptionally rich range of influences and to develop a distinctive style of his own.

This style crystallized in a house at Cadenazzo, completed in 1971 and characterized by a rectilinear volume of concrete blockwork set against the contours of a sloping site; spatial subdivisions in both plan and section controlled by a square module or bay; and the use of large openings to mediate the relationship – in terms of scale and view – to the surroundings and to modulate the entry of light. The latter, circular in Cadenazzo, were almost certainly derived from Kahn's 'ruins wrapped around buildings' (see the **Salk Institute**, page 138): they were to become a familiar feature of many of Botta's projects.

Situated outside the village on steeply sloping land above the shores of Lake Lugano, the House at Riva San Vitale is placed low down its site, and entered via a bridge at the uppermost level, lending it a somewhat military demeanour. Although manifestly tower-like, it is far from defensive: while eschewing the kind of structural gymnastics that might have 'destroyed' one or more of the corners, Botta effects a complete opening up of the form. Only about half the volume is occupied by indoor space and the landscape beyond can be glimpsed through the house from every side.

Square in plan, the design is an impressive demonstration of the spatial variety that can be derived from economy of geometric means. A square staircase is placed at the heart, but not geometric centre: displaced along one of the diagonals, it creates a subdivision between smaller service spaces to the northwest and living spaces and outdoor terraces and balconies to the southeast. Although the composition has affinities with the planar systems favoured by many Modernists, to Botta the process of carving out the space from a solid body is a means of relating the house back to its natural archetype, the cave.

The economy apparent in plan is equally evident in the choice of materials and colours. The walls are of concrete blocks, fair-faced externally, unplastered and painted white inside. The standard steel window frames are painted black, while the lattice structure of the entrance bridge, made of slender square steel sections and protected by steel mesh, is deliberately without any hint of structural cleverness: the point, here, is to establish a strong counterpoint with the masonry – visually light against visually heavy, vertiginous flexion against reassuring stability. Botta's attitude to materials and finishes, which seems to have much in common with the Italian Arte Povera movement, is to enhance the quality of 'poor' materials through precision of form and structure. In normal usage, both residents and visitors move directly from the entrance to the central stair, and this, like the bridge, is made of steel, hung within its enclosing walls and designed to flex slightly under the weight of your body.

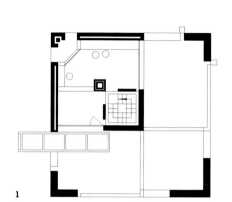

1

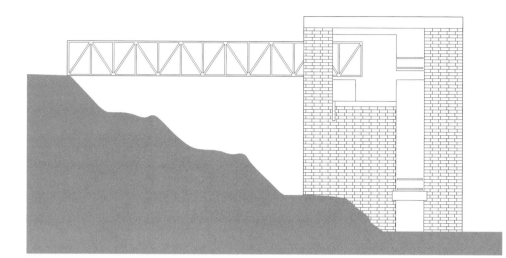

2

3

4

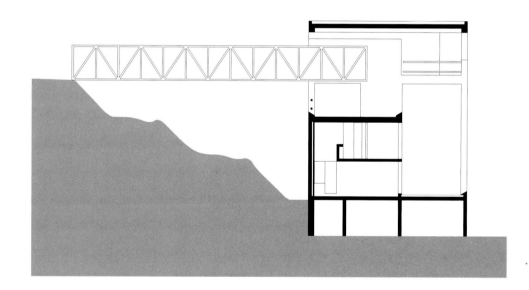

5

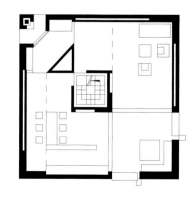

6

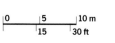

Mönchengladbach Museum

Hans Hollein, 1934–

Mönchengladbach, Germany; 1972–82

Hans Hollein came to attention young, courtesy of some striking, avant-garde images (an aircraft carrier sunk into a landscape and transformed into a megastructure being the most memorable) and a series of inventive shop-fronts and interiors in Vienna. The first of these, a tiny candle shop in Kohlmarkt, was designed in 1964. Its aluminium façade, with a keyhole entrance and matching pair of tiny, exquisite display windows that seemed as 'natural' to sheet metal as the peeled-back lid of a sardine can, was beguiling, but the hieratic displays of candles inside, like votive offerings to some god of light, struck many as too ironic to be admitted to the pantheon of architecture.

Even with the completion of this museum, the doubts about Hollein's intentions remained. His avant-garde allegiances and love of Pop, allied to an unease with the tradition of monumental architecture, drove him to adopt a strategy that challenged assumptions about what a public building should be like. Rejecting any system of overall order, he conceived the museum as a collection of disparate buildings that suggests, by turns, a miniature town, earthwork and ruin.

Visually, the interior is more unified – the finishes are mostly of the 'white box' kind then demanded for the display of modern and contemporary art – but spatially it is no less heterogeneous. And where the opportunity to introduce a surprising new scene or a disjunctive note presents itself, Hollein never disappoints: hence, for example, the perfectly framed picture of the Abteiberg offered by the projecting café, or the plush, red-and-blue colour scheme of the cylindrical lecture theatre.

As an environment in which to view art, Mönchengladbach is a delight. The principal galleries are square, but organized as diamonds, enlarging the apparent space and enabling Hollein to achieve an effortless integration of steps and ramps and provide security points supervising four galleries. On the two principal levels the galleries spill out into a loose, flowing, landscape-like space, along whose outer edge are ranged the discrete spaces that create – with the administration tower – the major 'events' of the miniature city. One of the latter is the main entrance, a cubic glass tower that presides, like Nike Apteros on the Athenian Acropolis, over the landscape below. It is reached via a deck across the adjacent road that connects directly to a pedestrianized shopping street, one of several connections into the existing town, including a secondary entrance into the main foyer below.

The lighting is as varied as the spaces. The main galleries have saw-tooth north-lights, set at 45 degrees to the orthogonal; the square temporary exhibition space has coffered lay-lights threaded through with a grid of neon tubes; and elsewhere Hollein deploys fluorescent tubes and spotlights in endlessly inventive ways. The cumulative effect not only ensures varied and appropriate light for the diverse artworks, but also reinforces the articulation of the interior into what Aldo van Eyck (**Amsterdam Municipal Orphanage**, page 120) called 'a bunch of places'.

By rejecting established building typologies and refusing to give the museum a monumental public presence in the city, Hollein ignored the fashionable wisdom of his time. To many his masterwork seemed too close to the literary, figurative interests of the more dubious kinds of post-Modern architecture, but at the beginning of a new century, when there is much talk of 'building atmospheres', it seems ripe for re-evaluation.

1

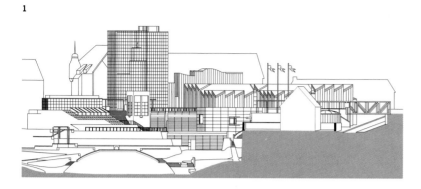

2

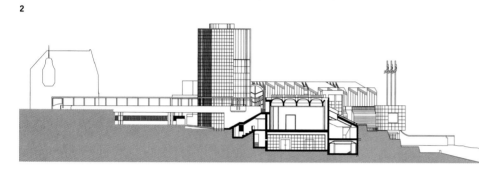

3

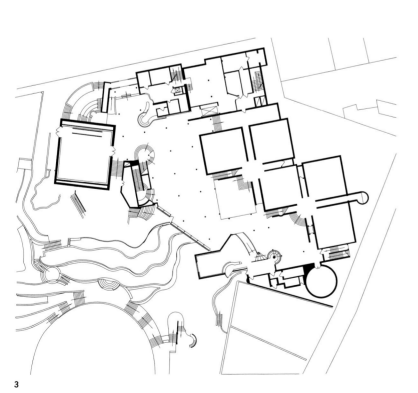

4

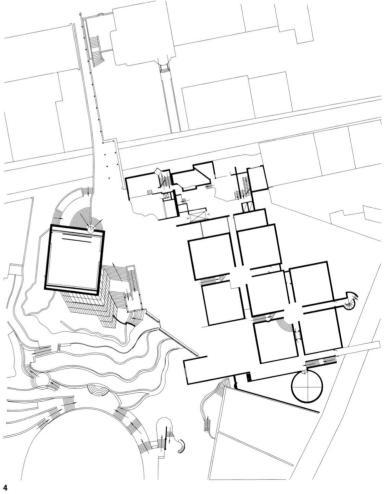

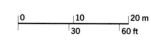

Can Lis

Jørn Utzon, 1918–

Porto Petro, Majorca; 1973

Sited on a strip of land between a narrow, pine-roofed road and a precipitous, 20-metre-high cliff plunging into the Mediterranean, Can Lis consists of a collection of small buildings and walled enclosures. As befits its setting, the design has obvious Classical roots – 'crystal clear forms on a site-adjusted base', as Utzon put it – but as with much of his work, the initial impulse for the design came from an experience of nature.

The site of the house stands in a small cave at the bottom of the cliff and Utzon realized that he wanted the architecture to re-create this archetypal sense of prospect and refuge: openness and light beyond; a deep, reassuring sense of enclosure behind. In response, like the ancient megaron form of house that fascinated Le Corbusier, he lit the rooms from one side only and, except in the kitchen and dining rooms – which stand behind a peristyle of columns – he gave the windows deep reveals, so large that they form tiny rooms.

In contrast to the almost monumental openings through which the house addresses the sea, the side facing the road consists of an entirely unremarkable series of casually angled walls framing small patios – you could almost mistake it for an example of Mallorquin vernacular building. You

enter via a covered porch beneath which stands, in a gesture of welcome as much symbolic as practical, a tiled bench. Beyond the plain wooden door lies a crescent moon: inspired by the name of the road, Media Luna, it offers a first glimpse of the sea. To the right lies the nine-square, colonnaded court, from which you confront the horizon from a stone platform that steps down towards a low wall: it feels ancient as the ruins of a Greek stoa. Turn left and you move into the first of the patios. Spatially, this forms an extension of the living room, to which it can be connected by opening a screen of timber doors, but it gives no hint of the drama that lies within.

As high as it is deep, and receding upwards into shade, the living room is articulated by a free-standing column into a square sitting space and narrow, L-shaped passage. Roughly, but not exactly, at the centre of the square Utzon placed three unequal tables – sectors of an implied polygon – and around them an almost semi-circular couch. Also made of stone, with dark-blue tiled nosings and snow-white cushions, it is large enough to gather the family before the spectacle of nature. The deep reveals and sloping soffits of the variously angled windows focus your gaze downwards

towards the meeting of sea and sky.

Sitting in the living room, the primal experience of the cave is at once domesticated and intensified, made almost theatrical in its impact – like prospecting the landscape that formed the backdrop of a Greek amphitheatre. In mid-afternoon the sun adds to the drama by staging what must be one of the most vivid expressions of its daily cycle in the whole of architecture. A patch of sunlight falls on the floor through a small glazed opening – too rudimentary to call a 'window' – placed high in the west wall. Minutes later, a diagonal slice of sun dusts the wall with light, intensifying into a stone-dissolving shaft only to recede in less than half an hour, leaving a glowing patch of orange light to linger in the opening until evening.

Utzon has described his second house on Majorca, Can Feliz, as 'a household altar' set up before the spectacle of nature. The description applies just as vividly to Can Lis, born as it is of his almost religious love of nature. The design equally clearly reflects his fascination with the elemental architectures of ancient cultures, and out of these twin passions was born a house that feels more completely of the Mediterranean than any other built in the twentieth century.

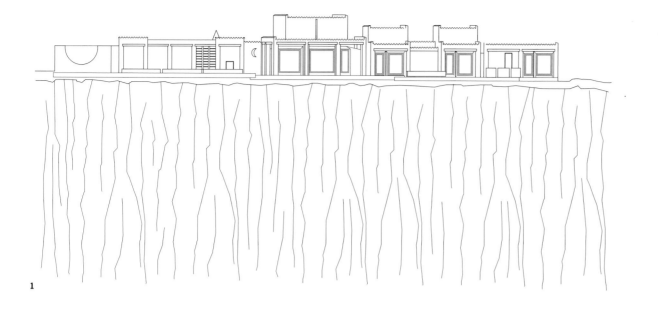

1

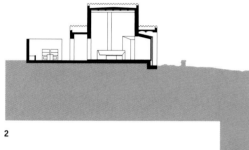

2

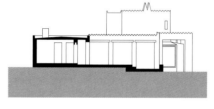

3

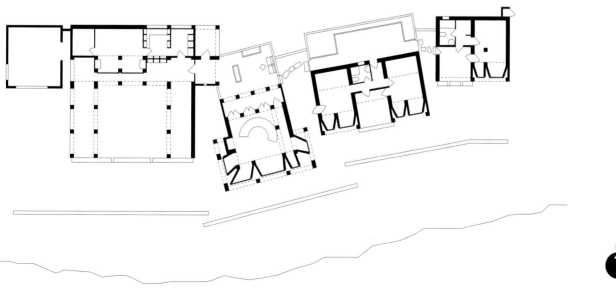

4

N

0   5   10 m
   15   30 ft

Museum of Modern Art

Arata Isozaki, 1931–

Gunma Prefecture, Japan; 1971–4

Gunma Prefecture is considered to be the birth-place of Eastern Japan and is home to major discoveries of clay Haniwa pottery figures as well as some 8,000 ancient burial mounds. The museum is sited close to the town of Takasaki, now almost a suburb of Tokyo, in Gunma-no-mori Park, which was established in 1968, on the site of former army munitions bunkers, to mark the centenary of the restoration to power of the Meiji emperor.

Like Arata Isozaki's architectural career, the design of the museum went through several radically different phases. His initial ideas exploited the surviving blast-deflection mounds by developing the museum as a series of partially sunken volumes surrounded by mastaba-like earthworks – in part, no doubt, the intention was to evoke memories of the region's traces of ancient settlement. A later variant envisaged a series of stepped, cubic pavilions with external beams that suggested a debt to Bo and Wohlert's Louisiana Museum in Denmark – itself, in turn, influenced by the echelon-planning of Japanese houses.

Following an intervention by the national Government, who were responsible for the whole park, the available site was reduced, and in response Isozaki developed the more compact

form of the final design. He also decided to ground the volumetric composition and architectural expression in the strongly conceptual approach he had begun to explore in slightly earlier projects, such as the Fukuoka Bank of 1971. Fascinated by the infinite, gridded surfaces of the Italian Superstudio group, and by the cubic modules of Sol LeWitt's Minimalist sculptures, Isozaki saw their extreme abstraction as offering a way forward from the technologically based Modernism of the Festival Plaza he designed for Expo 70 in Osaka. He now aspired to create an architecture that would appear to be a pure creation of the rational mind – as insubstantial and lacking in physical weight or 'presence' as the ideas that gave it birth.

These ideas were expressed by using a cubic module to generate a conceptual structure that governs everything, in defiance of gravity and conventional distinctions between vertical and horizontal. The reinforced concrete columns and beams all have more or less the same, structurally 'illogical' square section, and to reinforce its abstraction, the entire museum was made as transparent, or reflective – and therefore as seemingly weightless – as possible. Large areas of glass being impracti-

cal for the display of artworks, Isozaki opted for highly reflective aluminium panels and reinforced the 'floating' quality by suspending a section of it above a reflecting pool.

Isozaki saw the metal-clad cubes as literally 'framing', proscenium-like, the artworks, and this in turn promoted the feeling that the museum detaches both itself, and its contents, from the surroundings. This may have been an unwanted consequence, because he produced a drawing of the cubes as open frames through which the surrounding trees were visible in a manner reminiscent of the interaction of interior and garden or landscape in traditional Japanese architecture. However hard Isozaki may have aimed at a formal and material neutrality to express the conceptual basis of the museum's architecture, its supposed 'neutrality' remains visually assertive and insistent, turning it into a potent monument to the twentieth century's preoccupation with art as a transportable and exchangeable commodity, detached from place and at home everywhere a suitably conditioned 'white box' was available.

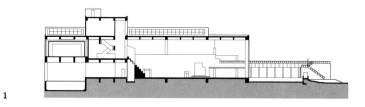

1

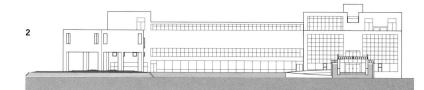

2 **South Elevation**

2

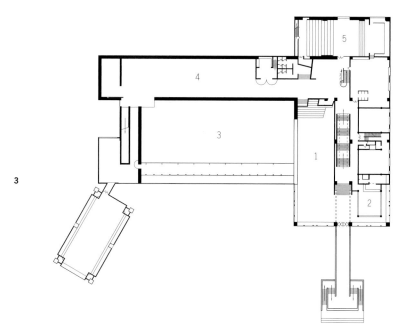

3 First Floor Plan

1 Void over Entrance
   Vestibule
2 Café
3 Void over Exhibition Space
4 Display Space
5 Lecture Theatre

3

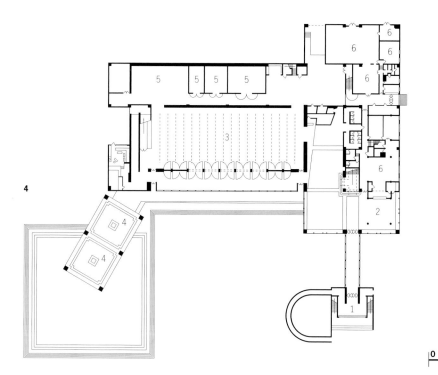

4 Ground Floor Plan

1 Entrance
2 Reception
3 Temporary Storage Area
4 Aedicule
5 Storage
6 Meeting Rooms and Offices

4

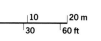

0   10   20 m
     30   60 ft

N

House VI

Peter Eisenman, 1932–

Cornwall, Connecticut, USA; 1975

Peter Eisenman, the most original of the 'New York Five' (see **Atheneum** and **Graves House**, pages 180 and 202), was preoccupied with the radical potential of the abstract formal language of early Modern architecture. House VI, as its laconic name suggests, is one of a series of designs in which he explored archetypal spatial relationships and systems. He was fascinated, in particular, by the 'horizontally vectored space' of De Stijl, emanating from a dense spatial core, and the frontally layered planes of many of Le Corbusier's early houses – most famously that at Garches, to a lesser extent the **Villa Savoye** (page 62) – which in turn were elaborated in the work of Giuseppe Terragni (**Casa del Fascio**, page 74).

The first four houses in the series were essentially transformations of white cubes, their spatial compositions derived from a series of formal operations performed on an initial set of what Eisenman called 'formal conditions' – typically an array of grids, planes and volumes that were variously shifted, translated and rotated to generate bewilderingly complex structures from which he could distil a sequence of habitable spaces. 'Such a logical structure of space,' he explained, 'aims not to comment on the country house as a cul-

tural symbol but to be neutral with respect to its existing social meanings.' Like the Minimalist sculptures of Sol LeWitt and Donald Judd produced around the same time, Eisenman's houses were hermetic, autonomous works: their form bore no relation to their site, nor did their organization spring from the pattern of activities that they might house.

To Eisenman, however, these early projects were still too 'culturally conditioned' by the familiar idea of house. In House VI, commissioned by the photographer Dick Frank and his wife Suzanne, an architectural historian, he set about inverting preconceptions about the nature of architecture. He again used 'diagrammed transformations', but now saw the house not as an end product of the process, but as a living record of it. The resulting solids and voids, columns and planes, were intended to be seen not as a static, resolved composition, but as an invitation to the mind to re-order them, and in the process question their 'meaning'. The house is permeated by vertical and horizontal slots, some glazed, some open, implying the existence of a 'virtual house' of absent columns and beams. Each 'house' even has its own staircase – a 'real' green one connecting the actual floors,

and a red one that goes nowhere and hangs in space as a 'sign'.

Suzanne Frank describes 'the series of slots, beams, and columns that unfold when viewed from the bedroom' as 'an effect as spellbinding as the movement of bits of glass on mirrors in a kaleidoscope', but even as a vacation home it proved problematic. A stray column made conversation around the dining table difficult; guests had to cross the master bedroom to reach the bathroom; the kitchen worktops were uncomfortably high – all the more inconvenient as Dick Frank photographs food and is a keen cook; and, most famously, a 'window' in the floor of the master bedroom required the clients to sleep in separate beds. In 1988 the Franks decided to renovate the house; it was leaking, and they had had enough of sleeping apart and putting up with some of the other idiosyncrasies. Eisenman declared that the house had lost its edge, but finally seemed to be reconciled to his work's new life.

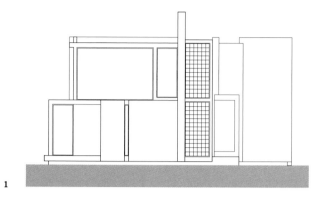

1

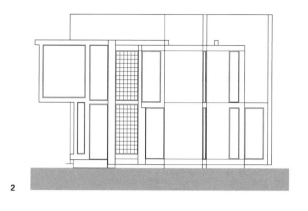

2

1 South Elevation

2 West Elevation

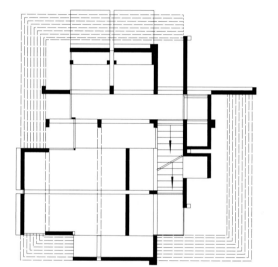

3

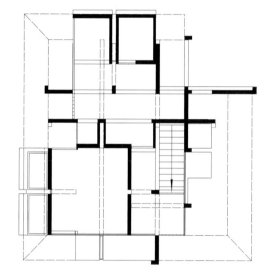

4

3 First Floor Plan

4 Ground Floor Plan

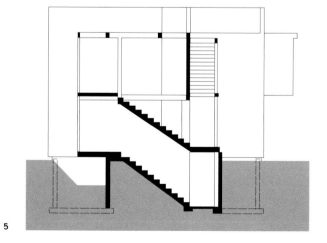

5

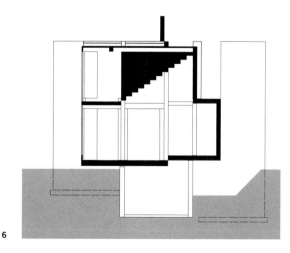

6

5 Section

6 Section

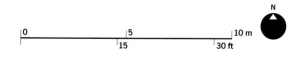

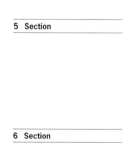

Atheneum

Richard Meier, 1934–

New Harmony, Indiana, USA; 1975–9

Of all the members of the New York Five, Richard Meier has pursued the most consistent and commercially successful line, developed from his abiding passion for the work of Le Corbusier. This commission to build what might, in a less elevated context, be described as a 'visitor centre' for the town of New Harmony gave him free rein to deploy his brand of 'white architecture' to full effect.

The vision of the Welsh social reformer Robert Owen, New Harmony was a utopian response to the problems of industrialization. He bought its 30,000 acres of farmland in 1825 from George Rapp, a like-minded German whose followers preferred Pennsylvania. Owen commissioned a grand new communal building, along the lines of the 'phalanstery' of Charles Fourier, but it was only partly built. He still managed to populate it with assorted teachers and sages and, rather against the odds, the town exerted a significant influence over the region's cultural life. It enjoyed a resurgence in the 1960s and began to attract many visitors – hence the Atheneum.

Sited in a floodplain just beyond the edge of town, the building sits on a low mound and derives its primary regulating lines from the context. First, and dominant, is the orthogonal grid of the town itself; cutting through this, shifted by five degrees and taking its cue from the skewed edge of the town and the river bank, is the line of the path that serves visitors arriving by boat and connects through the building to the town.

Approaching from the river you are greeted by a blank white plane, angled at 45 degrees and undercut to reveal the entrance, itself shifted at five degrees to the path to announce the primary grid within. As in Le Corbusier's **Villa Savoye** (page 62), principal spaces – orientation, exhibition, lounge, film theatre – unfold around a central ramped circulation system, through which light filters down from above. Part way up, the ramp regains the offset geometry of the path, setting grid against grid, spatial compression against spatial tension.

From the second floor exhibition you can look back, through staggered slots and internal windows, across the route already traversed and forwards to what lies ahead. Finally, on the rooftop terraces, you enjoy views of the landscape and town: the highest terrace, triangular like the prow of a ship, is on axis with the major monuments of New Harmony – the restored log cabins, pottery studio, roofless church designed by Philip Johnson and memorial garden to the theologian Paul Tillich. From there the route descends via another, stepped ramp out to the adjacent restaurant and amphitheatre and to the town that is the object of the visit.

Although small, the Atheneum is, arguably, the most complex of all Meier's buildings. His methods are, however, essentially picturesque, and for all its sophistication it does not achieve that tautness of composition and compression of spatial ideas found in Le Corbusier's designs. Although manifestly skilful as an exercise in three-dimensional visual composition, the Atheneum is also open to the accusation of being an essentially formalist exercise, deploying far more 'architecture' than either the brief or context required. Stretched to meet ever larger programmes, Meier's subsequent games with grids and vocabulary of abstract white planes – typically finished, as here, using coated metal panels – became increasingly overblown.

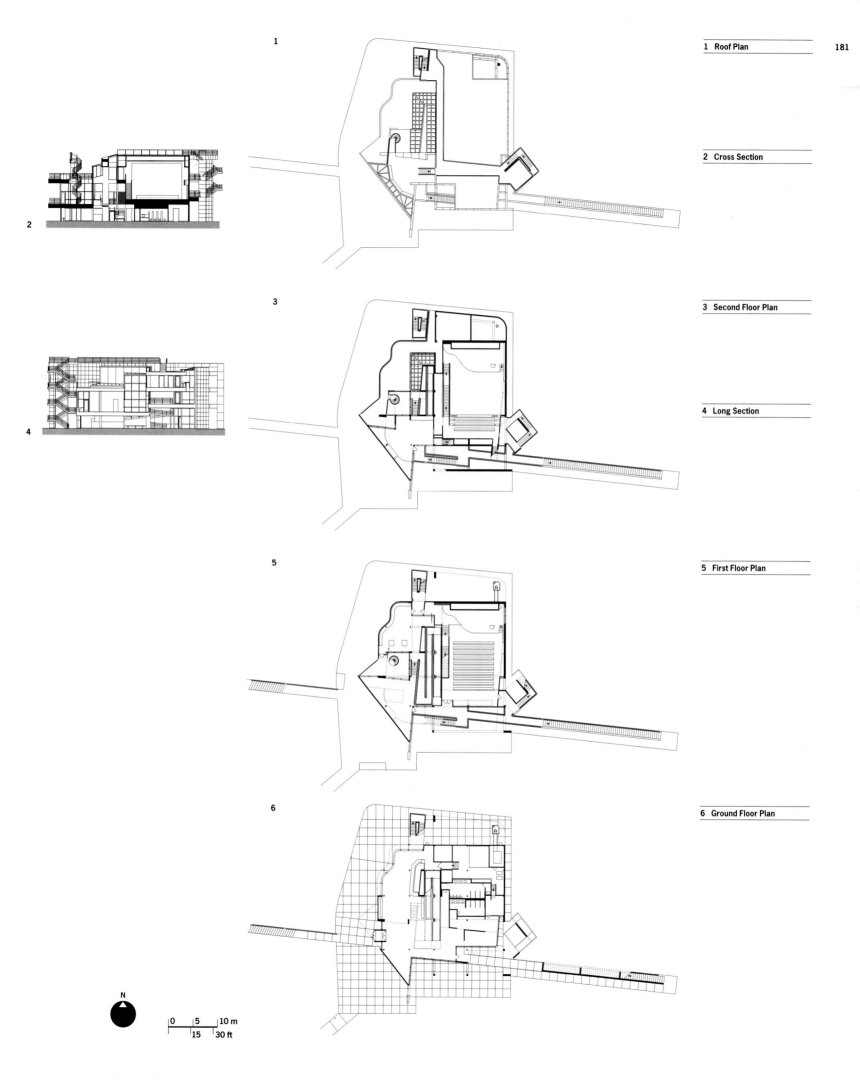

1   Roof Plan

2   Cross Section

3   Second Floor Plan

4   Long Section

5   First Floor Plan

6   Ground Floor Plan

N

0   5   10 m
15   30 ft

Staatsgalerie

James Stirling, 1926–92, and Michael Wilford, 1938–

Stuttgart, Germany; 1977–83

Following the sequence of 'object buildings' typified by the **Leicester Engineering Building**
(page 116), James Stirling became increasingly
concerned with the destruction of the traditional
city. In an unbuilt project for Derby Civic Centre,
made in 1970, a semi-circular arcade framed a
new public space and – in a witty commentary on
planning officers' foibles – a retained façade was
treated like an *objet trouvé* in a Cubist collage.
Seven years later, in a theoretical project to revise
the celebrated Nolli 'Plan of Rome' – instigated by
the city's mayor – Stirling famously scattered the
Eternal City with his own unbuilt projects.
Although not without irony, the project made a
serious point, akin to that of the book *Collage
City* written by his former teacher Colin Rowe and
Fred Koetter, which appeared the following year. In
place of the sterility resulting from 'comprehensive
redevelopment', Stirling argued that cities should
be compounded of heterogeneous fragments, variously adapted to the context. With the competi-
tion-winning design for the Stuttgart Staatsgalerie
he had the chance to put theory into practice.

The gallery extension occupies a steeply
sloping site between two roads – the lower one, a
major multi-lane highway – and two sections of

the city: the hillsides above, the city centre below.
It was a condition of the brief that a pedestrian
route be maintained through the site and this
seemingly minor, potentially awkward, requirement
became an armature of Stirling's design. The
accommodation is sub-divided into discreet buildings, organized around a U-shaped series of en-
suite galleries that echoes the arrangement of the
adjacent neo-Classical gallery. To the east, the
chamber theatre wing projects forward, while to
the north, matching the scale of the surrounding
buildings, are the library and offices.

At the centre of the composition is an open
rotunda, a 'ruin' – it was designed to be rapidly
engulfed by climbing plants – that might once, in
an imaginary past, have had a dome but now
forms both an outdoor space for the gallery and a
dramatic incident along the route through the site.
The path ramps its way down around one half of
the perimeter, continues via a straight ramp to the
raised deck above the car park and finally down a
further ramp or steps to the lower pavement level.
In the spirit of the Rome collage, the different
compositional elements are given varying charac-
ters according to context, function or whim. The
offices, for example, recall the larger of Le

Corbusier's two houses on the nearby Weissenhof
estate; the tiny music school is accommodated in
a piano-shaped volume; the symmetrical end of
the chamber theatre alludes to German Classicism
– almost a taboo subject following its adoption as
the state style by Adolf Hitler. These major variations are reinforced by the liberally scattered 'high
tech jewellery' of the brightly coloured canopies
(upside-down versions of a Corbusian type), fat railings and glazed screens, and by allusions to other
styles – the arched opening through the theatre
wing sports a 'graphic arch' that projects slightly
from the surface of the cladding.

The volumetric planning of the Staatsgalerie
was a virtuoso demonstration of Stirling's extraordinary compositional talent, but 20 years later the
witty, allusive collage of forms feels increasingly
devoid of conviction. Sophisticated and erudite it
may have been, but like most essays in Mannerism,
it marked an end, not a new beginning.

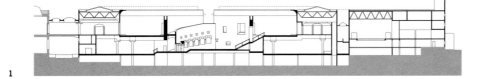

1

2

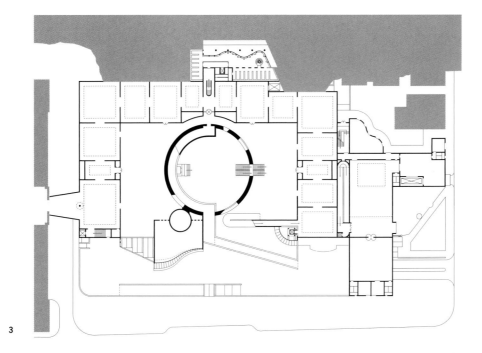

3

4

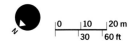

0 10 20 m
30 60 ft
N

Gehry House

Frank Gehry, 1929–

Santa Monica, California, USA; 1977–8

Half-finished tract houses are a familiar sight across the USA, and Frank Gehry was surely not the first to find more excitement in their exposed timber frames and temporary struts and props than in the finished buildings, politely dressed in assorted buyer-friendly styles. But he surely was the first to turn this feeling to serious architectural ends when, in 1977, he set about transforming the pink, two-storey, gambrel-roofed house he and his wife acquired on a corner site along Santa Monica Boulevard.

Although he had behind him more than two decades in practice, Gehry was then only beginning to build a reputation as an innovative designer. He had become fascinated by the formal possibilities of mundane materials such as corrugated metal, plywood, chain link and asphalt – as well as, of course, timber-framing – and so the old house was duly wrapped with a surprising new envelope. This rendered some previously external walls internal, allowing them to be stripped of their finishes and laid bare as part of a layered composition. Elsewhere, timber cladding was replaced with glazing, exposing the insulation and timber studs to view, while window frames were turned into 'exhibits' in the deconstructed walls.

Explaining the forms that crash through the extension, Gehry said he thought of them as the result of a series of large boxes – made of chain link or timber-framed glass – falling onto the house and coming to a precarious state of rest between it and the new wall. The wrap-around wall itself ran past the house, its free-standing end supported by a 'dynamic' pair of diagonal props and its surface cut open with a trapezoidal opening to frame a view of a large cactus.

As a description, the 'tumbling boxes' – rendered in different materials – certainly captures the extension's seemingly casual composition. But its almost throw-away quality does nothing to suggest the range of ideas, many drawn from the world of art rather than architecture, on which Gehry drew. The splits and ruptures we see in his house recall the work of the sculptor Gordon Matta-Clark, renowned for using a chainsaw to 'deconstruct' redundant buildings. Gehry himself has said that he wanted to emulate the unfinished quality found in the work of artists like Jackson Pollock and Willem de Kooning, and he was also fascinated by a group of contemporary Californian artists, part of his circle of friends, whose works involved the use of distorted and contradictory

perspectives as a means of forcing the viewer to address them as purely perceptual phenomena.

Gehry's distorted boxes also owed a debt to the Suprematist paintings of Kazimir Malevich. Much as Malevich deployed slightly distorted rectangles to suggest a 'higher' universe free of gravity, so the glass 'cube' above Gehry's new kitchen presents a similarly elusive form. Its front is a rectangle, not a square, while to the rear its face has been displaced sideways and upwards, so that – save for those in the rectangular front – no two members join at right angles. Cut adrift from the world of familiar figures and uses of materials, and denied the convenient shorthand of perspectival vision, we are invited to pay attention to the forms, spaces and surfaces of Gehry's house as purely visual phenomena, to immerse ourselves in their present reality, free of past associations.

5 **First Floor Plan**
1 Bedroom
2 Closet
3 Master Bedroom
4 Outer Deck

6 **Ground Floor Plan**
1 Bedroom
2 Living Area
3 Dining Room
4 Kitchen
5 Garage

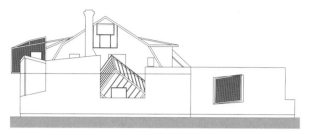

1

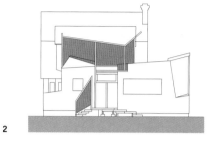

2

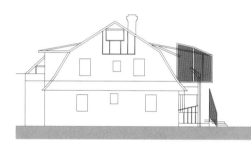

3

4

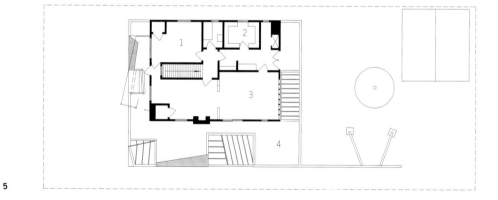

5

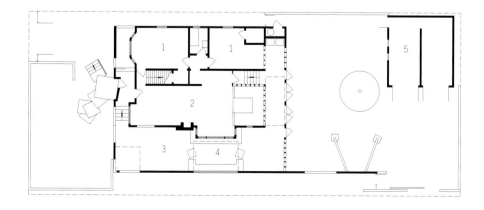

6

0   5   10 m
15   30 ft

Koshino House

Tadao Ando, 1941–

Ashiya, Hyogo Prefecture, Japan; 1979–81, 1983–4

Tadao Ando came to national attention in Japan in 1976, following the completion of his Row House Sumiyoshi in Osaka. The unrelenting severity of this reinterpretation of a traditional wooden terraced house provides a key to all his later work. Describing his houses as 'bastions of resistance' against the destruction of the native culture by Western consumerism, he saw them as means to help their occupants rediscover the traditional, direct relationship to nature. In the Row House, the street façade is a rectangle of concrete, bare but for a shallow top-lit recess that gives access to the first of two cubes of accommodation placed either side of an open court, across which runs a narrow, open bridge to connect the upper floors. Regardless of the weather, the occupants must go outside to move between rooms.

Dug into its site, the weekend house for the fashion designer Koshino is entered at the upper level. From there you descend into the double-height living room, off which the kitchen-dining room is placed under the master bedroom. A row of six children's bedrooms and two traditionally furnished *tatami* rooms for guests are housed in a parallel wing, ranged down a long, single-banked corridor. Compared with the rambling plan of a

traditional Shoin-style house like Katsura Detached Villa, Ando's appears relatively compact, but like a Japanese garden it is structured around a series of what he calls 'scenic locations' intended to heighten the awareness of nature. The concrete-paved terrace and steps, for example, are a reinterpretation of the traditional *kare sansui* or 'dry gardens' of gravel that celebrate the contrasting pleasures of sun and rain, while the two large openings in the living room allow views of the falling ground, trees and distant hills; as in a traditional Japanese house, they are placed low to invite the imagination to complete the scene.

Although critical of Western consumerism and determined to give new life to distinctively Japanese ideals, Ando was deeply influenced by Modernism, and all his work is marked by efforts to reconcile modernity and tradition. The carpet, for example, echoes the colour of traditional *tatami* mats, but the modular control of the spaces that they provided – Japanese rooms were identified by the number of mats – is assigned to the similarly sized (1.8 x 0.9-metre/6 x 3-foot) grid left by the concrete formwork. The concrete itself is of extraordinary quality, made with a blue-grey sand and rendered almost as insubstantial as

paper screens by the play of sunlight that enters a continuous slit of glazing between roof and wall: a raking slice of sun moves slowly across the eastern end wall and then finally dissolves the north-facing rear wall into a seemingly weightless screen.

In 1983 Ando was asked to add a studio. Placed completely underground to the north of the living room, the retaining wall is a quarter-circle in plan and lit by a narrow horizontal slit: the complex, intersecting curves of light and shadow are a perfect counterpoint to the orthogonal world of the original house, and the addition achieves the rare trick of making the whole feel more complete. The Koshino House made an international impact and Ando's work proved widely influential. Although frequently linked to the revival of interest in Minimalist art, it is best understood in the context of the archetypal forms of Shinto shrines and of the pared-down aesthetic of Zen Buddhism.

1 First Floor Plan

1 Study
2 Bedroom
3 Terrace

2 Section

3 Ground Floor Plan

1 Atelier
2 Living Room
3 Bedroom

4 Elevation

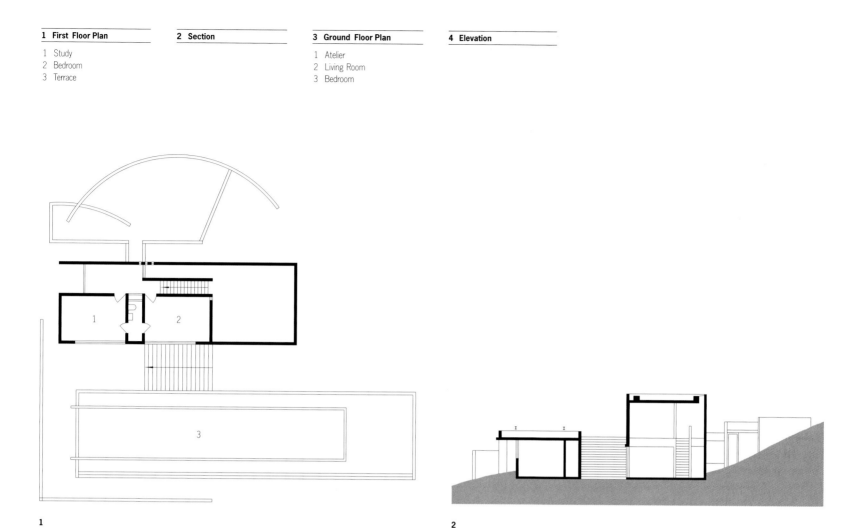

1

2

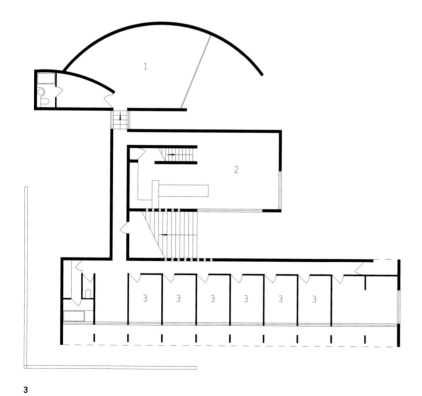

3

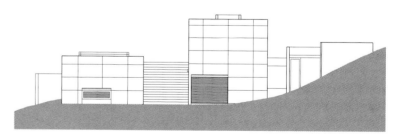

4

0   5   10 m
15   30 ft

187

Hong Kong and Shanghai Bank

Norman Foster, 1935–

Hong Kong, China; 1979–86

Built as the British lease on Hong Kong was coming to an end, the Hong Kong and Shanghai Bank was an affirmation of faith in its future as part of China. The client's brief called for 'the best bank building in the world' and the practical requirements alone were demanding: more than a million square feet were to be built in a relatively short time, suggesting that a high level of prefabrication would be needed.

In responding to these challenges Norman Foster reinvented the office tower – which by that time had typically become a formulaic affair of floor plates stacked around a central service core (for classic versions of the type, see **Lever House** and **Seagram Building**, pages 102 and 118), dressed in post-Modern clothes. The necessity of building upwards and downwards simultaneously led to the idea of a suspension structure consisting of pairs of steel masts arranged in three bays, from which the intermediate floors were hung in groups. Double-height 'sky lobbies' at each suspension level divide the building into 'vertical villages' served by a combination of high-speed lifts and escalators. Pushing the main structure out to the corners also gave greater stability against typhoons and enabled the service cores to be

moved to the perimeter, maximizing the flexibility of the floors – office layouts have been regularly reconfigured and a large dealing floor incorporated.

In section, the building was articulated into three individual 'towers', 29, 36 and 44 storeys high, giving floors of different depth, garden terraces on the roof of each tower and a vigorous, stepped profile to the east and west elevations. The lower, deeper office floors are stacked around a ten-storey-high atrium, and rather than the usual glass roof the space is lit by a mirrored ceiling that receives sunlight from a giant reflecting 'sun-scoop' outside the building. Until the costs proved prohibitive, it was hoped that this might be made to track the sun.

Site conditions – interpreted by a traditional Chinese geomancer – suggested that pedestrian circulation should be maintained through the site down towards the water. In place of a passage or arcade, Foster developed the area below the building as a public plaza. Apart from creating a public space, rare in Hong Kong, this enabled the plot ratio to be increased from the normal 14:1 to 18:1. Closing the atrium above with a glass floor gave the plaza not only ample daylight but also reflected sunlight: walking under the building is an

uncanny experience and at weekends it has become a popular place for picnics. The public entrance to the banking halls is via escalators that rise from the plaza and penetrate dramatically through the sag-curve of the glass floor into the atrium. Foster's drawings originally showed them parallel to the main axis of the building but the geomancer recommended a diagonal alignment, resulting in a more dynamic arrangement.

When presenting his work, Norman Foster rarely strays beyond the rational justifications for seemingly every design decision, but faced with a building like the Hong Kong and Shanghai Bank it is clear that his work draws on a wide range of influences, from Futurist and Constructivist fantasies to the 'architecture' of big engineering such as rocket-launching platforms. Facing across the water to the Chinese mainland, the bank was an exuberant statement of the potential of 'the Pacific century'.

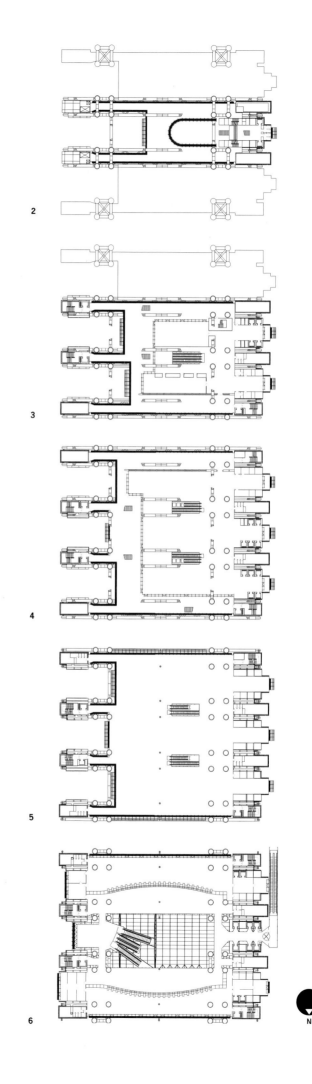

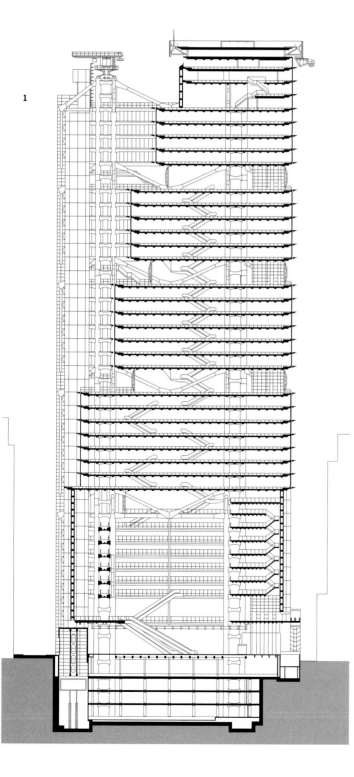

1

2

3

4

5

6

N

0   5   10 m

15   30 ft

Willemspark School

Herman Hertzberger, 1932–

Amsterdam, The Netherlands; 1980–3

One of a pair of almost identical buildings on the Apollolaan in Amsterdam, this school represented a significant shift in Hertzberger's work in response to the perceived weaknesses of the additive formal structure developed for the **Centraal Beheer Insurance Offices** (page 164): namely, that it lacked legibility and made no attempt to shape the exterior space. The site, although near the city centre, is in a mature, leafy area of detached houses. In response, the schools were designed as a pair of urban villas, placed at right angles to each other to frame, and open onto, a clearly defined urban space – an open plaza for access and play.

The almost Classical sense of composure externally is generated by a nine-square plan, with a classroom at each corner and a shared, top-lit space at the centre that doubles as assembly hall and circulation. The four intermediate 'squares' are made narrower to accommodate service spaces. At the lowest level, the classrooms are replaced by a music and gymnastics hall, reached from a gathering and play space below the central hall, and by the school administration area. The latter cuts into the volume, creating space for the external stairs. This simple diagram is transformed by setting in play what Hertzberger's teacher Aldo van Eyck

(**Amsterdam Municipal Orphanage**, page 120) called 'the mild gears of reciprocity'. In section, the plan is shifted by half a storey along one axis, placing pairs of classrooms on different levels and transforming the hall into a stepped mini-auditorium. In plan, the hall is enlarged to become a complete square whose corners overlap with the classrooms, creating a series of lower spaces that are continuous with the hall but manifestly 'belong' to the classroom.

The spatial richness resulting from this organization is matched by a systematic and clearly legible constructional system. The result is a delight, offering myriad opportunities for the children to occupy the building singly, in variously sized groups and as a complete community. The stepped hall becomes a place to assemble, play or read and around it are built-in desks for private study. The 'doorsteps' to the classrooms have their own writing desks, a glass cabinet for displaying work and solid, two-part doors like horse-boxes, enabling the teachers to allow different degrees of openness according to the activities in progress. Light filters everywhere, thanks to the generous rooflights and use of glass blocks for the stair treads.

Within the classrooms, window-transoms swell to receive potted plants and sills are transformed

into desks, while the sink and associated cupboards and shelves become monumental pieces of furniture, self-consciously figural in their symmetry. The same attention to the potential for interpretation through use is apparent externally in the detailing of the steps down which the children stampede to play or go home. The balustrade of the square landing swells to accommodate cantilevered seats, and from there a straight metal flight descends to a cascade of solid, curving steps that engage the circular column supporting the classroom above. The lowest step bulges in response to the column, creating – as Hertberger anticipated – an invitation to the children to play games around its base.

The fascination with use evident in the work of leading Dutch architects such as van Eyck and Hertzberger – not to mention in Rietveld's **Schröder House** (page 48) – is part of a tradition that values the domestic and has grown out of occupying a small country where the land, much of it man-made, requires constant management. Over-elaboration of such 'invitations to use' can feel dictatorial, but in the Willemspark School Hertzberger achieved a balance between the logic of the architecture and the manifold opportunities for interpretation the forms offer to the children and teachers.

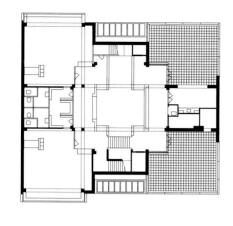

1

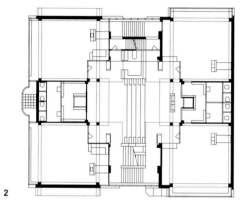

2

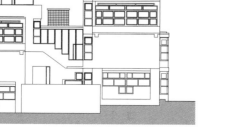

3

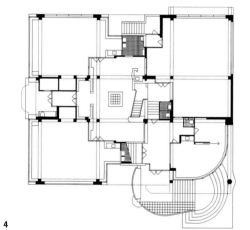

4

5

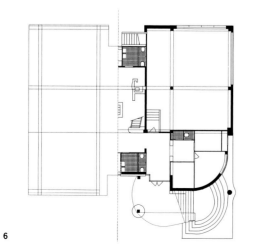

6

7

1　Third Floor Plan

2　Second Floor Plan

3　Site Plan

A　Montessorischool
B　Willemsparkschool

4　First Floor Plan

5　Section

6　Ground Floor Plan

7　West Elevation

```
|0    |5    |10 m
    |15   |30 ft
```

Ball-Eastaway House and Studio

Glenn Murcutt, 1936–

Glenorie, Sydney, Australia; 1980–3

Glenn Murcutt was introduced to building and architecture while still a boy, courtesy of his father who ran a small joinery business and worked as a builder and developer in Sydney. Murcutt Senior experimented with building houses using the Modernist vocabulary he discovered in various American magazines to which he subscribed. These included the influential *Architec-tural Forum*, and it was there that his son first encountered the building that was to prove the single most important influence on his work, Mies van der Rohe's **Farnsworth House** (page 92).

Almost from the outset of his formal architectural education at the then Sydney Technical College, Murcutt developed a keen interest in the work of leading Californian architects, especially of Richard Neutra and Craig Ellwood. He also got to know members of the so-called 'Sydney School', a disparate, romantically inclined group of architects committed to reinterpreting a range of European and American influences – including Wright, Le Corbusier, Aalto, and the English Brutalists – in terms of Australian sites, materials and building traditions. Amongst Australians of his own generation, he enjoyed a fruitful relationship with Richard Leplastrier, who had worked for Jørn Utzon and

shared Murcutt's interest in developing houses attuned to Australian landscapes and climate.

After his formal education, Murcutt worked in London and travelled extensively. In 1973 he went on a 'world tour' during which he finally met Ellwood and, even more crucially, visited the **Maison de Verre** (page 64) in Paris, where Chareau's ability to adapt and combine industrial products, and thereby turn the mass-produced into the unique, greatly impressed him.

Chareau's example is apparent in Murcutt's integration of vernacular materials and details – such as corrugated iron roofs, water butts and pivoting ventilation shutters of agricultural provenance – while the planning and tectonic disciplines of Mies van der Rohe and the California School are present in everything he designs, nowhere more so than in the Ball-Eastaway House. Here, a linear volume, structured by seven tubular-steel portal frames, is variously articulated by the entrance porch, the recessed deck that looks out to the landscape on the northwest side, and by the generous verandah that terminates one end of the volume and melds house and site.

In response to the intense Australian light and crisp, dry eucalpytus trees, with their vulnera-

bility to fire, Murcutt lifts the house off the site and provides external blinds, whose filigree character rhymes with the corrugated cladding. The delicate, almost fragile details are also calculated to exploit the play of light: members project and slide past each other and the roof is expressed as a shimmering plane of metal supported by slender steel purlins, revealed at the open ends of the volume. The construction is laid bare on the large verandah, where the floor peels away to disclose the layered structure and to reconnect the occupants to the ground. Internally, light is filtered and reflected, permeating the house to create a luminous whole: colours are homogeneous, textures unpronounced, and partitions meet the roof as transparent planes of glass to ensure continuity of vision and inter-reflection of light.

Poised above its site, its walls almost hovering in space, and reached via a suspended walkway, the Ball-Eastaway house suggests a precarious equilibrium with nature. As clearly as anything he has built, it exemplifies Murcutt's commitment to observing the Aboriginal injunction to 'touch this earth lightly'.

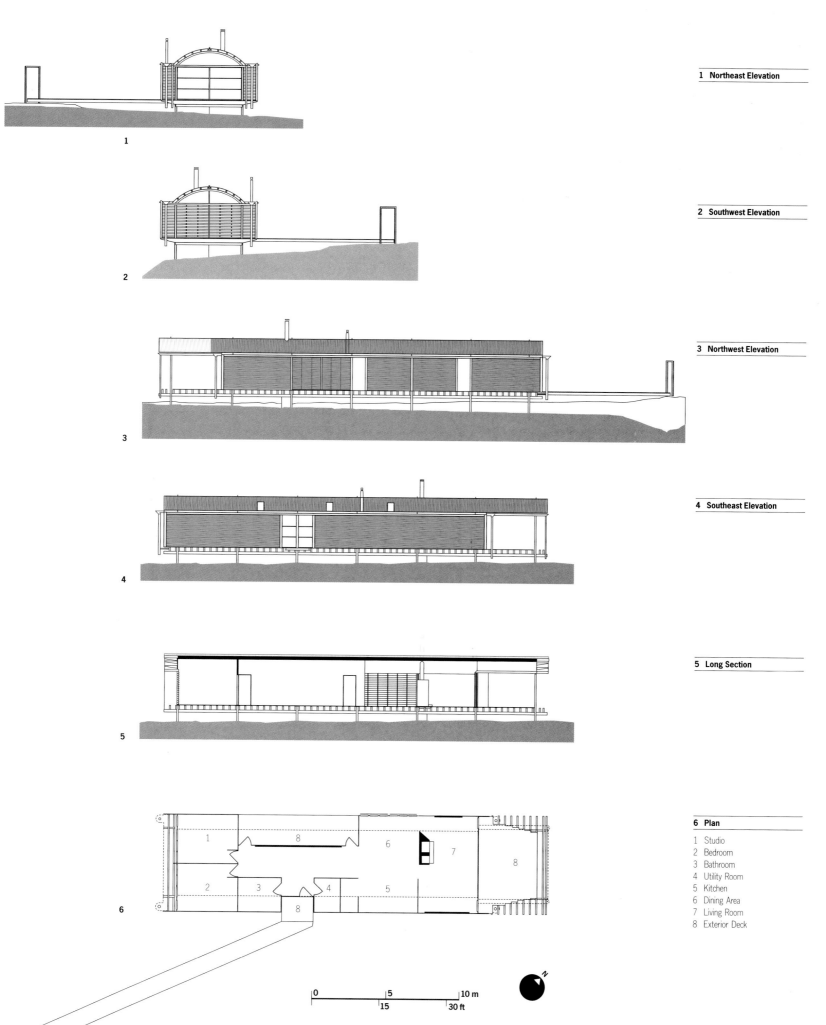

1 Northeast Elevation

2 Southwest Elevation

3 Northwest Elevation

4 Southeast Elevation

5 Long Section

6 Plan

1 Studio
2 Bedroom
3 Bathroom
4 Utility Room
5 Kitchen
6 Dining Area
7 Living Room
8 Exterior Deck

0   5   10 m
    15   30 ft

National Museum of Roman Art

Rafael Moneo, 1937–

Mérida, Spain; 1980–6

Founded in 25BC as Emerita Augusta by the Roman Emperor Augustus, the town of Mérida lies on the Guadiana river at the crossing of roads between Salamanca and Seville, Toledo and Lisbon. Thanks to its strategic position, it quickly became the capital of Lusitania and was enriched by numerous monuments. These constitute the best preserved collection of Roman remains in Spain and include, in close proximity to the museum, a theatre that has been brought back into use, a less well preserved amphitheatre and a major villa. Sited directly over ancient remains, the museum serves as the gateway to the excavations and home to a slowly growing collection of artefacts of all kinds, from statues to mosaic floors.

Moneo's challenge recalls, on a grander scale, that faced by Sverre Fehn in designing the **Archbishopric Museum of Hamar** (page 160). But whereas Fehn opted to expose the excavations throughout most of his interior, and to minimize the elements of structure touching them, Moneo did precisely the reverse. The excavations are preserved in an undercroft, accessible only by going outside, and are thereby experienced as continuous below the town in all directions, not local and unique to the museum. The slender concrete suspended floors above are supported on a series of massive, equally spaced brick walls. In the undercroft these form a rhythmic series of arches, like rearranged fragments of some ancient viaduct, while above, the succession of far larger arches, four storeys high, creates a monumental, asymmetrically placed nave with galleries to either side. Above ground the regularity is insistent, while below, wider arches are introduced to avoid building sections of wall directly through important ancient remains.

The new walls and arches are made in the Roman way, but with a twist: the brick skins act as permanent shuttering for a concrete infill, but the bricks are laid up without visible mortar, lending them a Modern, almost Minimalist, quality. Much the same could be said of the insistent repetition of the walls, which read serially in a way quite unlike the Roman, Gothic or more primitive prototypes they otherwise recall. Organized to create a succession of breathtaking vistas, the diverse spaces of the museum – they include a lecture room, library and workshops, as well as galleries – are linked around an open well, sliced through by an ancient path and connected, via a ramp, down to the excavation level, where a triangular lobby is closed along its hypotenuse by a fragment of the aqueduct of San Lázaro.

The interior is more brightly lit than the ancient-feeling arched walls might lead you to expect. But the light is constantly changing, and when shafts of sun rake in through high windows, or play across the tops of walls, the spaces acquire a Piranesian splendour worthy of comparison with the grandeur of Ancient Rome. Archaic in spirit, yet thoroughly modern in composition, Roman in materials and construction, yet not in the least Classical, Moneo's museum ranks with the museum at Hamar and Carlo Scarpa's transformation of the Castelvecchio in Verona as a seminal reconciliation of ancient and modern. It is also one of the most poetic products of the renewed interest in architecture as an embodiment of civic memory and history that gathered strength during the 1980s.

1   North (Rear) Elevation

2   Long Section Through Workshops

3   Ground Floor Plan: Central Nave Level

1   Void over Garage
2   Void over Remains of San Lázaro Aqueduct
3   Ramp from Access Level
4   Ramp down to Archaeological Precinct
5   Entrance to Museum over Archaeological Precinct
6   Museum
7   Workshops for Mosaic Restoration

4   Excavation Level Plan

1   Entrance to Theatre and Amphitheatre Ruins
2   San Lázaro Aqueduct Remains
3   Cafeteria
4   Storage and Garage Access
5   Cafeteria Storage
6   Access to Archaeological Precinct
7   Palaeochristian Basilica Remains
8   Roman House Remains
9   Tombs

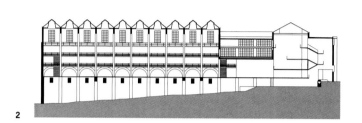

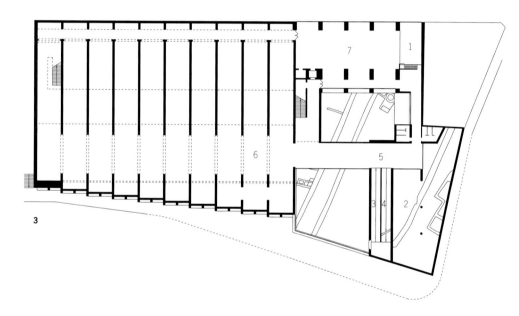

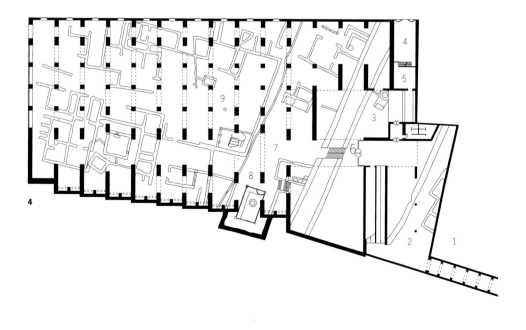

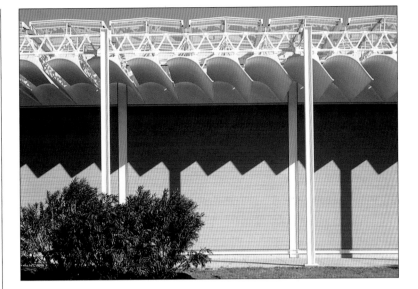

Menil Collection

Renzo Piano, 1937–

Houston, Texas, USA; 1981–6

Renzo Piano came to fame as co-architect of the defining monument of High-Tech, the **Pompidou Centre** (page 168). The subsequent work of his Building Workshop, as he styles his practice, has confirmed his fascination with the process of building, yet consistently transcends the technocratic reduction of architecture to mechanically serviced sheds.

In designing a gallery to house the primitive and Symbolist works that make up the Menil Collection, the chief problem to be addressed was modulating the intense southern light while allowing the interior to reflect its ever-changing qualities. Working with the lighting engineer Tom Barker, Piano developed a lighting system based on elegantly curved lamellae, shaped so that the light falling on the upper surface of one is reflected back onto the underside of the adjacent blade, and then diffused into the interior below. The result clearly owes something to Louis Kahn's **Kimbell Art Museum** (page 156), which was completed just over a decade earlier slightly further north in Fort Worth, and, as in Kahn's masterwork, the resulting quality of natural light creates an atmosphere far more animated than in conventional, north-lit galleries.

Unlike the overtly mechanical forms of much High-Tech architecture, Piano's lamellae immediately evoke associations with natural forms such as leaves or vertebrae. In addition to moderating the light, they form the lower, tensile members of wide-span trusses, and the organic quality is reinforced by the decision – taken with the structural engineer Peter Rice – to make them of ferrocement, enabling the cross-section to be delicately tapered in response to the forces at work. The same logic is extended to the choice of ductile iron for the stem-like upper sections of the triangulated trusses, and such were the technical demands that only two firms were considered equal to the task of making them – both across the Atlantic, in Britain, where hand-crafted technology still flourishes amidst the general decline of manufacturing industries.

In contrast to the sophistication of the roof, the gallery's steel-framed walls are deliberately almost prosaic, weather-boarded in timber like the Museum's suburban neighbours. The boards are slightly wider than usual and, at the Menil Foundation's insistence, the wood is heart cyprus from ancient, South Carolinian trees. And in place of traditional paint, which would need to be regu-

larly renewed, the finish is a pigmented weather-stain, intended to accelerate the natural weathering of the timber.

Like its neighbours, the Menil Museum is set amidst generous lawns on a shallow platform and entered under what amounts to a shady verandah. In his accounts of the project, Piano made much of these contextual qualities, but his work was worlds apart from the eclectic, 'referential' architecture that flourished in the 1980s as architects re-addressed the issue of building in historic contexts. The intricate 'cornice' of roof-blades, carefully studied proportions and light steel frame have more to do with those otherwise contrasting traditions of American post-war architecture represented by Mies's reinterpretation of Classicism (**Crown Hall,** page 106) and the relaxed domestic steel-frame tradition epitomized by the Californian Case Study Houses (the **Eames House**, page 90).

Piano has described his aim as being to 'return to the close association between thinking and doing'. In the Menil Museum he gave a compelling demonstration of how architecture could be renewed by working from the part to the whole, and of how a fascination with technology could be harnessed to serve broader architectural concerns.

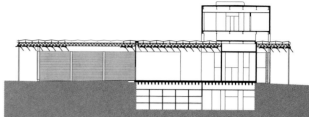

1

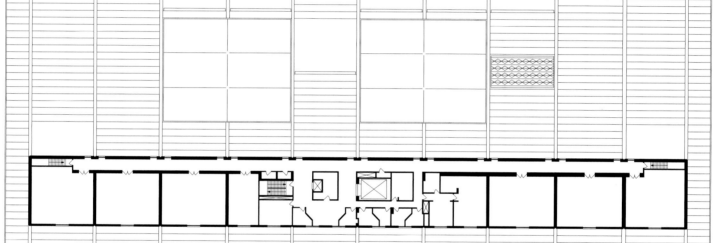

2

3

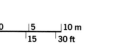

Spiral Building

Fumihiko Maki, 1928–

Tokyo, Japan; 1982–5

Having studied at Cranbrook and Harvard and worked for Skidmore, Owings & Merrill, it is not surprising that Fumihiko Maki's early work, like that of many Japanese architects of his generation, was deeply marked by Western Modernism. Then, around 1980, a disparate range of ideas began to cohere into a new approach that seemed perfectly attuned to expressing the elusive, fragmentary character of Tokyo. In part these ideas were drawn from Modernism – not from architecture, but from the paintings of Paul Klee, the novels of Marcel Proust, the films of Michelangelo Antonioni. What Maki found there were ways of expressing movement as an inherent condition of both the subject and the object, and this in turn enabled him to come to terms with the continual conflict between static and dynamic elements in the fabric and life of Tokyo – a city in which memories of Edo-period calm mix discordantly with clamorous intimations of the twenty-first century.

The Spiral Building is the most perfect expression of Maki's vision of the city. Built as a Media Centre for the lingerie manufacturer Wacoal, the brief called for such a complex mix of uses that it amounted to a city in miniature. These included a club, theatre, beauty salon, two restaurants and a café, shopping and assorted offices. Seen in drawings, Maki's organization of these spaces appears fairly conventional, but whereas in the West the atrium would almost certainly have been a central focus, bringing light into the heart of the plan, Maki places it at the farthest end from the entrance, a space to be reached only by passing through a succession of low and variously differentiated spaces. And the atrium is not a place of rest, but of transition, an incident along the route, which continues via a circular ramp. This, says Maki, is precisely how such spaces functioned in traditional Japanese architecture: 'instead of a "climax" … a collision between spatial events'.

The exquisite street façade is conceived as a collage of disparate elements unified by a deliberately limited palette of materials. The most obvious system of order is created by the 1.4-metre (4$^1/_2$-foot) grid of aluminium panels, within which square openings appear to float at random – from one, which frames a terrace, a delicate wire sculpture projects. White columns appear and disappear, hinting at the grid within, and a large, square, *shoji*-like screen projects out at an angle – framed in aluminium, it is clad with translucent fibreglass. A glazed volume slides down from above and next to it, framed by fragments of the aluminium-clad surface, sits a mysterious white cone.

Many of the elements of Maki's composition might almost be purified distillations of the surrounding buildings on Aoyama Boulevard, half-remembered fragments rather than new inventions, and they are assembled in a loose spiral movement that culminates in the lightning conductor at roof level. From a distance the façade appears almost uniformly white, but closer to you discover a startling diversity of materials – aluminium and steel, smooth and rough marble, fibreglass, shiny metal. In place of the uniformly clad, stratified boxes of orthodox Modernism, Maki offers us a shifting image compounded of abstract points, lines and planes and recognizable figures: as an image of the teeming vitality of the post-Modern city it has few equals.

3 Ground Floor Plan
1 Entrance Hall
2 Café
3 Gallery
4 Atrium

4 Fourth Floor Plan
1 Void
2 Hall Control Room
3 Studio
4 Studio Control Room
5 Video Studio

5 Sixth Floor Plan
1 Beauty Design Centre

6 Seventh Floor Plan
1 Salon

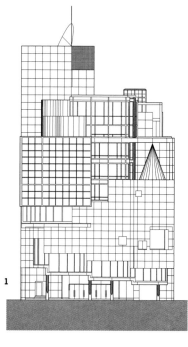

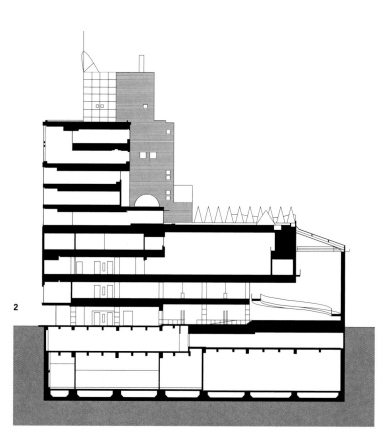

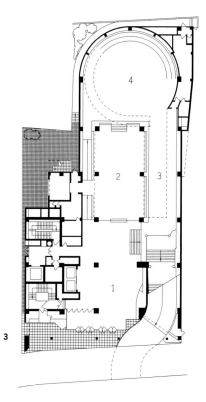

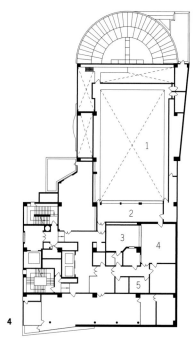

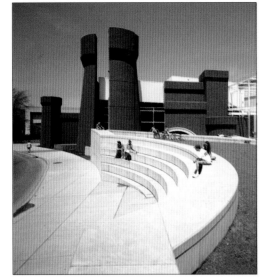

Wexner Center for the Visual Arts

Peter Eisenman, 1932–

Ohio State University, Ohio, USA; 1983–9

Having exhausted the potential of the hermetic formalism epitomized by **House VI** (page 178), Peter Eisenman began to explore a new approach to design based on complex 'mappings' of a project's site. His methods, however, had much more in common with his early interests than with the newly fashionable idea of 'contextual' design (see, for example, James Stirling's **Staatsgalerie**, page 182). Eisenman remained committed to the idea of architecture as an autonomous formal 'language', and in place of the planes, lines and grids that provided the raw material for his early houses, he used formal material derived from the site to provide the 'texts' upon which to perform his syntactical operations.

The first project in which these interests were fully expressed was a theoretical design for the Cannaregio in Venice made in 1978. The prime generator was not found in the physical 'facts' of the site, but taken from a previous 'text' – Le Corbusier's unrealized project for the Venice Hospital, whose grid Eisenman rotated and extended to create a new 'context'. This exercise in 'intertextuality' was in full accord with the then fashionable idea that languages have no necessary connection with a supposed 'real' world but are

merely the means by which we delude ourselves into thinking that such a world can be known. In 1983 Eisenman refined his methods in a proposal for a building at Checkpoint Charlie in Berlin. There, the configuration was generated by overlaying the Mercator grid – the most familiar means for mapping the earth – on the Berlin city grid, and by 'excavating' the site using historic maps to discover other systems of order from the eighteenth and nineteenth centuries.

The Cannaregio and Berlin projects became the primers for the Wexner Center for the Visual Arts, Eisenman's first opportunity to build on a large scale. Here, the Jefferson grid, imposed on Ohio in the eighteenth century, provided a primary reference, whilst on the university campus, the axis of the main open space – the Oval – was found to have been laid out just over 12 degrees off the city grid. Eisenman added to this already rich mix by aligning other elements of the composition on distant features, such as an airstrip, and then – as if to poke fun at more conventional 'contextual' concerns – by inventing a fictional historical façade: the fragments of the imagined 'fortifications' were then duly fragmented, wrenched apart and built in brickwork.

The planning of the Center began without a detailed brief or site, and rather than choose the conventional option – a freestanding building on an open plot – Eisenman opted to build between several possible sites and adjacent buildings. He calls the completed project 'a non-building, an archaeological earthwork whose essential elements are scaffolding and landscaping' – the latter, by Laurie Olin of Hanna Olin, plays a vital role in tying together the disparate parts.

The sophistication with which the multiple, site-derived layers of the Wexner Center are overlaid and expressed is visually stimulating, but the implications of Eisenman's methods are more problematic. Although intended as a critique of the social and economic forces that were destroying traditional conceptions of architecture and place, such Mannerist games were of a piece with them, parodying within the confines of the academic campus the arbitrariness that was increasingly apparent on every hand in the 'real world'.

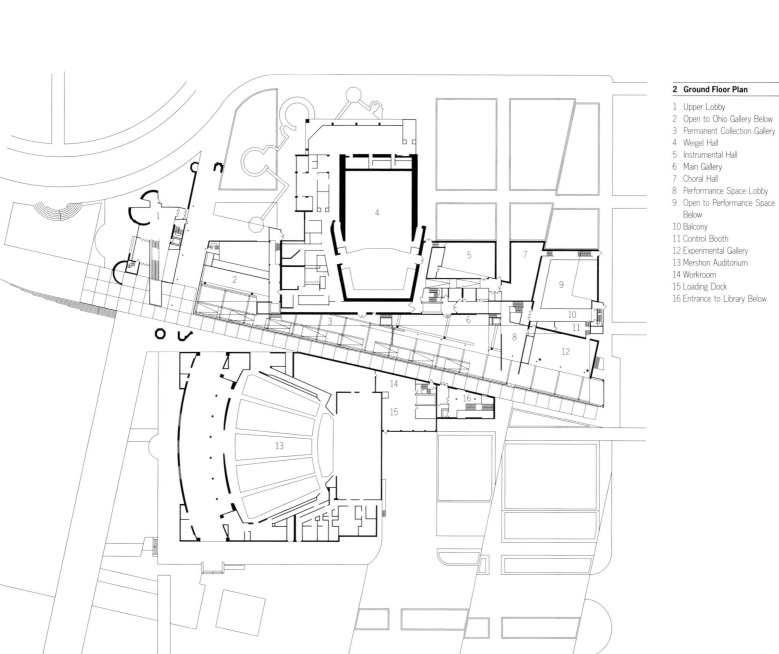

1

2 Ground Floor Plan

1 Upper Lobby
2 Open to Ohio Gallery Below
3 Permanent Collection Gallery
4 Weigel Hall
5 Instrumental Hall
6 Main Gallery
7 Choral Hall
8 Performance Space Lobby
9 Open to Performance Space
   Below
10 Balcony
11 Control Booth
12 Experimental Gallery
13 Mershon Auditorium
14 Workroom
15 Loading Dock
16 Entrance to Library Below

2

Graves House

Michael Graves, 1934–

Princeton, New Jersey, USA; 1986–93

Michael Graves came to international attention in the early 1970s as a member of the so-called 'New York Five' group that included Richard Meier (**Atheneum**, page 180) and Peter Eisenman (**House VI**, page 178). His early projects – dubbed 'Cubist kitchens' by his friends – were explorations of Le Corbusier's 1920s Purist style, but with the completion of the Public Services Building in Portland, Oregon, in 1983, Graves was hailed as a leader of that strand of post-Modernism characterized by a preoccupation with imagery and free use of historical – most commonly Classical – quotations. Stylistically, the leap appeared enormous, but in retrospect the two phases of his career are linked by the belief that architecture can be treated as a form of language.

Despite appearances to the contrary, Graves's own house is not a new building but a comprehensive re-working of a 1926 furniture repository built by Italian masons to serve the needs of Princeton University's academic staff whilst away on extended foreign study tours and of students who vacated their rooms for the summer. The 'Warehouse', as Graves calls it, had 44 rooms, none more than 3 metres (10 feet) long, but its combination of an Italianate frontage and more conventional, brick-built rear extension fascinated him. He acquired it in 1970, whilst still a junior professor at the university, and moved in seven years later. Its thoroughgoing architectural transformation, however, only began almost a decade later.

Like one of his architectural heroes, Sir John Soane, Graves is a fanatical collector and his house developed as both a home and a showcase for his furniture (mostly neo-Classical), artworks (including much-prized drawings by Gunnar Asplund) and artefacts. The original building was L-shaped and Graves made his first, makeshift home in the later, narrower wing, which, in the finished house, accommodates the secondary spaces. The house is entered through a small, room-like courtyard, beyond which lies a top-lit rotunda of Soanean inspiration. For the most part, the original spatial divisions have been eliminated, but in places the articulation is a 'memory' of the original: in the living and dining rooms, for example, the shallow alcoves framed by squat columns mark former subdivisions. Despite a probable debt to the book-lined, layered façade of Soane's own house-museum in London's Lincoln's Inn Fields, the library that terminates the suite of reception rooms is pure Graves. Its Classicism is conspicuous but far from canonic – the diminutive columns, layered in tiers, are wood-grained plastic: Graves likens the ensemble, aptly, to 'a miniature street lined with colonnaded buildings'.

With its use of symmetry, *enfilades* of distinct rooms, segmental windows and rudimentary Tuscan order, the house is undeniably Classical in spirit and in much of its detailing, but it feels looser and less self-conscious than most of Graves's *de novo* designs for clients. To Graves, its 'naturalness' was intended to evoke memories of summers spent amidst the rural buildings of Italy. The spaces flow easily from one to another and the use of symmetry is relaxed, controlling parts of the composition rather than imposing itself on the whole. Unlike the Portland building – which hostile critics referred to disparagingly, but not unjustifiably, as a 'billboard dolled up with cultural graffiti' – the Classicism here is neither skin deep nor uninformed by the freedoms of the modernity it might otherwise appear to reject.

1 First Floor Plan

1 Study
2 Courtyard Below
3 Master Bedroom
4 Closet
5 Bathroom
6 Storage
7 Bedroom

2 East Elevation

3 Ground Floor Plan

1 Forecourt
2 Entrance Courtyard
3 Foyer
4 Dining Room
5 Living Room
6 Library
7 Terrace
8 Bathroom
9 Storage
10 Kitchen
11 Breakfast Room
12 Service Room

4 Section

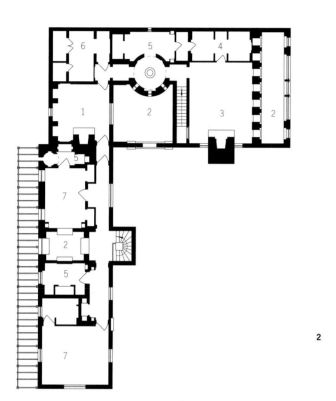

1

2

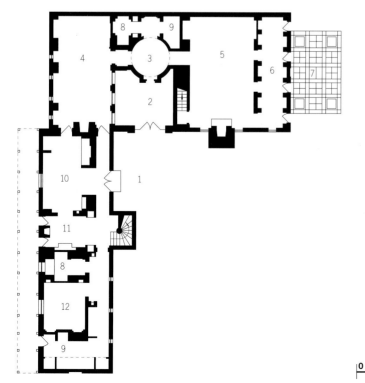

3

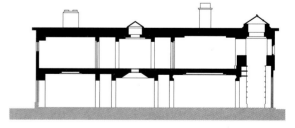

4

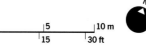

Thermal Baths

Peter Zumthor, 1943–

Vals, Switzerland; 1986–96

Apprenticed as a joiner before training as an architect, Peter Zumthor has enormous respect for 'the art of joining, the ability of craftsmen and engineers', believing that architecture should be renewed and extended by paying attention to its basic qualities – of material, structure and construction – rather than by ever more gymnastic form-making. He takes particular delight in materials – 'wooden floors like light membranes, heavy stone masses, soft textiles, polished granite, pliable leather, raw steel, polished mahogany, crystalline glass, soft asphalt warmed by the sun' – and aims at what he calls the 'corporeal wholeness' found in the architecture of the master builders. Despite some shared concerns evident in their work, this attitude is very different to that of Herzog and De Meuron (**Goetz Gallery**, page 206), who argue that an intellectual approach to materials is the only one now open to architects.

All Zumthor's interests are evident in these Thermal Baths at Vals. Located deep in a valley where the cows still wear bells and tourists are the primary source of income, they are owned by a large hotel built in the 1960s to exploit the hot natural springs that were diverted onto the site for therapeutic bathing in the nineteenth century.

Externally, Zumthor gives little away: the building resembles a vast monolith, an orthogonal version of the kind of cave-pocked cliffs that loom large in books of 'natural architecture'. It is scarcely visible from the hotel, being entered through a curving tunnel: this is no functional expedient, Zumthor's aim being to detach you from the quotidian world outside in preparation for the rituals of bathing.

The changing booths set the tone for the experience to come: screened by black leather curtains, they are panelled in highly polished red mahogany. Stepping out, you find yourself on a terrace overlooking the main pool, which is reached via a shallow, stepped ramp – a deliberately leisurely descent below a narrow gap in the roof that admits a strip of daylight. In plan, the pool appears to be simplicity itself, a square of water entered via steps of variable width that are framed by rectangular stone solids that pinwheel around its perimeter and contain hollowed-out, rectilinear caves housing hot, cold or scented pools. The cumulative effect, compounded by the pervasive presence of water, steam and wonderfully varied natural and artificial lighting, is labyrinthine.

The interior is unified by being clad almost entirely in one material – gneiss, sourced from a local quarry and exquisitely laid in narrow, stratified bands – but structurally it is a complex hybrid of in-situ concrete and load-bearing stone walls. The stone solids that frame the indoor pool, and house massage and other facilities around the perimeter, support their own section of roof: the various sections do not touch, but are separated by narrow, glass-capped fissures. The floor is similarly subdivided, with fissures marking thresholds or creating channels to drain away excess water. The hot and cold rooms are lined in pink and blue terracotta, respectively, and all the secondary elements – doors, rails, signage, even the sipping cups and their chains – are of bronze. Without Zumthor's rigour and restraint in handling such materials, the interior could easily have descended into a vacuous show of opulence. Instead, his constructed cave is a compelling, primal setting for communal bathing, designed to engage all our senses.

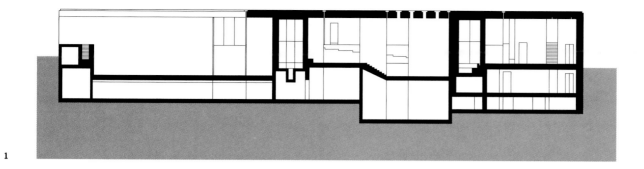

1 Long Section

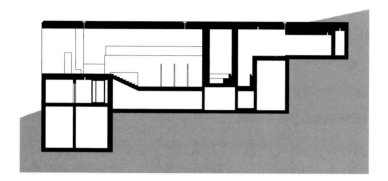

2 Cross Section

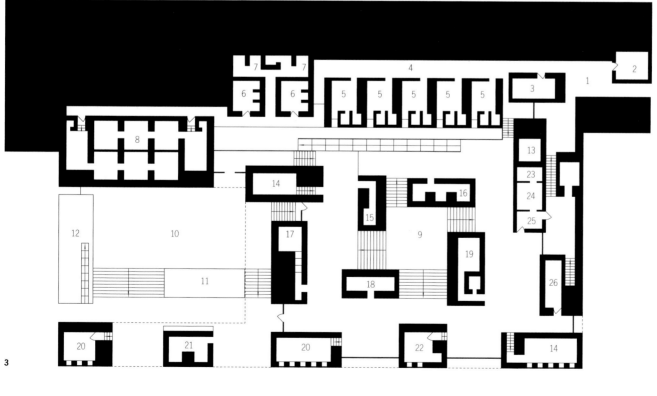

3 Ground Floor Plan

1 Entrance
2 Cleaner's Store
3 Make-up Room
4 Hall
5 Changing Rooms
6 Showers
7 Toilets
8 Turkish Baths
9 Indoor Pool
10 Outdoor Pool
11 Stone Island
12 Rock Terrace
13 Harmony Pool
14 Fire Bath
15 Cold Bath
16 Shower Stone
17 Drinking Stone
18 Sounding Stone
19 Flower Bath
20 Rest Space
21 Outdoor Shower Stone
22 Massage Room
23 Disabled Toilets
24 Cloakroom
25 Access for Disabled
26 Bath Attendants

0 5 10 m
15 30 ft

Goetz Gallery

Jacques Herzog, 1950– and Pierre de Meuron, 1950–

Munich, Germany; 1989–92

Having escaped the direct effects of the two world wars, Switzerland enjoyed a unique continuity in the development of its Modern architecture, or *Neues Bauen* as it was known. The quality of building and level of craft skills remain high by European standards, and architects retain a degree of control that has largely disappeared elsewhere. For architects of Herzog and De Meuron's generation this technical tradition was cross-fertilized with the ideas of conceptual artists such as Joseph Beuys and the American Minimalists, and with the work of Aldo Rossi (**Gallaratese Housing Block**, page 162), who had a brief but influential spell as a Professor at the ETH (Eidgenössische Technische Hochschule) in Zurich.

Herzog and De Meuron's international arrival was marked by an iconic building for Ricola completed in 1987. What might have been a mundane warehouse was made extraordinary by their exquisite handling of that most familiar material of industrial estates, fibre-cement siding. Diminishing in size from top to bottom and crowned by a cantilevered 'cornice', the panels recalled both the stacked timbers in the area's numerous saw mills and the strata of the adjacent rock faces — the building sat in a disused quarry. The repetition with

slight variation was mesmerizing, in much the same way as it can be in the Minimalist music of Philip Glass or the sculptures of Sol LeWitt.

Pushing a material 'to an extreme to show it dismantled from any other function than "being"' is central to Herzog and De Meuron's architectural approach, and in the Goetz Gallery — designed to house a private collection of modern art dating back no further than the 1960s — the building is reduced to contrasting bands of material and construction. Structurally, it consists of a timber box faced with birch-ply and resting on a reinforced concrete base. The latter is half buried so that only its almost fully glazed upper half is visible. This corresponds precisely in height to the matt glass strips, horizontally trimmed with untreated aluminium and wrapped around the upper section of the building, that allow glare-free daylight into the principal exhibition spaces.

Externally, this configuration appears decidedly enigmatic, not least because the entrance and office, visible through large, transparent sheets of glass, appear to form a conventional ground floor. In point of fact, they occupy the larger of two concrete tubes that span across the sunken volume, for which most of the ground floor glazing

acts as clerestorey lighting, identical to that in the galleries above. Internally, the spatial organization is correspondingly straightforward. The width of the volume and split-level arrangement are contrived to allow single-flight stairs to ascend and descend to the gallery levels, and the galleries themselves are simple *enfilades* of three rooms — identical cubes on the upper floor; a square, half-square and square-and-a-half in the basement, their heights varying in response to the 'tubes' overhead. The finishes and detailing are similarly pared down, the timber-lined stairways giving way to timber-strip floors and white-painted plaster.

Although responsive to changing light, the 'white box' interior creates an almost constant environment in which to view the artworks. The exterior, by contrast, is surprisingly elusive and fugitive, the clerestorey of glass forming, according to the ambient conditions, a frieze alive with the reflections of the surrounding trees or appearing almost to dissolve into the atmosphere.

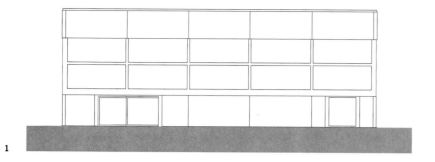

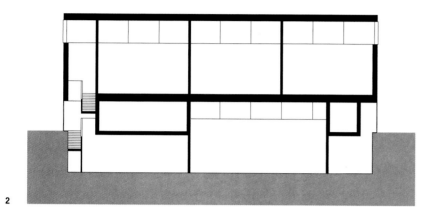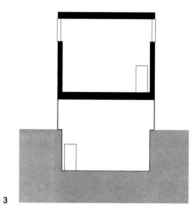

2 Section Through Galleries

3 Cross Section Through
   Galleries

4 First Floor Plan

1 Upper Gallery

5 Ground Floor Plan

1 Entrance and Bookshop
2 Void over Basement Gallery

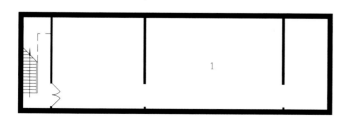

6 Basement Floor Plan

1 Basement Gallery

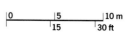

Kunsthal

Rem Koolhaas, 1944–

Rotterdam, The Netherlands; 1987–92

Rem Koolhaas formed the practice OMA (Office for Metropolitan Architecture) in 1975 and made his name with theoretical projects, notably 'Delirious New York' (1972–6; book 1978). His ideas developed out of a critique of the modern city and were informed by a fascination with the cinema as a quintessential expression of Modernity – hence his metaphoric use of frames, screens and 'clips' and incorporation of electronic projections in some projects. Compositionally, however, Koolhaas's major debt was to Le Corbusier's development of the free plan, with its grids, ramps and curvilinear, free-floating volumes.

The programme for the Kunsthal in Rotterdam called for three major exhibition spaces, capable of being used together or separately, an auditorium and an independently functioning restaurant. The site, on the edge of the city's Museum Park, presented two radically different conditions: green and restful to one side and, a full floor-level up, a frontage directly onto the busy Maasboulevard, a four-lane highway running on top of a dike. It was also crossed by a service road running parallel to the highway.

Koolhaas's response to the site was a square building divided into four unequal quadrants by two crossing routes, the service road running east-west and the north-south pedestrian ramp, which extends a primary route through the park up to the highway. The broad pedestrian ramp is split with a glass wall, dividing the freely accessible external route from the internal ramp. A second internal ramp runs parallel to the path but is inclined in the opposite direction: the entrance is located at its point of intersection with the sloping path. The internal ramp is terraced to form the auditorium and gives access to the lower, park-level gallery – an artificial landscape of jokily literal tree-columns. The restaurant is placed below the auditorium, whilst the ramped floor rises towards the park-side, bridges the external pedestrian route into the upper, top-lit gallery and offers a glimpse of a ramped roof garden that slices diagonally across the pedestrian path – and, frustratingly, always seems to be kept locked.

The pavilion-like character and exposed steel structure that the Kunsthal presents to the highway is a direct allusion to Mies van der Rohe's National Gallery of Art in Berlin and the entire project can be seen as a commentary on both Mies's building and, more generally, on the aesthetic consistency of the International Style. Where Mies offered a temple-like pavilion through which the visitor processes down into a crypt for art and then out into a sunken sculpture garden entirely protected from the depredations of the modern city, Koolhaas has created a multiplicity of routes, bewildering in their apparent complexity and tantalizing in the glimpses they afford of destinations that appear to be inaccessible. And in place of Mies's sunken sanctuary, the primary route through the Kunsthal culminates in an elevated steel-grate platform in full view of passing traffic.

Materially, the Kunsthal is equally iconoclastic. In place of the rendered surfaces designed to express the volumetric character of the spaces within, Koolhaas offers a disjunctive series of finishes. Glass 'Reglit' planks, badly stained concrete, profiled polycarbonate sheeting and deliberately cheap-looking stone cladding: all clamour for attention in a considered assault on our expectations of 'good design'. According to Koolhaas, what matters is the building's performance in use, not the quiet contemplation of outmoded aesthetic values.

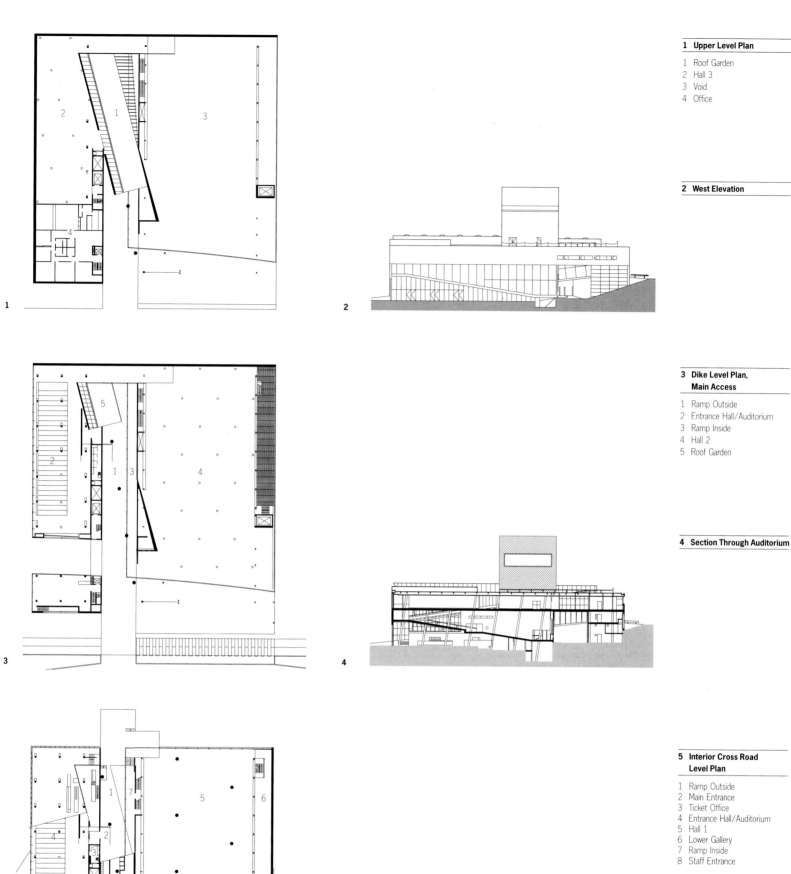

1 Upper Level Plan

1 Roof Garden
2 Hall 3
3 Void
4 Office

2 West Elevation

**3 Dike Level Plan,
Main Access**

1 Ramp Outside
2 Entrance Hall/Auditorium
3 Ramp Inside
4 Hall 2
5 Roof Garden

4 Section Through Auditorium

**5 Interior Cross Road
Level Plan**

1 Ramp Outside
2 Main Entrance
3 Ticket Office
4 Entrance Hall/Auditorium
5 Hall 1
6 Lower Gallery
7 Ramp Inside
8 Staff Entrance

```
0   5    10 m
    15   30 ft
```

Galician Centre of Contemporary Art

Álvaro Siza, 1933–

Santiago de Compostela, Spain; 1988–93

Amongst the most inventive early works of the Portuguese architect Álvaro Siza is a swimming pool sited on the coastline at Leça de Palmeira (1961–6), near his home town of Oporto. Siza's design consisted of an invented topography that effortlessly combined the angled cuts of wall, roof and ground planes with the given topography. The plan recalls Wright's Taliesin West, but the Cubist composition was equally clearly indebted to a range of European influences – most obviously, perhaps, Aalto and Le Corbusier. Siza would also draw on the work of Adolf Loos and the Spaniard José Antonio Coderch, but his mature work never appears remotely eclectic.

In the Galician Centre of Contemporary Art, Siza's early topographical interests again came to the fore, as a means of interpreting an historic site and responding to the disparate scales of the celebrated pilgrimage centre of Santiago de Compostela. The site was adjacent to a national monument – the Convent of Santo Domingo de Bonaval – and Siza was asked to set the new building as far back as possible and to 'hide' it. Rather than accept these negative constraints, he pointed out that the convent had never been fully visible, due to the presence of a high granite wall

through the site, and far from deferring weakly to the context he chose to strengthen it.

The new and old buildings converse across a clearly defined sequence of open spaces, while in response to the grain of the town the museum was articulated into three elements: the atrium and offices, facing the road; the auditorium and library, which angle back from it; and the exhibition halls, which range along the garden between the museum and convent. A triangular void between these volumes is a major source of light for the interior, while a second, smaller such void occurs externally, between the auditorium and the atrium: it appears merely residual on plan, but volumetrically acts as a taut hinge in the composition.

The internal walls are finished white throughout, and light enters from countless angles through an assortment of cracks, windows and rooflights. The complexity of the circulation routes Siza weaves through the interior is in striking contrast to the straightforward *enfilade* of galleries on the top floor. He had no time for the so-called 'flexibility' of spaces like those in the **Pompidou Centre** (page 168), and the dropped ceiling and clerestorey glazing ensure that objects on the walls are always more brightly lit than the visitors.

To clad the building, Siza first thought of white marble, but he was persuaded to use the local granite. The detailing engages in a complex game of concealing and revealing construction. Above the main entrance, for example, a long steel beam appears to support the stone above: in reality, as the detailing reveals, the stone is a cladding – which the beam does support, but only via concealed blockwork. Adjacent to this, a wall plane rests on a beam fabricated from two steel channels, supported by stubby columns. The wall appears, deceptively, to be made of solid stones: it is, in fact, a revetment of L- and U-shaped pieces, five centimetres (two inches) thick, and by hovering so unexpectedly above the ground it cleverly reinforces the dialogue between new and old – the planar new work, so to speak, lifting its skirts to allow a view through to the solid old walls.

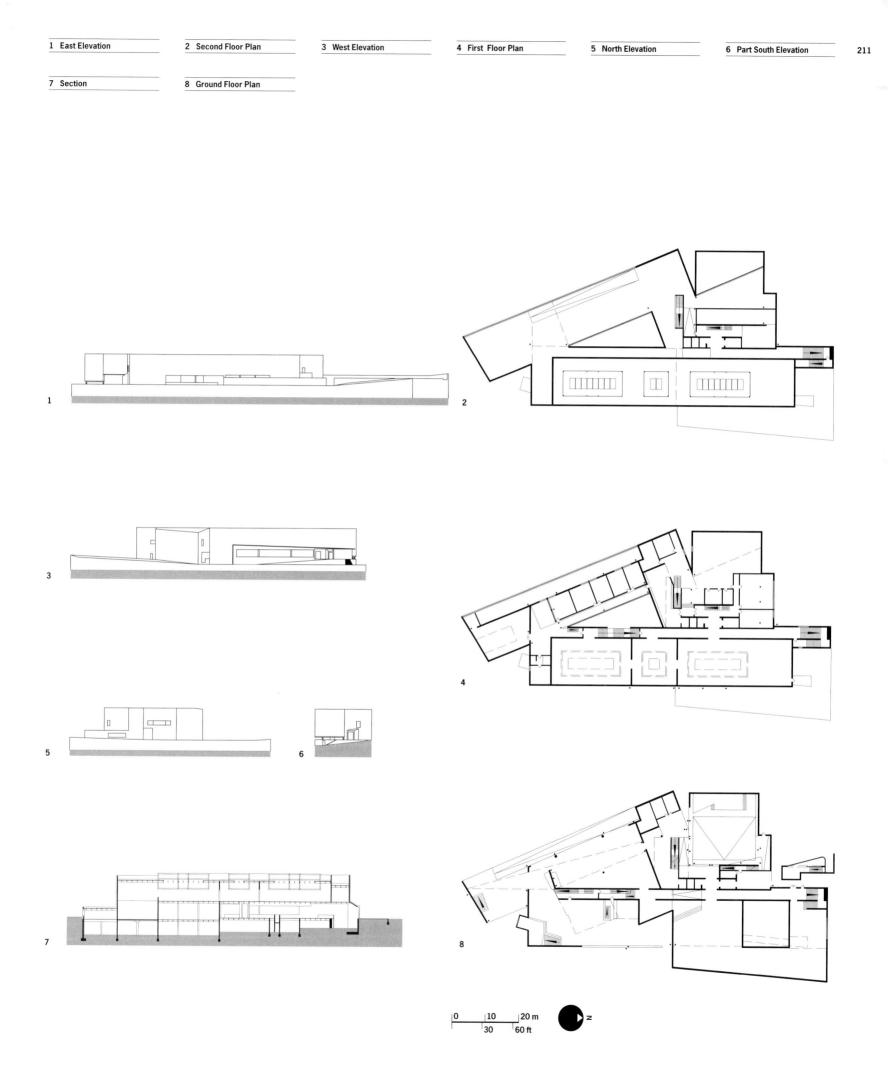

1

2

3

4

5

6

7

8

0   10   20 m

30   60 ft

N

Civic Centre

Enric Miralles, 1955–2000, and Carme Pinós, 1954–

Hostalets, near Barcelona, Spain; 1988–94

Although frequently linked to so-called Deconstructivism, the exuberant work of the Spanish architects Enric Miralles and Carme Pinós is better understood in the context of Catalan culture, and in particular the work of Antoni Gaudí. This early project in Hostalets, although not as well known as the Igualada Cemetery (1985–92) and Archery Range for the 1992 Barcelona Olympics, typifies their dynamic style in a compact building.

The Civic Centre occupies an old orchard located where the medieval main street of Hostalets straightens out to join the more regular nineteenth-century part of town. The basis of the design is a series of tapering 'beams' of accommodation that fan out from a pivot-point marked by a staircase and exit to the raised garden. These spatial 'beams' are also structural, framed by box girders in which the window frames double as webs between the floor and roof slabs – the latter in turn form stepped roof terraces overlooking the hard-surfaced sports pitch and garden.

Approaching down the main street, the visitor is greeted by a gently curved wall. The raised garden is accessible directly via the steps and gate at the corner of the site, while two adjacent entrances, both tall and relatively narrow, give

access to the club rooms above and directly to the triangular main hall. Tapering in plan and stepping down in section, this space might be oppressive in a more northerly climate, but here it is more than adequately lit by the long strip of angled clerestorey glazing, which fills the gap between the lowest 'beam' and the retaining wall that frames the hall's southern edge, and by borrowed light from the club rooms above. Views up into these spaces also allow the volume to expand vertically, countering the potentially oppressive effect of the closing down of the space in section.

The dynamism of the major moves in plan and section is reflected in the details. The opening lights, for example, are small-paned triangular casements set within the glazing of the beams. Facing south, they clearly need protection from the sun when closed, which Miralles and Pinós provide with shutters that fold up vertically and are cut at syncopated angles so that when partially opened they add yet more diagonals to the composition.

What made Hostalets and Miralles and Pinós's other projects so striking, especially given their relative youth, was the extraordinary control of all aspects of the architecture. In the late 1980s and early 1990s similarly 'dynamic' draw-

ings were to be seen on the boards of students around the world, not to mention in the offices of the self-styled avant-garde who figured in the New York Museum of Modern Art's 'Deconstructivist Architecture' exhibition of 1990. But whereas in so many of these projects the dynamism was as much graphic as spatial – and barely considered in terms of the structural and constructional means to realize it – with Miralles and Pinós it was manifestly thought through in material terms. Due to the sheer complexity of their spatial inventions, their drawings were often taxing to read, but they were also wonderfully economical in showing only spaces, forms and details that had been thoroughly worked out.

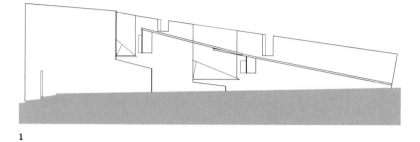

1

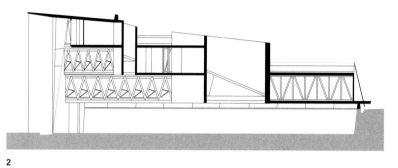

2

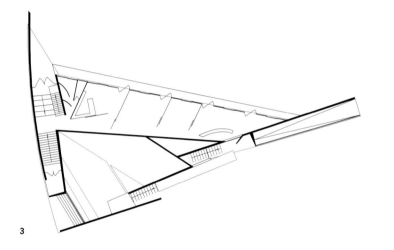

3

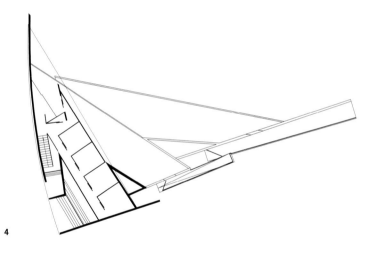

4

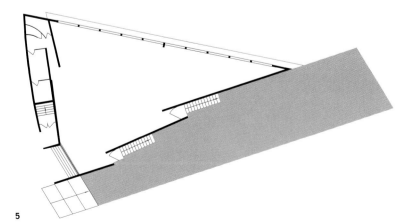

5

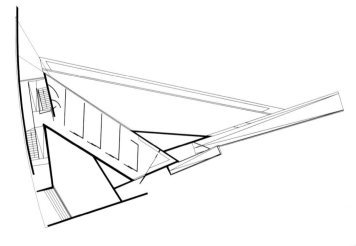

6

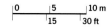

Menara Mesiniaga

Ken Yeang, 1948–

Subang Jaya, Selangor, Malaysia; 1989–92

Born in Malaysia and educated at the Architectural Association in London and at the universities of Cambridge and Pennsylvania – where he studied landscape architecture under the pioneer of ecological design, Ian McHarg – Ken Yeang is a leading figure in the search for a Modern architecture suited to the climates and cultures of Southeast Asia. He brings to the task a surprisingly disparate range of interests, from the technological fantasies of Cedric Price and Archigram, which played a decisive role in the conception of the **Pompidou Centre** (page 168), to a keen interest in native Malaysian architecture, about which he published a distinguished history in 1993.

Central to Yeang's vision of a regionally inflected Modern architecture for Malaysia, where British rule ended only in 1957, is the conviction that the built environment must be understood in relation to the natural systems of the biosphere – the subject of his doctoral thesis at Cambridge. In applying this broad-scale agenda to architecture, Yeang has identified two major approaches: sunpath projects and wind-rose projects. In the latter, the plan is typically broken down into clusters of accommodation to make the most of the ability of prevailing winds to provide natural ventilation,

assisted by such innovations as skycourts and 'wind walls' that draw air into innermost spaces, and by roof-level aerofoils that enhance stack-effect ventilation through the building's section.

With the sunpath projects, the arrangements of the service cores and disposition of glazing are determined directly in response to the sun's movement; extensive solar shading – often associated with balconies, skycourts and other buffer zones between inside and out – is provided; and planting is introduced across an entire elevation, creating what Yeang likes to refer to as 'hairy' office towers. Menara Mesiniaga, completed for IBM in 1992, is a classic example of this type. Planting spirals up the building from the earth mound around its base, through triple-height recessed terraces, and around the rooftop swimming pool, gymnasium and sun terrace beneath the dramatic trussed steel and aluminium solar-shade.

Curtain-walling is confined to the north and south elevations – both of which, in this tropical location, receive high-angle sun – while all the glazing facing east and west is protected by external aluminium louvres. The glazing details allow the glass to act as a ventilation filter, enclosing the interior without totally isolating it. Placed protec-

tively around the building's eastern edge, the service core also has direct contact with the outdoors: the lift lobbies, stairwells and toilets are all naturally ventilated and lit. Formally, Yeang's architectural language is firmly rooted in Western Modernism, but through his climatically informed manipulation of light, and use of delicate structural members and responsive, loose-fit skins, it acquires a character that feels both attuned to the tropical context and sufficiently fresh to offer an architectural identity for a rapidly developing Malaysia.

Despite the oil crisis of the early 1970s, and the growing recognition of the broad-scale impact of human development on the global climate that finally achieved formal recognition with the Earth Summit convened by the United Nations in Rio de Janeiro in 1992, many architects proved surprisingly reluctant to address bioclimatic factors as major determinants of architectural form. Ken Yeang was an early, and remains an unusually vigorous, exponent of what seems destined to be a major strand of architectural thought in the twenty-first century.

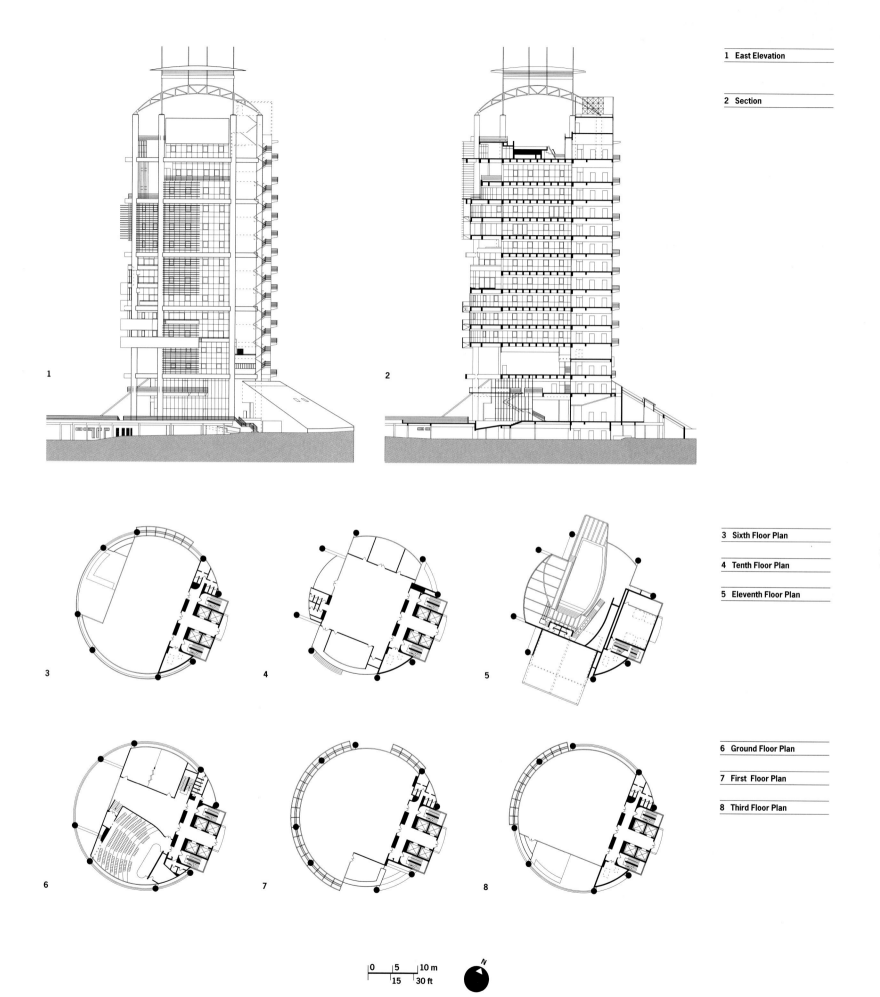

1   East Elevation

2   Section

3   Sixth Floor Plan

4   Tenth Floor Plan

5   Eleventh Floor Plan

6   Ground Floor Plan

7   First Floor Plan

8   Third Floor Plan

0   5   10 m
    15   30 ft

N

Cultural and Congress Centre

Jean Nouvel, 1945–

Lucerne, Switzerland; 1989–98

Following the arrival of the railway in the nineteenth century, the compact city of Lucerne has flourished as a tourist centre serving visitors to the surrounding Alpine landscape. High-quality cultural facilities developed to serve its affluent clientele, and this new Cultural and Congress Centre re-houses the city's long-established classical music facilities, and provides international-standard conference facilities and a museum for contemporary art. Jean Nouvel won the competition for the project in 1989 but for three years his proposal – in which the concert hall was to be built out into lake Vierwaldstättersee – fell out of favour.

Nouvel returned to the project in 1992. Realizing that building in the lake was politically unacceptable, he decided to divert the lake water across a new public piazza to channels inside the new Centre. He developed the design as a 'memory' of the shipyard that once occupied the site by grouping the major programme elements into vessel-like volumes. These in turn are unified by the plane of the vast copper roof, majestically cantilevered out over the water and finishing in a knife-edge thin line: given the drama of the setting, it offers one of the most compelling images in late twentieth-century architecture.

Lined with matt-grey aluminium panels, the roof's underside is dappled with reflections from the lake, a 1930s fountain and the twin channels that run deep into the building, framing the principal volumes. A reinterpretation of the classical portico, the roof is both a monumental symbol and a shelter for a new kind of open space. Named Europlatz, this is shaded and protected from rain but open to the landscape and, unlike so many recent purportedly 'public' spaces, freely accessible throughout the day and night.

The drama of the section is complemented by a plan of elegant simplicity consisting of three boxes, interstitial secondary circulation and service spaces, and a linear service wing connecting the back-stage areas. The largest, housing the main concert hall, is clad with red maple veneer and separated from the adjacent floors to reinforce its vessel-like qualities – an idea further emphasized by the curvaceous interior. The hall is entered from a four-level foyer, from which picture-postcard views of Lucerne and the surrounding landscape are framed by large windows with wide, raking jambs.

The central 'vessel' houses the smaller Middle Hall, while along the edge facing the railway station and Lucerne's celebrated crooked medieval bridge, Nouvel has placed a narrow, linear volume containing the restaurant, museum, offices and various conference facilities, including the smallest of the three auditoria. Its roof is an open terrace, from where the Alps are framed as if by a giant peaked cap.

Nouvel has long been fascinated by the cinema and the possibility of dematerializing architecture, and at Lucerne, more convincingly perhaps than in any other of his completed projects, he realizes the feeling of floating between volumes in apparent defiance of gravity. This is achieved in part by making the spatial volumes themselves support the seemingly hovering roof, and, more importantly, by the extensive use of glass to produce both horizontal and vertical transparency. With the continuous movement of people around the centre's many facilities and the fugitive, constantly changing play of light reflected from water, the result is a compelling image of perpetual flux.

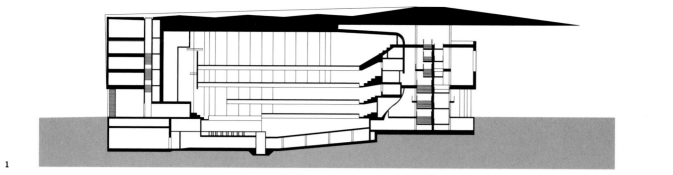

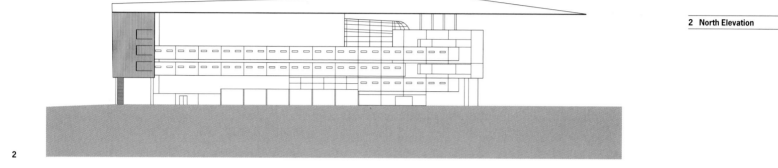

2 North Elevation

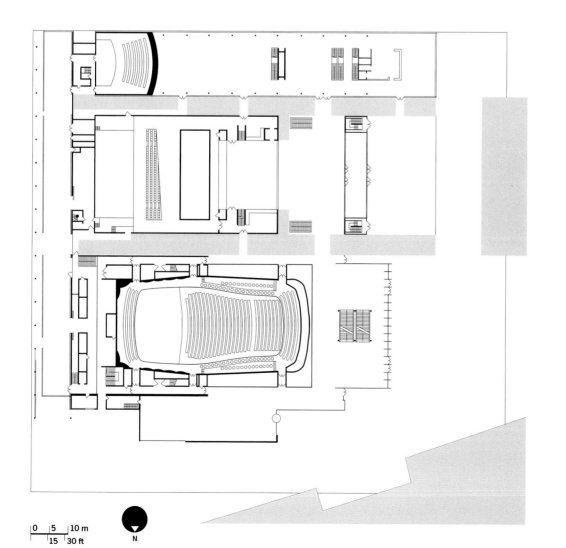

3 Ground Floor Plan

0 5 10 m

15 30 ft

N

Jewish Museum

Daniel Libeskind, 1946–

Berlin, Germany; 1989–98

One of the most acclaimed buildings of the 1990s, the Jewish Museum completed Daniel Libeskind's transition from theoretician to practitioner. As a teacher at the Cranbrook Academy of Art in Michigan, USA, he developed a complex, hermetic calligraphy of interwoven lines. From this evolved an architectural language of tilting volumes that, formally, owed something to the Russian Constructivism of the 1920s, albeit less than was implied by the catch-all label of 'Deconstructivism', invented in the late 1980s to describe a disparate range of architects, including Peter Eisenman, Frank Gehry and Zaha Hadid, who shared an interest in fragmented forms.

The design for the Jewish Museum has its roots in Libeskind's 1987 City Edge project for Berlin, in which new spatial structures, responding to the presence of the Berlin Wall, ripped through the existing fabric. Sited on Lindenstrasse, it is near the Rondel, once a celebrated Baroque intersection of Wilhelmstrasse, Friedrichstrasse and Lindenstrasse, and adjacent to the Collegienhaus that now houses the Berlin Museum, of which Libeskind's construction is, officially, the 'Jewish Department'. The physical 'memory' of Berlin's past is one of several sets of 'traces' Libeskind wove into the design. A second came from creative figures whom he saw as forming a link between German and Jewish history, others from the music of Schönberg, writings of Walter Benjamin, and records of Jews who were deported and murdered in the concentration camps.

The complex, zig-zag geometry was generated in part from an 'irrational matrix' – as Libeskind describes it – created by finding the addresses of Jewish cultural figures who had lived in Berlin, and drawing connecting lines between them to generate intertwining triangles. These in turn coalesced into a distorted Star of David – reminiscent of the yellow star that Jews were forced to wear in Hitler's Germany.

The extension begins beneath the existing museum and criss-crosses below ground before emerging as a seemingly autonomous, alien construction. To represent the invisible, the murdered, the absent, Libeskind created a Void that runs as a straight but discontinuous slot through the zig-zag of accommodation. The building was not, he explained, 'a collage or a collision or a simple dialectic, but a new type of organization which is organized around a centre which is not, around what is not visible. And what is not visible is the richness of the Jewish heritage in Berlin, which is today reduced to archival and archaeological material, since physically it has disappeared.'

The presence of multiple systems of order is emphasized on the building's skin by wrapping it with a single material – zinc – and then seemingly arbitrarily slashing and slicing it open. In places the openings hint at more conventional, orthogonal systems within, while others remain as inscrutable traces of the 'lay lines' that underpin the configuration. Although his methods were akin to the neo-Formalist strategies of Peter Eisenman (**House VI**, page 178) and other members of the neo-Modernist avant-garde, Libeskind produced in the Jewish Museum a complex architectural metaphor for the void left in Western culture by the Holocaust. It impressed itself on most visitors and critics as a chillingly authentic meditation on one of the most apocalyptic episodes in human history, but it remains to be seen if this will be undermined by Libeskind's subsequent use of a similar formal language for more prosaic building programmes.

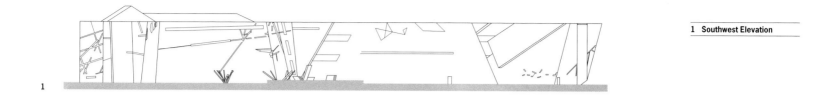

1 Southwest Elevation

2 Long Section

1

2

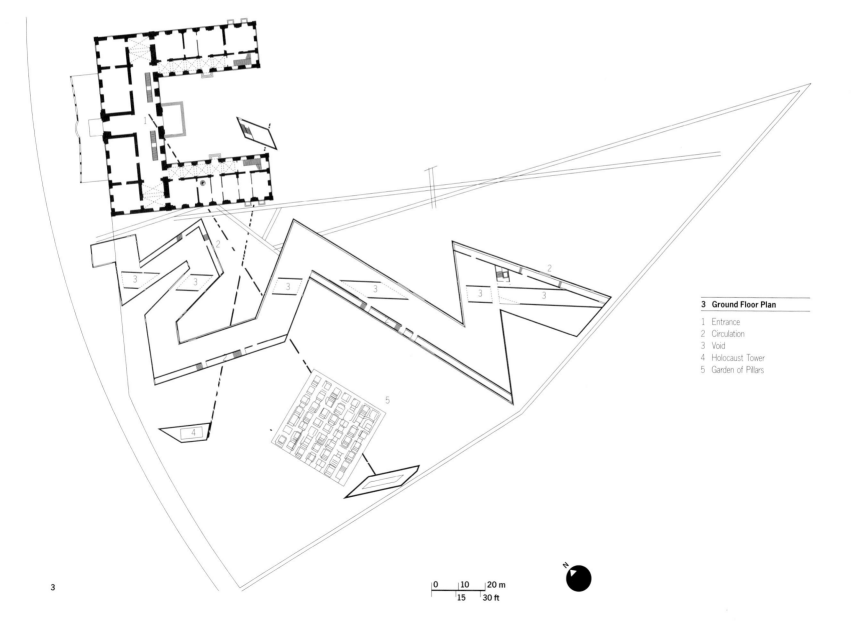

3 Ground Floor Plan

1 Entrance
2 Circulation
3 Void
4 Holocaust Tower
5 Garden of Pillars

3

| 0 | 10 | 20 m |
| 15 | 30 ft | |

N

Barnes House

Patkau Architects, 1978–

Nanaimo, British Columbia, Canada; 1991–3

The pioneers of Modern architecture looked forward optimistically to a 'Machine Age' in which industrially produced buildings would both solve practical problems, such as the shortage of decent housing, and provide an architectural expression of the emerging industrial civilization. Although the building industry proved more resistant to change than many anticipated, mass-produced components and assemblies have inexorably displaced traditional craft-based methods. The homogenization of building production and progressive loss of control over detailed aspects of construction that inevitably followed has, predictably, produced a counter-reaction. During the 1980s and '90s a growing number of architects began to explore ways in which construction could recover its expressive potential. Canadians John and Patricia Patkau, who founded their practice in 1978 in Alberta, are distinguished exponents of this new interest in 'tectonic expression' in architecture.

As if in response to the flat, prairie landscape of Alberta, the Patkaus' early work was homogeneous and gridded in character. Following a move to Vancouver in 1984, however, it quickly took on a radically different character. Responding to the rugged coastline of British Columbia, they

became fascinated by the particular ways in which each location challenged them to articulate the relationship between buildings and nature. Every project now begins with 'investigations into the particular' from which they aim to uncover the 'found potential' in the physical, social and cultural dimensions of the brief and site. Rejecting the universal models of Classicism and Modernism, and with them accepted building typologies, they seek to ground their designs in the uniqueness of place, programme and materials, and to make them part of a continuum with the natural world.

The Barnes House marked the culmination of almost a decade of work during which the Patkaus gradually clarified their search for the particular. Sited on the edge of an open, rocky outcrop in five acres of forested land, it enjoys outstanding views of the Strait of Georgia and mainland British Columbia to the north, and of the rocky shoreline of Vancouver Island to the northwest. The irregular, compacted form of the house is itself boulder-like, and entered through a glazed fissure at the lower level. The complex, site-adjusted geometry of the plan might almost appear to have been developed simply by wedging the spaces into the tapering ravine, but as the plans

and sections show, the design also artfully juxtaposes two geometries, two kinds of space: orthogonal and non-orthogonal, figurative and abstract, strong and weak.

A key inspiration for the Patkaus' approach, it seems reasonable to conjecture, is to be found in the work of Alvar Aalto (**Seinäjoki Library**, page 148), and their work also has much in common with those other northern masters, Jørn Utzon and Sverre Fehn. A key aim is to heighten the experience of the landscape and the feeling of interiority. The walls of the orthogonal spaces are thickened by built-in cabinets and define cave-like retreats, while the geometrically weaker, non-orthogonal zones direct the eye to the views and defer to the landscape that forms their visual boundary. Similar contrasts are cultivated in the construction: delicate steel railings and connections contrast with the heavy, monolithic surfaces of the concrete floors, stucco-clad, timber-framed walls and substantial roof timbers, while a centimetre-thick steel-plate canopy projects dramatically beyond the large opening to the northwest — a thin, perfectly horizontal surface in literally sharp contrast to the thick folded planes of the roof.

| 1 Upper Floor Plan | 2 Cross Section | | 3 Lower Ground (Entry Level) Plan | | 4 Long Section | |

1 Upper Floor Plan   **2 Cross Section**   **3 Lower Ground (Entry Level) Plan**   **4 Long Section**   221

1 Living Room
2 Master Bedroom
3 Dining Room
4. Kitchen
5 Utility Room
6 Terrace
7 Barbecue
8 Firepit

1 Entrance
2 Studio
3 Bathroom
4 Guest Room

1
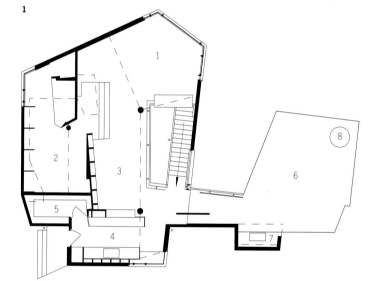

2
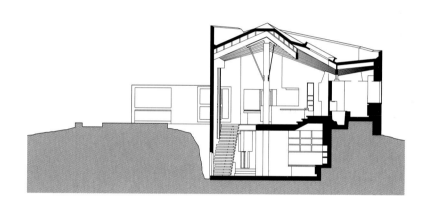

3
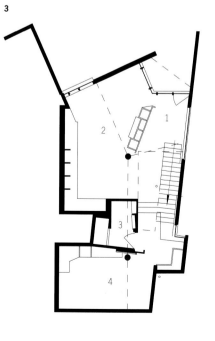

4
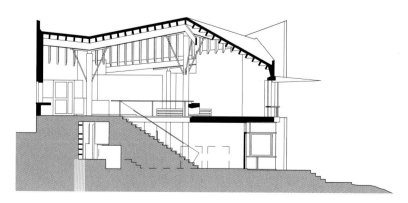

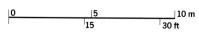

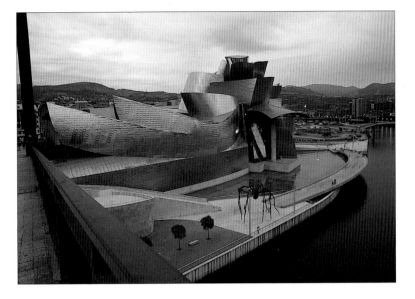

Guggenheim Museum

Frank Gehry, 1929–

Bilbao, Spain; 1991–7

Arts projects were widely exploited as catalysts for urban regeneration in European cities during the 1990s, and nowhere more successfully than in Bilbao. Located in the nationalistic Basque region of northern Spain, this was a collaboration between the Basque Country Administration and the New York-based Solomon R. Guggenheim Foundation, which provided the core art collections. The museum marks the centre of a 'cultural triangle' formed by the old Museum of Fine Arts, the university and the Old Town Hall, and its site, adjacent to the Nervion River, is crossed by the Puente de la Salve Bridge that connects the town centre with the suburbs, making the Museum a gateway to the city.

Frank Gehry's response to the project's pivotal location was to develop a new plaza to encourage pedestrian movement between the Guggenheim Museum and the Museum of Fine Arts. The Guggenheim's major public facilities – auditorium, restaurant and shops – are grouped around this plaza and belong as much to the city as to the museum, being accessible directly from it, as well as from inside the museum.

The Foundation required spaces for three different kinds of exhibition: a permanent collection, a temporary collection, and exhibits of the work of living artists. These are all arranged above a platform of service areas, and in response to the variety of exhibition types Gehry opted to provide three radically different kinds of space. The permanent collection occupies traditional, square rooms stacked on the second and third levels. The temporary collection is in a more dramatic, elongated rectangular space. Extending to the west, this passes under the bridge and culminates in a tower, locking the bridge into the composition: imposing in scale and column-free, it is designed to cope with major installations. Finally, 11 distinct galleries, each unique in spatial character, are provided for the exhibitions by living artists.

All the exhibition spaces are accessible from a large central atrium. Among the most dramatic spaces in late twentieth-century architecture, this connects the galleries on three levels via a collection of curvilinear bridges, glass lifts and stair towers. Rising to more than 45 metres (150 feet) above the river, the atrium is a towering volume crowned by a sculptural roof that opens, like giant metallic flower-petals, to flood the interior with light. Externally, in a manner reminiscent of **Sydney Opera House** (page 126), the building is

clad in just two materials: a Spanish limestone for the platform and rectangular volumes and titanium panels for the freely sculptural shapes. The latter were developed through a series of increasingly refined physical models and then converted into digital data using a laser-scanning system and special software developed for use in the aerospace industry. The structure, a deformed grid made up of numerous small steel sections and calculated using digital finite element techniques, is entirely subservient to the sculptural forms through which Gehry articulates his vision of architecture as a formal spectacle ruled only by the logic of his eye.

The Bilbao Guggenheim proved hugely successful as a flagship for the city's post-industrial regeneration, drawing vast numbers of tourists to this hitherto unknown backwater. Politically and culturally, however, it was more controversial, being seen by some as a form of cultural imperialism that, by imposing a version of a globalized Modern art, worked to the exclusion of local culture.

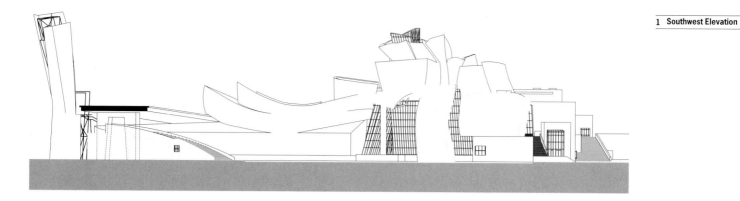

1 Southwest Elevation

1

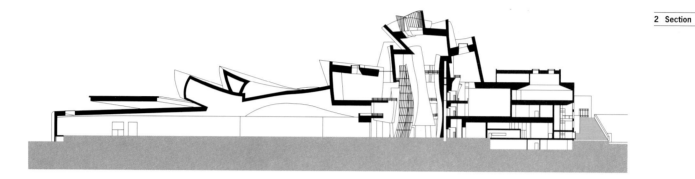

2 Section

2

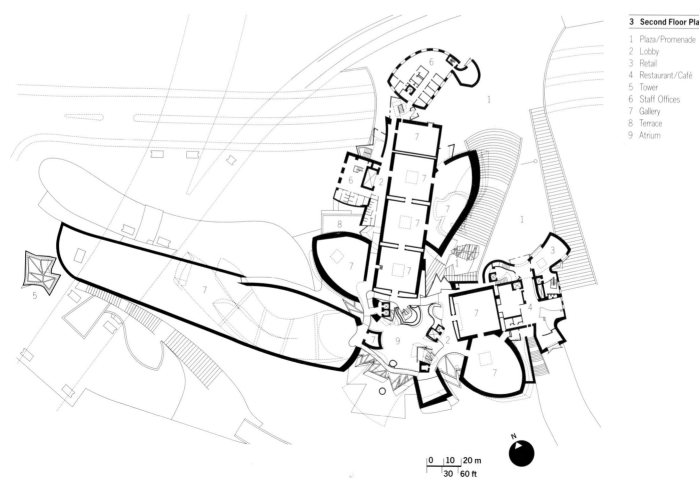

3 Second Floor Plan

1 Plaza/Promenade
2 Lobby
3 Retail
4 Restaurant/Café
5 Tower
6 Staff Offices
7 Gallery
8 Terrace
9 Atrium

3

0 10 20 m
30 60 ft

N

Tjibaou Cultural Centre

Renzo Piano, 1937–

Nouméa, New Caledonia; 1991–8

New Caledonia has been an overseas territory of France since the mid nineteenth century, held against local opposition because the main island is the world's third largest supplier of nickel. The native Kanak people's struggle for independence during the 1980s resulted in the Matignon accords. Negotiated by their leader, Jean-Marie Tjibaou, these granted greater recognition to the local culture, but not independence – and because of this, Tjibaou and some of his followers were killed by Kanak extremists in 1989. In response, President Mitterrand proposed this Centre, the last of his '*grands projets*', a lavishly funded celebration of a culture that itself produced no permanent buildings or monuments.

The design was the subject of an invited international competition and the chosen site, on a promontory just east of the capital, Nouméa, was spectacular. On visiting it, Renzo Piano was struck by the beauty of both the landscape and of the Kanak huts woven from its plants. He quickly decided on a policy of minimum disturbance, developing the plan along an existing path that curved along the promontory's ridge and restricting construction to three already bare patches that extended down to the lagoon.

Working with the ethnologist Alban Bensa, an expert on Kanak culture, Piano's design team explored the organization of traditional villages. This was reflected directly in the competition design, which proposed an elongated communal/circulation space, tracking the existing path, along which were ranged the major spaces, framed by 'cases' of wooden ribs modelled, perhaps too literally, on the form of the Kanak huts. The cases were intended to act as climatic modifiers, functioning as both wind scoops that harnessed the almost mono-directional trade winds, and as convection chimneys.

In the built scheme, the cases were simplified structurally and, although less obviously hut-like, articulated in a way that proved more resonant to the Kanak clients. There are ten cases of three different sizes, but all made in the same way using two three-quarter-circle rings of ribs made from laminated iroko, a stable, termite-resistant hardwood. The inner ring is vertical and supports the roof, while the outer, gently curved, rises higher and carries screens of wooden slats. Computer simulations and physical testing in a wind tunnel enabled the forms to be refined into a highly sophisticated system of passive environmental control. Their shapes may still suggest giant baskets, but almost every detail, from the varied spacing of the timber slats to the high- and low-level louvres in the inner walls, is calculated to maximize the capacity of the trade winds to provide natural ventilation or, when the wind is light, to achieve a similar result using convection currents.

The openness of the main floor to the landscape was made possible by sinking all the rooms requiring solid enclosure below ground, and even this drastic transformation was effected without losing any major plants on the site or disturbing areas of valuable topsoil. Approached from a distance, the timber cases rise majestically above the vegetation to be seen against a backdrop of sky or mountain. Rooted in local traditions and inseparable from the surrounding plants, yet designed and built using sophisticated, Western technologies, Piano's distinctive, unforgettable forms strike many as being among the most provocative harbingers of a World Architecture for the twenty-first century.

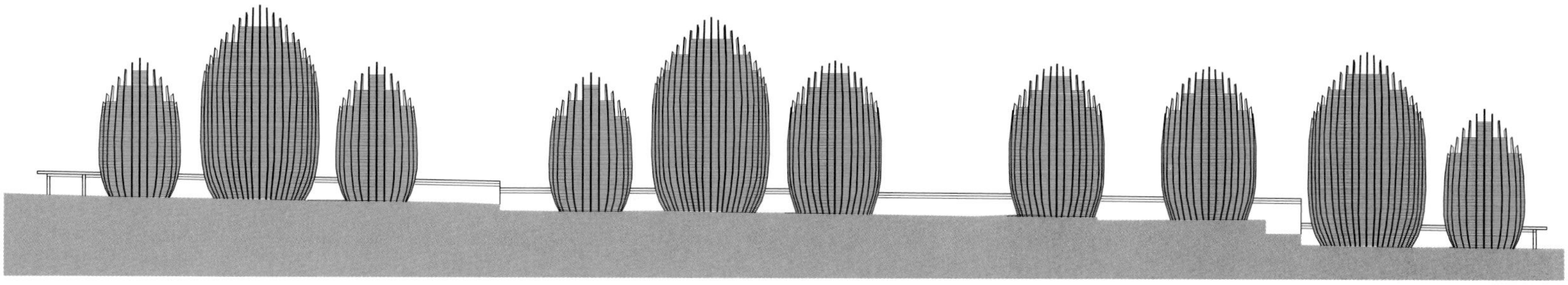

1

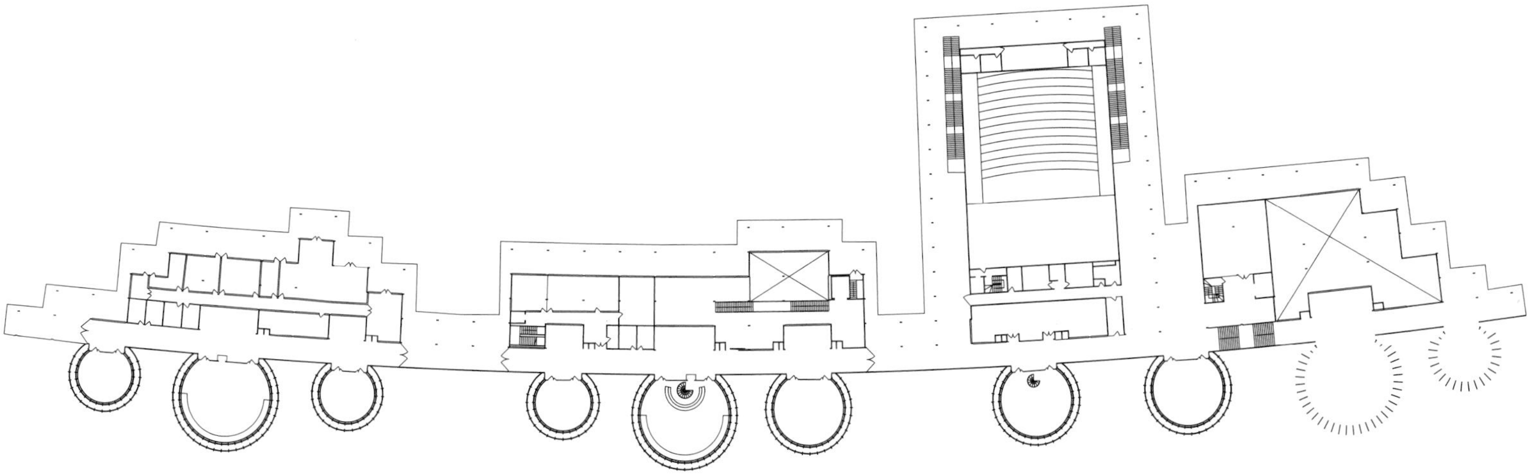

2

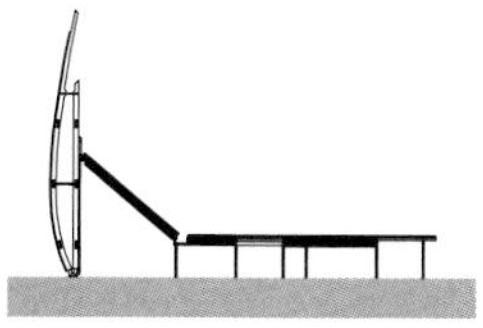

3

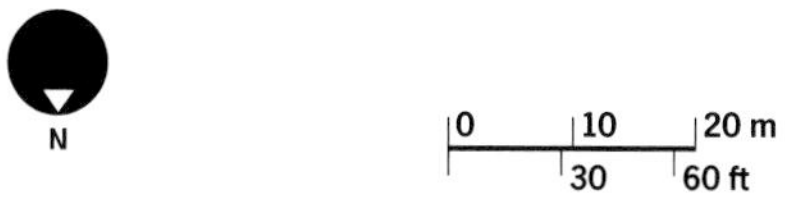

N

0   10   20 m
      30   60 ft

Chapel of St Ignatius

Steven Holl, 1947–

Seattle University, Washington, USA; 1994–7.

Towards the end of a century dominated by ideas of abstraction, and of space as the primary architectural 'material', a renewed concern with the physicality of buildings became the focus of interest among a new generation of architects. In Europe this was associated particularly with the Swiss School represented by Peter Zumthor (**Thermal Baths** at Vals, page 204) and Herzog and De Meuron (**Goetz Gallery**, page 206), while in the USA its leading exponent is Steven Holl. Like the Minimalist artists of the 1960s, Holl has drawn productively on the ideas of the French phenomenologist Maurice Merleau-Ponty, who argued that we can know ourselves only through our relationship with the environment, through what we see and touch. For Holl, therefore, architecture must engage all our senses, not primarily our eyes, and it should use materials that are palpably 'real' – tactile, worked, weathered, stained.

The starting point for the Chapel of St Ignatius – built for a Jesuit college's urban campus in Seattle – was a watercolour representing 'seven bottles of light in a stone box', a metaphor inspired by St Ignatius's vision of the inner, spiritual life as characterized by numerous competing interior 'lights' and 'darknesses'. Each 'bottle' cor-

responded to a different part of the programme of Jesuit Catholic worship – the Mass, the choir, a small Chapel of the Blessed Sacrament, etc – and Holl saw their diversity as a metaphor for the Jesuits' 'spiritual exercises' that offer alternative approaches to suit different people's needs.

Translated into architecture, the 'bottles' become six discreet volumes of space, variously lit, while the seventh is represented by the reflecting pool that forms part of the processional sequence to the entrance. The volumes are contained by a rectangular plan, and its simplicity belies the spatial complexity achieved as the volumes explode upwards in search of light. In the narthex and entry procession, the light is natural, the play of shadows familiar. But as you penetrate deeper, it is mysteriously transformed by pairing coloured glass lenses with large areas of clear glass, through which light enters and is coloured indirectly, by reflection off painted surfaces concealed by baffles. In places, these juxtapositions of different colours are startling: in the confessional, for example, orange light enters through the glass lens into a field of reflected purple.

Externally, the chapel is unassuming, made of yellow ochre-coloured interlocking concrete pan-

els, which were cast on the ground slab and tilted up into place. The beautiful, hand-tooled door and sinuously curved, purpose-made handles hint at the sensory delights – rough plaster, cast glass, hewn wood, gold leaf – that lie in store. Spatially, the interior oscillates between appearing to be carved from the solid or assembled from planes, and externally, too, Holl's detailing is calculated to promote a similar ambiguity, the obvious weight and revealed thickness of the concrete panels being offset by the knife-edge joints and edges of the tautly detailed zinc roof.

At night, the principal time of gathering for Mass in the college, the building is dramatically transformed. Externally, the indirect artificial lighting is reflected outwards, turning the roof-lights into glowing, multi-coloured beacons addressing all corners of the campus. The interior becomes contrastingly dark and brooding: with the numerous pendant lamps and sconces dimmed to the intensity of candles, the rite unfolds against a backdrop of mysterious, sumptuous colours.

3 Plan

1 Procession
2 Narthex
3 Vesting Sacristy
4 Bride's Room
5 Reconciliation Chapel
6 Altar
7 Choir
8 Baptistry
9 Blessed Sacrament Chapel

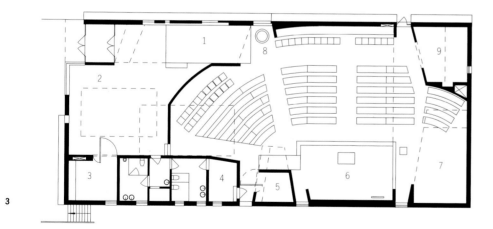

1

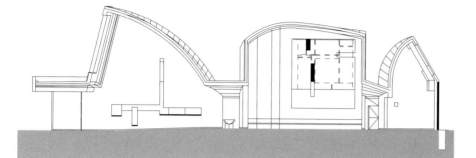

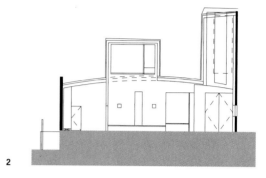

2

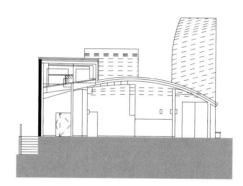

4

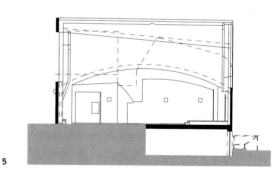

3

5

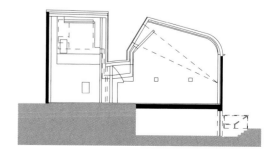

6

0	5	10 m
15		30 ft

LF1, Landesgartenschau

Zaha Hadid, 1950–

Weil am Rhein, Germany; 1997–2000

Born in Iraq and educated at the Architectural Association in London, Zaha Hadid came to fame by winning the Hong Kong Peak competition – for the design of a social club – in 1983. Formally and functionally stratified into a series of discrete layers, its gravity-defying 'beams' and voids seemed as much geological as architectural, as if some seismic shift had uprooted and re-structured the mountaintop site. Hadid's presentation was similarly dramatic. In addition to (relatively) conventional drawings, she represented the scheme in giant paintings, in which the fragmentation and dissolution were emphasized by showing parts of the club invading downtown Hong Kong. The message was clear: as well as a highly site-specific design, this was also an urban proposition applicable to any modern metropolis, its abstract, shard-like forms pointing towards a general reconfiguration of space. And this in turn grew out of her preoccupation with early Modernist ideas about the dissolution of subject and object exemplified by Cubist paintings.

Hadid's first opportunity to build permanently using something akin to the formal language of the Hong Kong Peak project came with the 1990 commission for the Vitra Fire Station. Situated at Weil am Rhein in Germany, it forms part of a collection of buildings – by architects as diverse as Frank Gehry, Tadao Ando and Alvaro Siza – commissioned by the furniture makers Vitra International. This commission for a small exhibition building came as a result of local admiration for the Fire Station. But whereas that seemed to strain every muscle to suggest the image of a shattering world that had become Hadid's trademark, this is altogether more unassertive, reflecting the increasing fluidity of spaces and forms that seem to have grown out of her growing preoccupation with landscape. Where forms were once aggressively angular and fragmented, by the mid 1990s they were beginning to flow like rivers, to move in and out of the land, not float above it or break violently out.

Seen from a distance, LF1 borders on invisibility. More ground-form than building, it might almost be a slice of the surrounding, gently rolling landscape. The design brief had the simplicity favoured in schools of architecture that allow students freedom to concentrate on the formal and spatial qualities of their work, and Hadid took full advantage, turning it into a composition of routes woven from four parallel, partially interlocked spaces 'trapped' by a bundle of paths and internal and external ramps. The geometry seems to emerge effortlessly from the site and the ramps relate directly to the adjacent gravel pit, restored for exhibition purposes. To reinforce the links to the land, gravel-covered strips extend out from the roof of the building into its immediate landscape.

Although, thanks to their abstraction and unmistakable 'signature' quality, Hadid's drawings suggest an almost complete detachment from the waves of fashion – the oft-remarked affinities are with the floating planes of Russian Suprematism – her realized buildings are very much more of the moment. Vitra felt industrial and urban, and as such very much of the 1980s, whereas LF1 is more playful and relaxed, combining disparate versions of authentically 'modern' style with a similarly disparate range of materials – in-situ concrete, frameless leading glazing, timber, white-painted plaster (complete with 'High Modern' shadow gaps) and slate flooring.

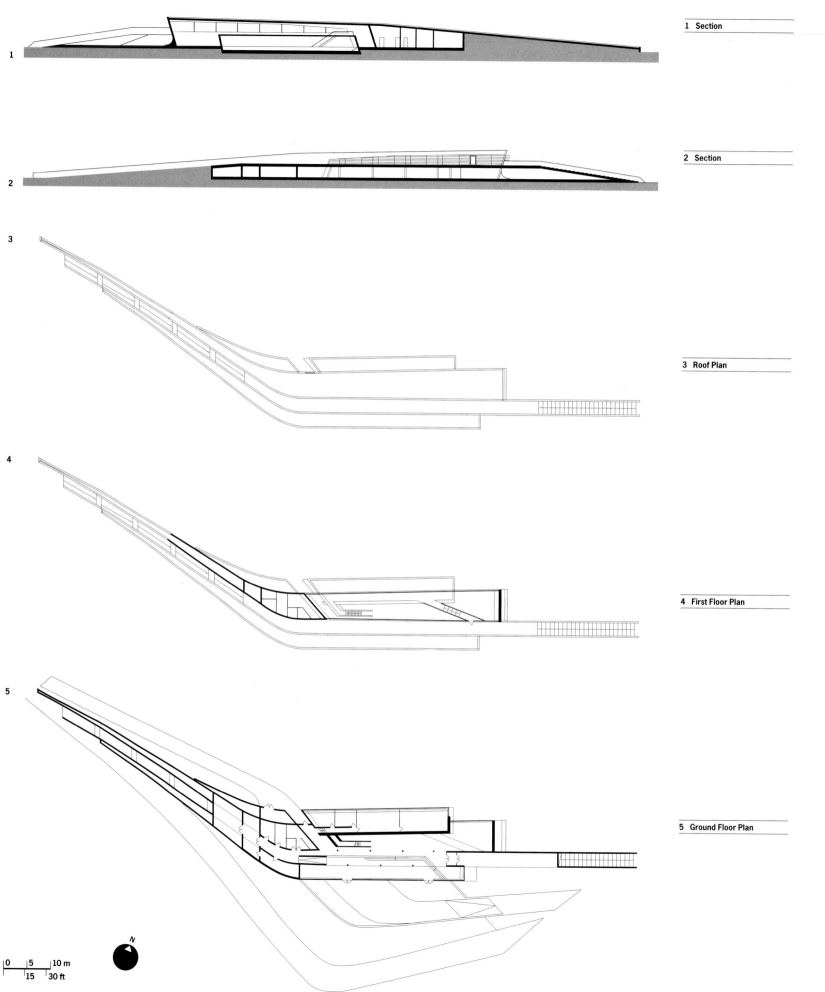

1 Section

2 Section

3 Roof Plan

4 First Floor Plan

5 Ground Floor Plan

0 5 10 m
15 30 ft

Sendai Mediathèque

Toyo Ito, 1941–

Sendai-shi, Japan; 1997–2000

In striking contrast to Tadao Ando, who views designs like the **Koshino House** (page 186) as 'bastions of resistance' against the depredations of consumerism, Toyo Ito conceives his buildings as lightweight screens laid over the bewildering complexity of Japanese cities. He makes extensive use of glass and transparency, but the effects he seeks are mediated by the qualities of traditional Japanese light filtered by paper screens. Spatially, he aspires to the fluidity of the **Barcelona Pavilion** (page 58), which, he suggests, exhibits 'not the lightness of flowing air but the thickness of molten liquid. … it makes us feel as if we are looking at things underwater, and would be better described as translucent. What we experience here is not the flow of air but the sense of wandering and drifting gently underwater.'

Written in 1997, this description might equally well have been a statement of intent for the Sendai Mediathèque, in which the feeling of being underwater is made almost palpable. In essence, the design is a direct re-working of Le Corbusier's 'Five Points of a New Architecture' (**Villa Savoye**, page 62), and comes complete with a public roof garden. But the changes Ito makes to the Corbusian schema transform the building into something new. Most obvious is the dematerialization of the vertical pilotis into permeable bundles of steel tubes that resemble high-tech basketry. Swerving and swaying their way up through the floors, they provide structural support and harbour services — lifts, stairs and conditioned air. Ito thought of them as 'seaweed-like' and the simile is reinforced by the feeling that they are held captive by glass, as if in a giant aquarium.

Ito's response to the freedoms of the free plan is more radical than in any of Le Corbusier's buildings, but recalls the latter's 1938 proposal for Algiers, in which several floors of 'artificial ground' were capped by an elevated highway. Just as Le Corbusier envisaged people building houses of various sizes and styles on these 'support structures', so Ito allows each floor to assume a distinct character. For the ground floor, Karin Rashid proposed organically shaped and boldly coloured pieces of furniture-sculpture. On the first floor, the space can be subdivided with synthetic white curtains that barely interfere with the spatial continuity. The second and third levels, which house the library, are mostly a double-height volume, with mezzanine-level reading rooms to north and south. The fourth-floor exhibition space can be subdivided by sliding partitions, whilst that on the fifth is open plan. Finally, on the sixth floor — the Mediathèque proper — a full-height curved wall of translucent glass wraps around the auditorium, meeting room, offices and cafeteria.

On the east and north elevations the floor slabs project slightly to create dark horizontal bands and the cladding changes from storey to storey. For the west elevation the necessity of providing fire escape stairs led Ito to develop a semi-transparent structure with an outer layer of vertical slats of perforated aluminium screening the stairs behind. The main façade is a lightweight screen of glass, double-skinned to provide ventilation and designed to reflect the sun by day. At night, however, it seems to disappear, bringing vividly alive Ito's vision of the building as an aquarium of liquid space teeming with the random experiences of the metropolis and its ceaseless flows of digital data.

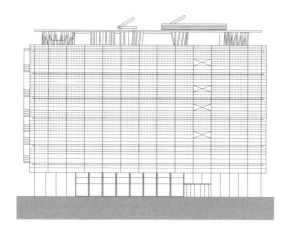

1

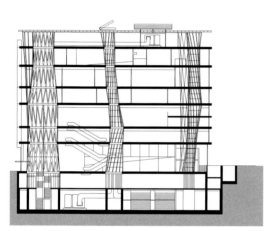

3

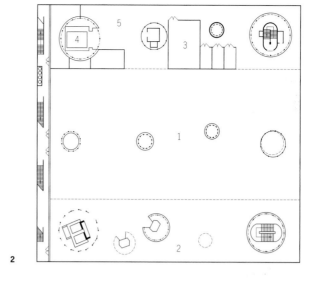

2

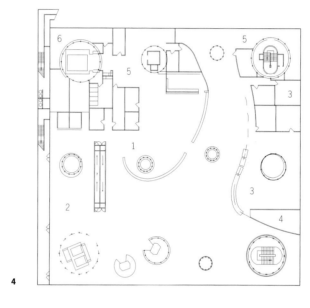

4

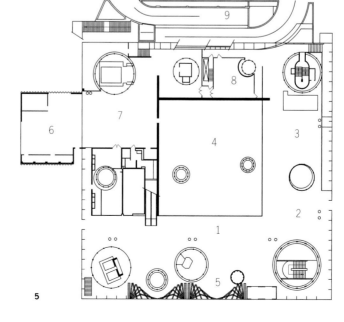

5

1 South Elevation

2 Fifth Floor

1 Exhibition Spaces
2 Foyer
3 Display Storehouse
4 Freight Elevator
5 Unpacking Area

3 Section

4 First Floor

1 Children's Library
2 Meeting Room
3 Offices
4 Voluntary Workers' Office
5 Service Space
6 Deposit for Children's Library
7 Service Elevators

3 Ground Floor

1 Information
2 Commercial Space
3 Cafeteria
4 Internal Plaza
5 Sliding Glass Walls
6 Loading Area
7 Unpacking Area
8 Storeroom
9 Access Ramps

N

0 5 10 m
15 30 ft

Bordeaux Villa

Rem Koolhaas, 1944–

Bordeaux, France; 1998

In this villa, built on a hillside just outside Bordeaux in part of the *jardin anglais* of an old mansion, Rem Koolhaas mounts as compelling an assault on the tyranny of gravity as any in twentieth-century architecture. The idea for the design is a vertically stratified composition that, perhaps, remotely recalls the contrasted layers — *piano rustica*, *piano nobile* and roof terrace or belvedere — of many Classical buildings. The three levels are connected by a large hydraulic lift, 3 x 3.5 metres (10 x 11½ feet), the silently moving room or 'station' of the father of the family who commissioned the design — shortly after approaching Koolhaas he was left paralysed following a car crash, unable to walk and barely able to talk.

The lowest, entry floor is a square compound, clad in travertine and with a central area large enough for cars to park and turn in, framed on one side by a rectilinear volume for the housekeeper and guests and on the other by a similar volume sunk into the slope. This acts as the entrance to the house above and, in a series of small, cave-like spaces, houses the main stair, wine cellar and a small TV room. Above the 'built cave' is an open, fully glazed floor and terrace: shiny and metallic, it has been stripped of most of the

accoutrements of living. And hovering over this is a concrete sleeping bunker with porthole windows placed to capture particular views from the beds and subdivided in a manner that recalls the freedoms of the Corbusian *plan libre*.

Koolhaas asked the engineers Ove Arup and Partners to make the massive concrete bunker appear to levitate in space. Their team, led by Cecil Balmond, decided to confuse normal expectations of structure by displacing two pairs of columns laterally, and in opposite directions, swastika-like, so that one column in each lies inside the house and the other outside. One pair of columns supports a highly visible shelf beam, and the other a steel roof girder, from which the bunker appears to hang precariously. Here, a tension cable replaced the external column, and balance was originally to have been restored using a rock visibly hanging from the cable above ground. This proved too expensive and the post-tensioned cable now disappears into the ground through a plate. Cost cuts also dictated a lighter but deeper girder, but this happily added to the drama.

In his briefing, the disabled owner told Koolhaas, 'This house is my world; please make it as complex as possible': the design more than

met his aspirations. The interlocking of inside and out is more like a Chinese puzzle than orthodox spatial continuity, and the spaces unfold like a labyrinth along which you encounter a bewildering array of experiences: the refinement of travertine and lightness and polish of aluminium; cave-like spaces, which simulate natural erosion; earth-coloured concrete of determined rawness; and the polished, transparent world sandwiched between. Most surprising is that it seems everywhere to court danger, with unexpected drops: there is no enclosed lift shaft — it rises against a three-storey-high library, but leaves a vertiginous void when it departs from a particular level. It is the antithesis of what most politically correct versions of 'universal access' deliver, and all the more liberating as a result. It will surely be reckoned one of the century's great houses.

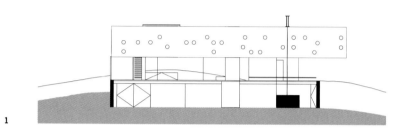

1

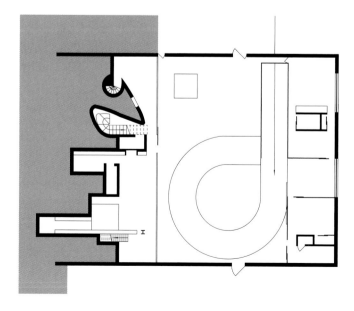

2

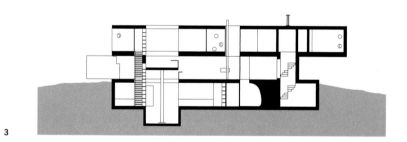

3

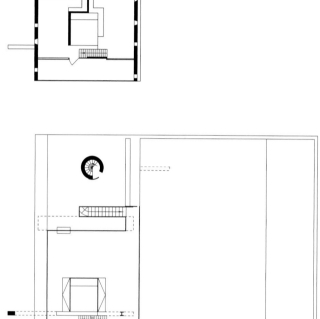

4

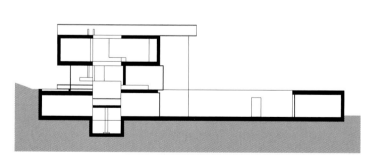

5

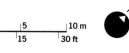

6

0   5   10 m
    15   30 ft

N

Further Reading

General Histories

Banham, Reyner, *Theory and Design in the First Machine Age* (Oxford: Architectural Press, 2nd Edn. 1962)

Benevolo, Leonardo, *A History of Modern Architecture Volumes 1& 2* (Cambridge, Mass.: MIT Press, 1971)

Collins, Peter, *Changing Ideals in Modern Architecture 1750–1950* (Montreal: McGill-Queens University Press, 2nd Edn. 1998)

Curtis, William, *Modern Architecture Since 1900* (London: Phaidon Press, 3rd Edn. 1996)

Frampton, Kenneth, *Modern Architecture: A Critical History* (London: Thames and Hudson, 3rd Edn. 1992)

Giedion, Sigfried, *Space, Time and Architecture* (Cambridge, Mass.: MIT Press, 5th Edn. 1967)

Hitchcock, H. R. and Johnson, Philip, *The International Style: Architecture Since 1922* (New York: Museum of Modern Art, 1932)

Jackson, Lesley, *Contemporary* (London: Phaidon Press, 1994)

Jencks, Charles, *Modern Movements in Architecture* (Harmondsworth: Penguin, 2nd Edn. 1985)

Jencks, Charles, *Language of Post Modern Architecture* (London: Academy Editions, 6th Edn. 1991)

Pevsner, Nikolaus, *Pioneers of Modern Design from William Morris to Walter Gropius* (Harmondsworth: Penguin, 2nd Edn. 1991)

Spier, Steven and Tschanz, Martin, *Swiss Made* (London: Thames and Hudson, 2003)

Weston, Richard, *Modernism* (London: Phaidon Press, 1996)

Weston, Richard, *The House in the Twentieth Century* (London: Laurence King, 2002)

Monographs

Aalto, Alvar Weston, Richard, *Alvar Aalto* (London: Phaidon Press, 1995)

Aalto, Alvar Reed, Peter, *Alvar Aalto: Between Humanism and Materialism* (New York: Museum of Modern Art, 1998)

Ando, Tadao Futagawa, Yukio, *Tadao Ando* (Tokyo: A.D.A. Edita Ltd, 1987)

Asplund, Erik Gunnar Holmdahl, Gustav (ed.), *Gunnar Asplund Architect 1885–1940* (Stockholm: Byggförlaget, 1981)

Asplund, Erik Gunnar Cruickshank, Dan (ed.), *Erik Gunnar Asplund* (London: Architects' Journal, 1988)

Atelier 5 Atelier 5, *Atelier 5* (Zurich: Amman Verlag, 1986)

Barragán, Luis Riggen Martínez, Antonio, *Luis Barragán* (New York: The Monacelli Press, 1996)

Behrens, Peter Anderson, Stanford, *Peter Behrens and a New Architecture for the Twentieth Century* (Cambridge, Mass.: MIT Press, 2000)

Botta, Mario Pizzi, Emilio, *Mario Botta: The Complete Works Volume 1: 1960–1985* (Zurich: Artemis, 1993)

Bunshaft, Gordon Herselle Krinsky, Carol, *Gordon Bunshaft* (Cambridge, Mass.: MIT Press, 1988)

Chareau, Pierre Vellay, Marc and Frampton, Kenneth, *Pierre Chareau: Architect and Craftsman 1883–1950* (London: Thames and Hudson, 1985)

Duiker, Jan Molema, Jan, *Jan Duiker* (Barcelona: Gustavo Gili, 1996)

Eames, Charles and Ray Kirkham, Pat, *Charles and Ray Eames* (Cambridge, Mass.: MIT Press, 1995)

Eisenman, Peter Dobney, Stephen (ed.), *Eisenman Architects: Selected and Current Works* (Victoria: The Images Publishing Group, 1995)

Fehn, Sverre Norberg-Schulz, Christian and Postiglione, Gennaro, *Sverre Fehn: Works, Projects, Writings, 1949–1996* (New York: The Monacelli Press, 1997)

Foster, Norman Lambot, Ian (ed.), *Norman Foster Volumes 1–4* (London: Watermark Publications, 1991–1998)

Gaudí, Antonio Martineu, César, *Gaudí: His Life, His Theories, His Work* (Barcelona: Editorial Blume, 1975)

Gehry, Frank Dalco, Francesco and Forster, Kurt, *Frank O. Gehry: The Complete Works* (New York: The Monacelli Press, 1998)

Gehry, Frank Andrews, Mason, *Frank Gehry Buildings and Projects* (New York: Rizzoli International, 1985)

Graves, Michael Powell, Kenneth, *Graves Residence: Michael Graves* (London: Phaidon Press, 1995)

Gropius, Walter Isaacs, Reginald, *Gropius* (Berlin: Gebr. Mann Verlag, 1983)

Hadid, Zaha Hadid, Zaha, *Zaha Hadid: The Complete Buildings and Projects* (London: Thames and Hudson, 1998)

Hertzberger, Herman Lüchinger, Arnulf, *Herman Hertzberger* (Den Haag: Arch-Edition, 1987)

Herzog and de Meuron Special Issue of *El Croquis*, no.109/110, 2002. 'Herzog and de Meuron: the nature'

Herzog and de Meuron Special Issue of *Architecture and Urbanism*, 2002. 'Herzog and de Meuron 1978–2002'

Hoffman, Josef Sekler, Eduard F., *Josef Hoffman: The Architect's Work* (Princeton: Princeton University Press, 1985)

Holl, Steven Holl, Steven, *Parallax* (New York: Princeton Architectural Press, 2000)

Hollein, Hans Special Issue of *Architecture and Urbanism*, 1985. 'Hans Hollein'

Isozaki, Arata Norment, Kate, (ed.) *Arata Isozaki Architecture 1960–1990* (New York: Rizzoli International Publications Inc., 1991)

Ito, Toyo Maffei, Andrea (ed.), *Works, Projects, Writings: Toyo Ito* (Milan: Electa Architecture, 2002)

Kahn, Louis Brownlee, David B. and De Long, David G., *Louis I. Kahn: In the Realm of Architecture* (New York: Rizzoli International, 1991)

Kahn, Louis Ronner, Heinz and Sharad, Jhaveri, *Louis I. Kahn Complete Work 1935–1974* (Basel, Birkhäuser, 2nd Edn. 1987)

Koolhaas, Rem Koolhaas, Rem and Mau, Bruce, *Small, Medium, Large, Extra-Large* (Rotterdam: 010 Publishers, 1995)

Koolhaas, Rem Special Issue of *Architecture and Urbanism*, 2000. 'OMA@work, A+U'

Koolhaas, Rem Herausgegeben von Aurora Cuito *Rem Koolhaas* (New York: te Neues, 2002)

Le Corbusier Benton, Tim, *The Villas of Le Corbusier, 1920–1930* (New Haven and London: Yale University Press, 1987)

Le Corbusier and Pierre Jeanneret Boesiger, M., Bill, M., Stonorov, O., (eds.), *Oeuvre Complète in 8 Volumes: 1910–1929; 1929–1934; 1934–1938; 1938–1946; 1946–1952; 1952–1957; 1957–1965*, (Zurich: Girsberger 1929–1970)

Le Corbusier Curtis, William J. R., *Le Corbusier: Ideas and Forms* (London: Phaidon Press, 1986, reprinted 2001)

Lewerentz, Sigurd Flora, Nicola, Giardiello, Paolo and Postiglione, Gennaro *Sigurd Lewerentz 1885–1975* (Milan: Electa Architecture, 2000)

Libeskind, Daniel Belloli, Andrea P. A. (ed.), *Radix-Matrix: Architecture and Writings* (Munich: Prestel, 1997)

Loos, Adolf Gravagnuolo, Benedetto, *Adolf Loos Theory and Works* (Milan: Idea Books, Wien, 1982)

Loos, Adolf Schezen, Roberto, *Adolf Loos: Architecture 1903–1932* (New York: The Monacelli Press, 1996)

Lutyens, Edwin Weaver, Lawrence, *Houses and Gardens by E. L. Lutyens* (London: Country Life, 1913)

Mackintosh, Charles Rennie Steele, James, *Charles Rennie Mackintosh Synthesis in Form* (London: Academy Editions, 1994)

Maki, Fumihiko Maki and Associates (ed.), *Fumihiko Maki Buildings and Projects* (London: Thames and Hudson, 1997)

Meier, Richard Ockman, John (ed.), Richard *Meier Architect* (New York: Rizzoli International Publications Inc., 1984)

Mendelsohn, Erich James, Kathleen, *Erich Mendelsohn and the Architecture of German Modernism* (Cambridge: Cambridge University Press, 1997)

Mies van der Rohe, Ludwig Lambert, Phyllis (ed.), *Mies in America* (Montreal: Canadian Centre for Architecture, 2001)

Mies van der Rohe, Ludwig Neumeyer, Fritz, *The Artless World: Mies van der Rohe on the Building Art* (Cambridge, Mass.: MIT Press, 1991)

Mies van der Rohe, Ludwig Riley, Terence, *Mies in Berlin* (New York: Museum of Modern Art, 2001)

Miralles, Enric Tagliabue, Benedetta, *Enric Miralles: Works and Projects 1975–1995* (New York: The Monacelli Press, 1996)

Miralles, Enric and Pinós, Carme Buchanan, Peter, Montaner, Josepmaria, Dollens, Dennis and Kogod, Lauren, *The Architecture of Enric Miralles and Carme Pinós* (New York: Lumen Books, 1990)

Moneo, Rafael Fernández-Galiano, Luis, *Rafael Moneo 1986–1992* (Madrid: Arquitectura Viva, 1992)

Murcutt, Glenn Fromonot, Françoise, *Glenn Murcutt Buildings and Projects* 1962–2003 (London: Thames and Hudson, 2003)

Nervi, Pier Luigi Joedicke, Jürgen, *The Works of Pier Luigi Nervi* (London: The Architectural Press, 1957)

Neutra, Richard Boesiger, W. (ed.), *Richard Neutra 1961–66* (London: Thames and Hudson, 1966)

Neutra, Richard MacLamprecht, Barbara, *Richard Neutra Complete Works* (Cologne: Taschen, 2000)

Niemeyer, Oscar Underwood, David, *Oscar Niemeyer and the Architecture of Brazil* (New York: Rizzoli International Publications Inc., 1994)

Nouvel, Jean Bonet, Llorenç (ed.), *Jean Nouvel* (Düsseldorf: te Neues, 2002)

Nouvel, Jean Special Issue of *El Croquis*, 1998. 'Jean Nouvel 1987–1998'

Patkau Architects Carter, Brian (ed.), *Patkau Architects* (Nova Scotia: TUNS Press, 1994)

Piano, Renzo Buchanan, Peter, *Renzo Piano Building Workshop Volumes 1–4* (London, Phaidon Press, 1995–2000)

Plečnik, Jože Prelovšek, Damjan *Jože Plečnik 1872–1957* (New Haven: Yale University Press, 1997)

Rietveld, Gerrit Kueper, M. and Van Zijl, I., *Gerrit Th. Rietveld: The Complete Work: 1888–1964* (Amsterdam: Architectura and Natura, 1993)

Roche, Kevin and Dinkeloo, John *Global Architecture* No. 29, 1974. 'Kevin Roche and John Dinkeloo Associates'

Rogers, Richard Powell, Kenneth, *Richard Rogers Complete Works Volumes 1 & 2* (London: Phaidon Press, 1994–2001)

Rossi, Aldo Arnell, Peter and Bickford, Ted, *Aldo Rossi: Buildings and Projects* (New York: Rizzoli International, 1985)

Rudolph, Paul Domin, Christopher and Paul, Joseph King, *Rudolph: The Florida Houses* (New York: Princeton Architectural Press, 2002)

Saarinen, Eero Román, Antonio, *Eero Saarinen: An Architecture of Multiplicity* (New York: Princeton Architectural Press, 2003)

Scarpa, Carlo Albertini, Bianca and Bagnoli, Sandro, *Architecture in Details* (London: Architecture Design and Technology Press, 1988)

Scharoun, Hans Blundell Jones, Peter *Hans Scharoun* (London, Phaidon Press, 1995)

Schindler, Rudolph Steele, James, *R. M. Schindler* (Cologne: Taschen, 1999)

Siza, Alvaro Frampton, Kenneth, *Alvaro Siza Complete Works* (London: Phaidon Press, 2000)

Siza, Alvaro Jodidio, Philip, *Alvaro Siza* (Cologne: Taschen, 1999)

Smithson, Alison and Peter Krucker, Bruno, Complex Ordinariness: *The Upper Lawn Pavilion by Alison and Peter Smithson* (Zurich: ETH Hönggerberg, 2002)

Smithson, Alison and Peter Smithson, Alison and Peter, *The Charged Void: Architecture* (New York: The Monacelli Press, 2002)

Stirling, James Krier, Leon and Stirling, James, *James Stirling Buildings and Projects 1950–1974* (London: Thames and Hudson, 1975)

Taut, Bruno Thiekötter, Angelika, *Kristallisationen, Splitterungen: Bruno Tauts Glashaus* (Basel: Birkhäuser Verlag, 1994)

Terragni, Giuseppe Zevi, Bruno, *Giuseppe Terragni* (London: Triangle Architectural Publications, 1989)

Utzon, Jørn Weston, Richard, *Utzon* (Hellerup: Edition Bløondal, 2002)

Van Eyck, Aldo Lefaivre, Liane, *Aldo Van Eyck Humanist Rebel: Inbetweening a Post-War World* (Rotterdam: 010 Publishers, 1999)

Van Eyck, Aldo Ligtelijn, Vincent, *Aldo van Eyck Works* (Basel: Birkhäuser, 1999)

Venturi, Robert Constantinopoulos, Vivian, *Venturi Scott Brown and Associates on Houses and Housing* (London: Academy Editions, 1992)

Wagner, Otto Geretsegger, Heinz and Peinter, Max, *Otto Wagner 1841–1918* (London: Academy Editions, 1979)

Wright, Frank Lloyd McCarter, Robert, *Frank Lloyd Wright* (London: Phaidon Press, 1997)

Wright, Frank Lloyd Levine, Neil, The *Architecture of Frank Lloyd Wright* (Princeton: Princeton University Press, 1996)

Wright, Frank Lloyd, Aalto, Alvar and Eames, Charles and Ray McCarter, Robert, Steele, James and Weston, Richard, *Architecture in Detail: 3 Twentieth Century Houses* (London: Phaidon Press, 1999)

Yeang, Ken Yeang, Ken, *The Skyscraper Bio Climatically Considered* (London: Academy Editions, 1996)

Zumthor, Peter Zumthor, Peter, *Peter Zumthor Works: Buildings and Projects 1979–1997* (Baden: Lars Muller, 1998)

Index

Picture Credits

About the CD

The attached CD can be read on both Windows and Macintosh computers. All the material on the CD is copyright protected and is for private use only. All drawings in the book and on the CD were specially created for this publication and are based on the architects' original designs. Drawings for buildings marked with asterisks in the list below are © DACS 2004. Drawings of works by Luis Barragán are © Barragán Foundation, Switzerland /DACS 2004. Drawings of works by Le Corbusier are © FLC/ADAGP, Paris and DACS, London 2004. Drawings of works by Frank Lloyd Wright are © ARS, NY and DACS, London 2004. Drawings by Adrian Scholefield with Michael Court, Nikki Hilton, Samuel Austin, Christopher Richards, Katherine Collins, Emma Taylor, Thomas Jordan, Oliver Moore, Kern Young, Richard Stollar, Samuel Utting, Giuseppe Amesbury and Nathen Avard.

The CD includes files for all of the plans, sections and elevations included in the book. The drawings for each building are contained in a numbered folder as listed below. They are supplied in two versions: the files with the suffix '.eps' are 'vector' Illustrator EPS files but can be opened using other graphics programs such as Photoshop; all the files with the suffix '.dxf' are generic CAD format files and can be opened in a variety of CAD programmes.

The generic '.dxf' file format does not support 'solid fill' utilized by many architectural CAD programs. All the information is embedded within the file and can be reinstated within supporting CAD programs. Select the polygon required and change the 'Attributes' to 'Solid', the colour information should be automatically retrieved. To reinstate the 'Walls'; select all objects within the 'Walls' layer/class and amend their 'Attributes' to 'Solid'.

All the drawings are to the same scale of 1:200.

The numbered folders correspond to the following buildings:

1. Glasgow School of Art, Charles Rennie Mackintosh
2. Deanery Garden, Sir Edwin Lutyens
3. Larkin Building, Frank Lloyd Wright
4. Post Office Savings Bank, Otto Wagner
5. Unity Temple, Frank Lloyd Wright
6. Palais Stoclet, Josef Hoffmann
7. Robie House, Frank Lloyd Wright
8. Turbine Factory*, Peter Behrens
9. Casa Milá, Antoni Gaudí
10. Glass Pavilion, Bruno Taut
11. Stockholm Public Library, Erik Gunnar Asplund
12. Einstein Tower, Eric Mendelsohn
13. Schindler-Chace House, Rudolf Schindler
14. Schröder House*, Gerrit Rietveld
15. Bauhaus, Walter Gropius
16. Open Air School, Johannes Duiker
17. Lovell 'Health House', Richard Neutra
18. Church of the Sacred Heart, Jože Plečnik
19. Barcelona Pavilion*, Mies van der Rohe
20. Tugendhat House*, Mies van der Rohe
21. Villa Savoye, Le Corbusier
22. Maison de Verre, Chareau and Bijvoet
23. Tuberculosis Sanatorium, Alvar Aalto
24. Müller House*, Adolf Loos
25. Swiss Pavilion, Le Corbusier
26. Schminke House, Hans Scharoun
27. Casa del Fascio, Giuseppe Terragni
28. Gothenburg Law Courts Annex, Erik G. Asplund
29. Fallingwater, Frank Lloyd Wright
30. Jacobs House, Frank Lloyd Wright
31. Johnson Wax Building, Frank Lloyd Wright
32. Baker House, Alvar Aalto
33. Villa Mairea, Alvar Aalto
34. Guggenheim Museum, Frank Lloyd Wright
35. Eames House, Charles and Ray Eames
36. Farnsworth House*, Mies van der Rohe
37. Kaufmann Desert House, Richard Neutra
38. Barragán House and Studio, Luis Barragán
39. Unité d'Habitation, Le Corbusier
40. Säynätsalo Town Hall, Alvar Aalto
41. Lever House, Gordon Bunshaft of SOM
42. Chapel of Notre-Dame-du-Haut, Le Corbusier
43. Crown Hall*, Mies van der Rohe
44. Maisons Jaoul, Le Corbusier
45. Parliament Building, Le Corbusier
46. Niemeyer House, Oscar Niemeyer
47. Monastery of La Tourette, Le Corbusier
48. Leicester Engineering Building, Stirling and Gowan
49. Seagram Building*, Mies van der Rohe
50. Amsterdam Orphanage, Aldo van Eyck
51. Halen Housing Estate, Atelier 5
52. Philharmonie Hall, Hans Scharoun
53. Sydney Opera House, Jørn Utzon
54. Richards Medical Laboratories, Louis Kahn
55. Palazzo dello Sport, Pier Luigi Nervi
56. Dulles International Airport, Eero Saarinen
57. Milam Residence, Paul Rudolph
58. Querini Stampalia Foundation, Carlo Scarpa
59. Salk Institute, Louis Kahn
60. Economist Building, Alison and Peter Smithson
61. Vanna Venturi House, Robert Venturi
62. Fredensborg Housing, Jørn Utzon
63. St Peter's Church, Sigurd Lewerentz
64. Seinäjoki Library, Alvar Aalto
65. Ford Foundation Building, Roche and Dinkeloo
66. Roman Catholic Church, Aldo van Eyck
67. Condominium at Sea Ranch, MLTW
68. Kimbell Art Museum, Louis Kahn
69. Bagsvaerd Church, Jørn Utzon
70. Museum of Hamar, Sverre Fehn
71. Gallaratese Housing Block, Aldo Rossi
72. Centraal Beheer Offices, Herman Hertzberger
73. Willis Faber & Dumas, Norman Foster
74. Pompidou Centre, Piano and Rogers
75. House at Riva San Vitale, Mario Botta
76. Mönchengladbach Museum, Hans Hollein
77. Can Lis, Jørn Utzon
78. Gunma Museum of Modern Art, Arata Isozaki
79. House VI, Peter Eisenman
80. Atheneum, Richard Meier
81. Staatsgalerie, Stirling and Wilford
82. Gehry House, Frank Gehry
83. Koshino House, Tadao Ando
84. Hong Kong & Shanghai Bank, Norman Foster
85. Willemspark School, Herman Hertzberger
86. Ball-Eastaway House, Glenn Murcutt
87. National Museum of Roman Art, Rafael Moneo
88. Menil Collection, Renzo Piano
89. Spiral Building, Fumihiko Maki
90. Wexner Center, Peter Eisenman
91. Graves House, Michael Graves
92. Vals Thermal Baths, Peter Zumthor
93. Goetz Gallery, Herzog and de Meuron
94. Kunsthal, Rem Koolhaas
95. Galician Centre of Art, Álvaro Siza
96. Hostalets Civic Centre, Miralles and Pinós
97. Menara Mesiniaga, Ken Yeang
98. Cultural and Congress Centre, Jean Nouvel
99. Jewish Museum, Daniel Libeskind
100. Barnes House, Patkau Architects
101. Bilbao Guggenheim Museum, Frank Gehry
102. Tjibaou Cultural Centre, Renzo Piano
103. Chapel of St Ignatius, Steven Holl
104. LF1, Landesgartenschau, Zaha Hadid
105. Sendai Mediathèque, Toyo Ito
106. Bordeaux Villa, Rem Koolhaas